D0796832

PAGE STREET

by

MARK J. BOSKOVICH

Book Time Staff,
+ hope you enjoy
reading Page Street as
much I did writing it

Mark J. Boskovich
9/19/93

Edited by
VICKI HESSEL WERKLEY

Illustrated by
THERESA M. ROBERTSON

ABALONE PUBLISHING COMPANY
Half Moon Bay, California

I

PAGE STREET

BY

Mark J. Boskovich

Editor: Vicki Hessel Werkley
Illustrator: Theresa M. Robertson
Published by: ABALONE PUBLISHING COMPANY
Post Office Box 3138
Half Moon Bay, CA 94019-3138 USA

Library of Congress Catalog Card Number: 93-71592
ISBN 0-9635958-0-6

II

TO

LUKA AND ANTOINETTE

ACKNOWLEDGMENTS

Thank You to all those who helped with
PAGE STREET, but most especially:
To Luka and Antoinette "Let's take that walk on the beach."
To Mewanina for all your encouragement and to David Shortt.
Thank you, Charlotte, my dearest friend. You make life so sweet.
To Misty, who put up with me through a dozen rewrites and was
the inspiration for creating Flora and Antone.
To Cassandra for help making decisions & choosing the logo and
to Christena for keeping the dream alive.
To Sister Christena, O.C.D. (and the others at Carmel of the Infant
Jesus) for being there when my mother needed them.
To my friends Elias Pacheco, Hank Sciaroni,
Rod Cardinale and Linda Wilson.
To Jim at Fog Press and Tammy at Coastside Photography.
To Marijana Stipanov and Theresa M. Robertson.
To W. Mark Sawrey & Eric A. Gotfrid at Dimensional Computer.
To Penny Arnett and Gaelyn & Bram Larrick.
To Jean Laidig, Madeline Hartmann, and Sandra L. Smith.
To Dr. Harold Olmo & Dr. Vernon Singleton at the UC Davis
Department of Viticulture and Enology and to
Kathy Redman at Wildhurst Vineyards.
To the staffs of the libraries at Half Moon Bay, Sonoma County,
Lake County and its Redbud Branch.
And to the Editor-From-Heaven,
Vicki Werkley.

Pronouncing the Croatian Words

Vowel sounds do not vary from word to word
and are uniformly pronounced:

a: as in father (ah)   *o:* as in orb (oh)
e: as in ever (eh)   *u:* as in room (oo)
i: as in is (ih)

Consonant sounds are pronounced as in English,
with the following variations and combinations:

c	(ts)	: as in lots	*j*	(y)	: as in year
č	(ch)	: as in church	*lj*	(ly)	: as in million
ć	(tch)	: as in tube	*nj*	(ny)	: as in news (like ñ
d	(d)	: as in do			in Spanish mañana)
đ	(dj)	: as in judge	*s*	(s)	: as in seed
dž	(j)	: as in job	*š*	(sh)	: as in sheep
g	(g)	: as in goat	*z*	(z)	: as in zero
h	(gh)	: as in ach	*ž*	(zh)	: as in pleasure

a few examples...
janje (lamb) = YAHn-yeh
dušho moja = DOO-shoh MOH-yah
(literally—my soul; free translation—my life)
Vučak (the name Wolf) = VOO-chack
Ružena (Slavic name) = ROO-zheh-nah

In some places in *PAGE STREET*, the following abbreviations
have been used:

Gosp. = Gospodin (Mr.)
Gdja. = Gospodja or *Gospođa* (Mrs.)
Gdjica. = Gospodjica or *Gospođica* (Miss)

CHAPTER 1
SANTA CLARA VALLEY, CALIFORNIA — 1885

Ever after, for all her days, Flora Bogdonovich would remember just the way it happened, the precise moment on Wednesday, March 11, 1885 when everything changed. She could never pinpoint exactly what might have served as a catalyst—unless it was simply the nearness of spring—but for whatever reason, in the space of one breath, one heartbeat, her life and her world changed forever.

She had been standing in the yard on the south side of the house, feeding the chickens, speaking aloud to them to practice her English. Mama and Papa never wanted to try learning more than the most necessary words—clinging instead to the language of their native land on the Dalmatian Coast—so now that Flora was no longer in school, she had few opportunities to practice.

"I was born here in America," she reminded the chickens, "and an American should speak English as well as Croatian, don't you think?" On occasion now, Flora found herself forming opinions different from her parents' and felt excited because it was proof she was no longer a child.

"Life here is different from where **they** grew up," she told the big, black rooster, who eyed her speculatively—as if hoping he'd get an extra portion of grain for listening carefully. "And these are modern times—1885, not the 1830s!"

She paused, looking away from the chickens to the east—where the sun was climbing the bright blue sky above the apricot orchard—and her dreams, as always, were of a life full of more than just a happy marriage and as many children as God would give her. She also wanted interesting friends and adventures that would take her traveling beyond this valley where she'd lived all her sixteen years.

But on a glorious day like this, Flora thought, closing her eyes to open her other senses, *who could think of being anywhere but here?* She welcomed the feel of the gentle sunlight on her upturned face and the warming earth beneath her bare feet as she listened to the chorus of birdsong and bees droning in the apricot trees. She could smell the perfume of those blossoms, woodsmoke rising from chimneys across the valley, and the spicy-sweet scent of frying sausages.

Her eyes opened fast when the rooster pecked her foot to remind her of her duties. "Hey!" Flora yelped and shooed him with her skirts before she dumped the rest of the grain on the ground. The hens swarmed over it, and only a few kernels were left by the time the rooster rushed back for his share. He cocked one yellow eye at Flora and glared balefully at her before shaking his black feathers and stalking away.

Flora stood with the empty bowl in her hands. The task was finished, but she couldn't bring herself to go back inside the house. Who wanted to be cleaning and mending on a day like this? Life must be lived in moments, and the precious moments of spring could slip by untreasured if one didn't take the time to savor them.

What eyes could resist such a feast? The morning's thick fog had lifted and dissipated until only a few wisps clung to the hills in the east, but below those peaks, the apricot trees in full bloom looked like great white billows of mist, each tree an explosion of white—incapable, it seemed, of opening one more blossom. From where she stood, Flora couldn't see their stand of plum trees, which she knew must be just as resplendent in pink blossoms.

Indeed, across the road, the plum and cherry trees of the Mellini family were like torches of pink all the way to the fence where their vineyards began. There were no leaves yet on the pruned trunks and arms of the grapevines, and Flora thought they looked a bit like rows of dark, twisted little soldiers with their arms held out to their sides and their feet obscured in a tide of yellow flowers. For the earth of the vineyards was covered with wild mustard blooming so profusely it blotted out the green beneath it and appeared to be a lemon-colored sea. Like a child intoxicated by too many sweets, Flora let her eyes caress the different fields of color: blue sky, green hills, orchards of white and pink, and back to the grape soldiers in their sea of yellow—a color so intense Flora felt she could actually see it in the pit of her stomach.

It wasn't her usual practice to stare across the road at the Mellini farm. Though the two families had lived there since before she was born, she barely knew the people by sight. They were, after all, Italians, and everyone knew what **they** were like. Or so Mama and Papa always said. The Mellinis—Gian and Lucia, their two sons and his orphaned younger brother—made a small family compared to most along the west side of Page Street.

For here in the beautiful valley called Santa Clara—where rich soil and perfect temperatures allowed seeds from around the world to flourish—people were drawn together from many European countries, each group determined to maintain its own identity. And here on Page Street, which extended south through the countryside from the town of Santa Clara, the west side was peopled with Mellinis and Ciceros and Gutras, all staring directly across the road at families named Bogdonovich and Tesla and Stanich.

Both the Italians and the Slavic peoples left their homelands for similar reasons, fleeing to America in hopes of better lives, but those around Flora always talked more about the differences of the cultures than what might make them alike. She was sure it must be the same in the homes across the road.

Thinking this, Flora stood still gazing over at the Mellini farm, and so she saw the horse as soon as it emerged from the barn and moved toward the house. What a beautiful animal! A mare, she decided, noting its delicate lines, physical grace, and easy manner. The mane and tail were the same color as the body coat—all a golden honey-brown. Flora could see four white socks, and she thought there was probably some kind of white marking on the face, but she couldn't tell from this angle, for the mare's head was turned attentively toward the person leading her. And Flora couldn't tell who that was because he was walking on the far side of the mare, half-hidden by the head and neck.

It was unusual to find such a splendid animal—obviously a saddlehorse—on one of the Page Street farms. They all had their draft teams, of course, for pulling wagons and plows. The Bogdonoviches had their pair of grey Belgians, who had come with the names Bob and Dan, but Flora had never felt any more interest in them than in Ilka, the Jersey milkcow. But this horse! She looked intelligent and affectionate, nuzzling her handler as she was led. So beautiful to watch in motion! Flora found herself drawn closer for a better view, but she didn't wish to be caught staring at her neighbors, so she moved into the garden in her front yard. Stooping, she set aside the bowl she was holding and began to attack the latest crop of weeds in her mama's iris beds. From that position, she could watch the activities across the street between the slats of the picket fence.

The horse was led into the Mellinis' front yard, which—unlike the Bogdonoviches'—was bare and untended. It was just another of the ways Page Street divided the Italians and the Slavs. To catch the afternoon sun, the west-facing Slavic homes had their vegetable gardens in their front yards, while the Italians planted theirs in back of their east-facing houses. But beyond that, there was no Mellini to beautify the front yard with flowers, like the huge lavender irises that would soon bloom here. Papa said Italians were lazy, but Flora had never seen that proven by the clan across the street. Gian Mellini and the three boys seemed always hard at work tending the animals, the fruit trees, or the vines, and one or all of them must also handle the household tasks of cooking and cleaning, for Mama Mellini had been bedridden as long as Flora could remember; she never even ventured out onto the porch to enjoy the fresh air.

The sun was high enough now that both front yards were bathed in sunlight, and Flora watched the honey-colored mare toss her head as she was tied to a post in the yard. Whose horse was she? The Mellinis already had their team of draft horses and two others suitable for riding. Where and why would they get such a fine animal? And who was that with her?

The person who had led and tied the mare was still obscured from view, even as he turned and walked away around the side of the house. Stooped in her yard, peering between the fence slats as she pretended to concentrate on the weeds, Flora squinted her eyes, trying to identify the man before he disappeared. He wasn't bent enough to be old Gian, and he didn't limp like that much-younger brother Gregorio who'd come to live there when he was orphaned. He was too thin and lithe to be the older son Bruno, but surely the youngest of the clan, Antone, couldn't be that tall?

In a moment the fellow returned, and since he faced her now, Flora could

3

see it was, indeed, young Antone. Of course, he **was** two or three years older than she was, but the time she'd seen the most of him was back when they were in school and she was ten years old. He and all the boys his age—Italian or Slavic or whatever—had seemed so immature with their practical jokes and lack of attention to their studies. Their suddenly gawky bodies and cracking voices could only intensify their awkward shyness, and Flora couldn't imagine why she would ever be interested in such creatures.

But this was not the boy she remembered. This Antone must be nearly as tall as her own father, and he moved with an easy, athletic grace that made it impossible for Flora to look away. He wore an immaculately white shirt, open at the throat and with the sleeves rolled up above his elbows, revealing quite a lot of his dark skin. His hair was very black and curly, a little longer than any Croatian man would wear it, but it looked clean and shiny, and Flora decided she liked it that length.

Antone carried a full bucket of water in one hand and what looked like a brush and a clean cloth in the other. As he approached, the mare turned toward him and whickered a greeting, and he laughed aloud and spoke to her, but Flora couldn't hear what he said.

She watched as he began to brush and wash the mare's golden coat. She noted the gentleness of his touch and the soft way he continued talking to the horse as he worked. Flora found herself mesmerized by the movement of his body and the way the muscles of his arms and legs strained against the fabric of his clothing. Now that he was closer, Flora could see his forearms were furred with fine, dark hairs, and more showed on his chest where his shirt was opened. She found herself wondering what he would look like without the shirt.... Would all his chest be covered with that fur? Would it cover his belly as well? And what of his back—might that not be covered too? She gave a little shiver, but she realized it was not of revulsion. Her Papa had hair on his chest, like soft little threads of gold when the sun touched them, and she'd always thought her own future husband would look much the same. Why would she want something different than her mother and grandmothers before her? But there was something mysterious and exciting in the thought of how Antone would look without his shirt—images that made her heart speed up and her breath more difficult to get into her lungs—and Flora found herself wondering what it would be like to touch those strong forearms, that chest and back, to trace her fingers through that dark fur—

And at that precise moment, Antone turned and looked straight at her, pinning her with his eyes like a butterfly on a mounting board. She gasped with the shock of it and felt hot, embarrassed color washed up into her face. What to do? Look away and pretend she hadn't been watching him? It wouldn't fool him; her blush was all the confirmation he'd need. What then? Continue to crouch here like a terrified rabbit or a humiliated schoolgirl?

4

No! Flora thought. *I won't give him the satisfaction.* She wouldn't allow him to tell his fellows how he'd caught his Croat neighbor staring at him but then she just cowered in the weeds.

As if the hand of God had grabbed her by the nape of her neck, she sprang up from her crouch and glared across at Antone, her teeth gritted together, fists clenched full of weeds, her breath coming hard. And she forced herself to look boldly and directly into his eyes.

They were black; it was impossible that they could be any darker. And yet, they were very expressive. She watched as the initial surprise sparked into anger at being spied upon. But that quickly melted into amusement as he savored her embarrassment, and those full lips parted in a disdainful grin. His teeth were very white and perfect, but it was his eyes that held hers, and as she stared into them, she saw the next subtle shift of emotions. As the amusement and insolence drained away, there was a dawning of something very different, and Flora saw in Antone's eyes a mirror of her own sudden sense of surprise and wonder and a kind of recognition . . . as if they'd known each other well in some distant time or place—though that, of course, was impossible.

And as Flora Bogdonovich stood staring across Page Street into Antone Mellini's eyes, it seemed the Universe paused and held its breath, and in that moment, Flora's whole world changed forever.

As Antone led the honey-colored mare from the barn to the front yard, his thoughts were entirely upon the horse. He could not believe his good fortune. That **he**—the youngest of the household—would possess such an animal! Papa didn't need her, Bruno was a little afraid of horses and avoided riding whenever he could, but Uncle Gregorio wanted her and was furious.

There'd been a big argument three nights ago after they'd learned the mare was up for sale. It wasn't about buying her or the price; they'd already decided they needed another saddlehorse so Antone could better discharge his new duties away from the area, and she was worth three times what Donati Podesta—a family friend—was asking. The argument was about whose horse it would be. Gregorio insisted—as eldest of the three young men—he was entitled and Antone could continue riding Rosa. But Papa stood firm in his convictions, saying, "No, it's Antone who must do the traveling in these new business matters, and he has ridden that old sack of bones over the mountains to the coast many times. He needs a faster horse, not so tiring to ride—one that will make a better impression. And he should be rewarded for the fine work he has done; he is the one with a head for business, and none of us can match his English. It is decided. Antone will have the new horse as his own."

Walking now beside his new mare, Antone shivered as he remembered the black stare Gregorio had leveled at him. He had learned at an early age that this orphaned uncle—barely seven years older than he was—could be very dangerous to anger.

"Not to worry," Antone whispered to the mare, wishing his voice sounded more convincing. "You belong to me, and I will take very good care of you." She nuzzled him affectionately as if she not only understood, but also believed him. He stroked the white stripe down her forehead and touched the little white spot above her left nostril, thinking how well she'd been named. He murmured her name—Dolce—prolonging the vowels: "Dole-chay, my Dole-chay. The color of honey and twice as sweet, aren't you?" She blew her soft breath on his cheek, and he laughed in delight. He couldn't have felt happier—or prouder.

As he tied Dolce to the post in the yard, Antone was little aware of his surroundings; he did have the vague impression one of his neighbors was working in the garden, but that was across the street, and those Croats were of little interest to him. Patting the mare's neck, he told her, "Wait now. I'll be right back." He went quickly around the house and gathered up the items he'd left by the pump—a brimming bucket of water, a large, soft piece of cloth, a dandy brush—and carried them back to where she was waiting. As soon as he rounded the house, the mare turned to look at him and whickered a greeting. Antone laughed aloud and asked, "Did you miss me so much? I was only gone a moment."

He moved around to her near side, with his back to the street, and began to brush the dust from her coat, continuing his one-sided conversation. "Ah, my sweet lady, I think my friend Donati has spoiled you. Maybe you think you are just a large dog? If I'm not careful, you'll be trying to follow me into the house to curl up by the fire, won't you?"

There wasn't much dust to be brushed loose, and surely it wasn't necessary to wash the mare, but this attention was more a ritual of new ownership and a way of establishing his bond with Dolce, so Antone began to wipe her coat with the dampened cloth. All the while, he talked to her, telling her how beautiful she was and how glad he was to have her and what wonderful adventures they'd share together.

And slowly as he worked, enjoying the pull in his muscles and the heat of the sun on his head and shoulders, he began to feel as if he were being touched. He suddenly felt sure someone was watching him. He was used to that: Gregorio often stared at him for long periods of time, and Antone had no wish to know the dark thoughts behind his uncle's furrowed brows as he did so. But he knew Gregorio had gone into town an hour ago, and this felt different. This was not the chill fingers he felt touch his spine when Gregorio watched him. In fact, if there was a sense of temperature, he would have to call it warm . . . as if hot eyes moved across his back and shoulders. The watcher would have to be across the street then—one of those Bogdonoviches. Well, let 'em look! Let 'em envy his beautiful new horse!

But somehow Antone felt sure the gaze was focused on **him**, not Dolce. *Why?* he wondered. *And who?* He ignored it as long as he could, not wanting to give such a rude person the satisfaction of knowing he'd been disturbed, but the pressure of those eyes became unbearable, and Antone had to know . . . .

He whirled—his own eyes narrowed—and saw her immediately, crouched down, peering at him between the slats of that picket fence. At first he thought it might be the mother, but then he saw it was the girl. Flora, her name was. He remembered her from school: quiet, studious, a little shy perhaps, and not amused by boyish pranks, though she never tattled when she had the chance. Antone had left school when he turned fourteen and had rarely noticed her since. He had more than enough work on the farm to keep his attention, and it was common practice to ignore anyone across the street. After all, they were only Slavs.

Antone saw the hot red color flame up across the girl's face. *Good!* he thought. *She **should** be embarrassed.* Was she just going to hide there and act like she was invisible and nothing had happened? As if she'd read his thoughts— or as if a giant hand had hauled her to her feet—she sprang up and faced him, her jaw set defiantly, her fists crushing the life out of the weeds she had pulled.

Reveling in her embarrassment, he stared into her red face and gave her his most condescending smile. *Let her squirm! Any second now, she'll run away and go crying to her mama about that rude guinea boy across the street.* But he was wrong about that. Flora Bogdonovich just stood there, matching his level stare, and with a little shock, Antone realized this was not the little girl he remembered.

Like most of the women from Dalmatia, Flora was tall and broad-shouldered, but her body was more sculptured than most. Her modest waist was accentuated by her wide hips and full breasts, and—even staring into her eyes—he was aware how those breasts rose and fell with her hard, quick breathing. Her auburn hair was pulled up atop her head in the traditional bun, but Antone could imagine what it would look like loose, covering those shoulders and those breasts like a reddish cape. As her blush faded away, Flora's skin returned to its natural ivory hues, and Antone marveled at such pale beauty, so different from the olive-skinned girls he knew.

But it was her eyes that held him: large and deeply set; their color reminded him of the rich brown fur of otters he'd seen playing in the rivers on his travels to the coast. Beautiful, expressive eyes conveying both defiance and apology . . . and more. Antone found he could not look away from those eyes, not even to survey the landscape of that beautiful body. When he was forced to leave school, he'd made the time each evening to continue his education with whatever books he could obtain, but there were many words and phrases he could not comprehend, and there was no one to explain them. Now he truly understood what it meant to be "in thrall"—to feel a slave to some other power—and as he stared in breathless wonder, he remembered the way her gaze had felt on him when she thought he wasn't aware. He himself had ogled enough girls to know what thoughts might accompany such a stare.

But what a surprise to find **himself** the object—and from this unexpected direction! And though Antone was not an arrogant youth, he knew with great certainty that her gaze had been admiring him. Something in this realization—and his own new awareness of this ripe beauty of a near neighbor—kindled passion within him, such a wave of emotion, he thought his heart might jolt out of his chest. A part of him with a more detached view decided wryly it was very much like being struck by lightning.

How could he fall in love with a Slavic girl? He could just hear his parents—and Gregorio! And if they only knew the way she'd been looking at him, if they could see what he saw in her eyes right now . . . . He struggled with the storm of conflicting feelings within him and finally silenced the voice that sneered, *If she looks at a man like that, she must be a true sgualdrina . . . slut . . . and a brazen one at that!* No, her admiration of his physical body and the lushness of her own did not overshadow the essence of purity about her, that appealing air of innocence and willingness to trust.

And Antone need only look at his own innocence to find the truth of it. Certainly he wanted to have a woman, and he lived a wanton life in his fantasies and dreams, and God knows, he'd had his opportunities. Donati's sister Concetta had certainly made herself available, had indeed made it difficult for him to decline on a number of occasions. She was an attractive and provocative girl, but for some reason, Antone had always felt it would be worth waiting for the right girl—someone he truly loved. His older brother Bruno—who dallied with any girl who'd let him (and there were many who appreciated his sweet nature)—thought he was crazy but didn't pressure him. Uncle Gregorio, on the other hand, was forever trying to get Antone to accompany him to one of the brothels in town, as if it were a personal goal to help Antone break his resolve. If Bruno was around at these times, he would come to his brother's rescue and say, "Leave the boy alone. When he's ready, he won't have to pay for it. And neither would you if you were nicer to the girls." That usually made Gregorio mad enough to drop his badgering or cajoling of Antone and storm away to saddle a horse for the ride into town, but it never resolved the situation.

And what if Gregorio could see him now, staring across the street as he fell in love with what his uncle would call a *putana slava!* The thought stabbed Antone with actual terror, but he didn't look away from Flora's eyes. For here he found what he'd been hoping for and the strangest sense that he already knew this woman . . . that they'd known each other forever. That detached part of him noted, *Falling in love can make you think the most ridiculous things!*

Be that as it may, in those awe-filled moments as Antone was jolted by dawning awareness and passion and terror, there was also a sense of the inevitable, as if he knew in some way that he was like metal, struck on an anvil by the hammer of destiny.

Flora stood transfixed, reading Antone's eyes, thinking that nothing could ever make her look away. But then she heard her father's voice.

"Flora! What are you looking at?"

She pivoted, almost falling from her lightheadedness and surprise. There was her father, coming toward her from the road, his arms full of packages, back from his shopping in town. What had he seen? What did he guess? With her heart pounding so loudly she could hardly hear her own words, she said, "The Mellinis have a new horse. She's beautiful, isn't she?"

Her own quick glance back across the street revealed that not only had Antone turned away, but he'd also slipped under the mare's neck to begin washing her other side. Flora was sure Papa wouldn't be able to tell which of the Mellini men it was.

Papa stopped and squinted across the road at the honey-colored mare. Luka Bogdonovich stood well over six feet tall, a rugged-looking man with big weather-beaten hands. It was amazing to think that those thick fingers—always scraped and scabbed from his hard work—could also coax lively tunes from the buttons of a concertina. His once-golden hair and finely trimmed mustache were whitening now, making his face look even more tanned. "Yes, yes, a good horse," he agreed, but he had more important things on his mind, and he turned to her with his blue eyes alight. "You'll never guess who I just met!"

Flora felt the small stone of sadness in her chest as she realized Papa'd had quite a lot to drink in town. But perhaps that had worked to her advantage. If he were himself, he would've noticed that brazen tableau in a moment. Still shaky after her close call, Flora asked, "Who?"

"People from home! From Dalmatia. Not from Dubrovnik—but from Hvar. Close enough, though, huh?"

"Yes, Papa," Flora answered, wondering when her heart would slow to a comfortable rhythm.

"I invited them for supper." With his chin, he indicated one of his paper-wrapped packages and said excitedly, "I got a nice piece of shark fresh at the market for your mama to cook with her special recipe, but she'll need some basil and thyme. So why don't you throw down those weeds and pick some for her, hey?" A couple of parcels were beginning to slip, and he wrestled good-naturedly with them.

Flora managed to unclench her fists and let the weeds drop as she stepped to help him. Drawing close to her father, she could smell the whiskey on him. "That's my girl," he said, leaning to kiss her forehead as she settled the paper bundles in his arms. "Can't cook our shark with weeds, now can we?" And he laughed at his own joke.

"No, Papa," she murmured.

"There now, I'm set," he told her. "Pick those herbs and get out your best Sunday dress. They have a son about your age." Without waiting for a reply, he started off around the house toward the kitchen door, calling, "Philomena! Get ready for company!"

Flora rubbed her hands together—they were stained green by the weeds she'd strangled—and thought, *The last thing I need is some boy from the old country looking me over as a prospective wife!* There was only one boy in the world she wanted to think about. She never questioned that it might be wrong for her to fall in love with an Italian boy—or experience such heady thoughts and emotions. God would guide her. He always had.

As she stooped to pluck the herbs, she couldn't help glancing over into the Mellini yard. It was absurd to think he might still be there watching her, but she was unprepared for the stab of disappointment as she saw him leaving the yard, leading the mare back toward the barn.

With a sigh from the very center of her being, Flora dropped the herbs in the bowl that'd held chicken feed what seemed like eons ago. As she carried it to the kitchen, she wondered how long it would be before she could arrange to meet Antone face to face.

T. ROBERTSON

CHAPTER 2
SANTA CLARA VALLEY — 1885

When Flora delivered the herbs to her mother in the kitchen and asked what she could do to help, Philomena Bogdonovich answered in a low, tight voice—but not unkindly, "Just stay out of my way, *janje.*" (Mama always called her *janje*. . . lamb . . . as a pet name, because her own mama had called **her** that, and passing along traditions was very important in her family.) Then Mama said, "I suppose you could straighten up the parlor—since we're to have company."

Flora knew her mother was furious. As much as she loved cooking and showing off with her special recipes from the homeland, she'd never appreciated Papa's penchant for inviting total strangers on a moment's notice. But she was probably madder still that he'd been to one of the saloons in town and had drunk so much so early in the day. Papa's drinking seemed to be getting steadily worse, and the fact that he made his own wine didn't help the situation.

At first, it was only on special occasions that he drank too heavily. But now it was a nightly affair that would begin as soon as he came in from the orchards. And Flora was beginning to suspect his drinking began even earlier—perhaps he kept a keg hidden somewhere out among the trees—for she could smell it on his breath when welcoming him with a hug. Surely Mama must have noticed this too, but she'd never said anything to Flora. In fact, she said little when she was mad; she just pressed her lips together tightly, as if trying to keep the words from coming out. Much of the time these days, her mouth looked like a hard thin line across her face where there had once been wide, loving smiles.

At least, Flora thought, *Papa isn't mean when he drinks.* Not like their neighbor Vlach Stanich. Flora had often heard him yelling and breaking things, and when his wife Eliska was still alive, it was rare to see her without some kind of bruise on her face or arms. Even now, three years after her death, Flora still remembered the haunted look in those pale eyes. He also beat his son Mattiza, who was a gentle boy only two months older than Flora, and she felt sure those beatings increased when Eliska wasn't there to protect the boy by taking on the pain herself.

Flora's parents never spoke of this to her, but once when she was barely ten, she overheard them talking about it in hushed whispers. She entered the room, surprising them, and cried, "What can we do to help Matty and his mama?"

Both her parents looked uncomfortable, but it was her father who said, "Nothing, Flora."

"Why not?" she demanded.

"She is his wife. That is his son and his house."

Flora was incredulous. "And that makes it all right?"

"No," Papa said tiredly. "But it is not our business." In disbelief, Flora turned to her mother for support, but that gentle lady only opened her hands, shrugging helplessly, and looked away from her daughter's eyes.

And the thing that baffled Flora most was the way Eliska and Mattiza would make excuses for the old man. She'd known Mattiza all her life. They'd played together as infants, learned to walk together, had shared secrets and dreams; Flora helped him with his schoolwork, and he carved beautiful little wooden trinkets for her. But when she tried to talk to him about his father's behavior, he always dismissed it or tried to change the subject. When she pressed, he would say the same things Flora heard from Eliska: "His work at the mill is very hard—no wonder he gets so mad" or "Everyone in his family has a bad temper; he can't help it" or "He only hits me when he's been drinking."

"It's not right," Flora told him one day as they walked to school, but he only gave that infuriating shrug. He was a tall, sweet-faced boy, blond and grey-eyed, with a jagged little scar on his left cheekbone. "Why do you let him do it, Matty?"

Again the shrug. "Sometimes I deserve it. I'm not quick with my work the way I should be . . . and sometimes I forget things." Flora tried that day—and on many other days—to convince Mattiza that no one deserved to be beaten like that, but even at the times she got him to agree with her, still he would do nothing to defend himself.

Flora loved her childhood friend, but she found it hard to respect him as much as he deserved. All his good qualities seemed to slip from view in the face of this inability to protect himself. Sad as this situation was, it created in Flora an iron resolve: *Never will I tolerate such abuse—not from anyone!*

Thankfully, Papa was a happy and foolish drinker. He would roar with laughter and loved playing silly games that embarrassed and infuriated Mama. At first, when the heavy drinking was only an occasional thing, Mama didn't seem to mind so much and often even joined in some of his silly pranks. But lately, she was not so tolerant. Even when there was company, she would sit to one side—stony-faced as if not wanting to encourage him with even a smile—waiting patiently for Papa to make a fool of himself before passing out.

Moving around the parlor, dusting wood surfaces and straightening the bright woolen shawls draped over various pieces of furniture, Flora wondered what this evening would be like—what kind of people her papa had invited. And what of this boy, this son who was "about her age"?

On the north side of the room, flanking the bay window, were two framed sketches of Dubrovnik, which Mama had made before leaving Dalmatia. There were a few other examples of her fine work in other rooms of the house, but never in her life had Flora seen her mother do a single drawing. "I'm just not inspired anymore," Mama always said. "And when would I find time?"

Flora checked to make sure the four kerosene lamps were full and the wicks ready to be lit. There were six lamps in all—one for each bedroom and four in the parlor—and they were Mama's most prized possession. A gift from her mother before she left Dalmatia for America, they'd been hand-crafted of pure silver there in Dubrovnik. Hvar, homeland of the guests they were expecting, was an island not too far northwest of that coastal city, and some of Flora's distant relatives used to live there. Thinking of Hvar brought her thoughts back to the boy she was about to meet and how lately her parents had gone out of their way to make sure she met any eligible bachelor of Slavic ancestry.

All the time she and Mattiza were growing up, she was half-aware that everyone expected they would marry one day. Back then, she hadn't given it a thought. Marriage was decades away and held little interest for her. She'd always loved her friend Matty, but her feelings never flowered into anything beyond sisterly affection.

And after Eliska died, Flora's parents treated Mattiza exactly the same, but they stopped referring to marriage with Flora. They never spoke about it, and if Flora asked any questions, they turned them aside. Flora wondered if they had suspicions about Eliska's death. Of course, the woman had not been well in years; she always looked pale and thin, as if there wasn't enough blood in her body, and no matter what she ate, she just kept losing weight. But still, the death seemed rather sudden, and everyone in the community avoided talking about it—at least as far as Flora could see.

Perhaps her parents feared Mattiza would turn out to be like his father. Or that he'd be too much like his mother and unable to protect those he loved. Either way, Flora's parents seemed to be looking elsewhere for a son-in-law. But of the Slavic boys Flora knew, there was no one she could imagine falling in love with. Especially not now . . . after her experience with Antone.

She moved to the front window and peered through the lacy white curtains toward the Mellini house across the street. There were boys in her ethnic community intelligent enough and educated enough and certainly some were pleasant enough to look at, some from prosperous families or with solid prospects of their own, but all their images slipped from her thoughts when she remembered what she'd felt gazing into Antone Mellini's eyes.

You must be out of your mind! she told herself. You can't possibly believe you can marry that boy!? As if these thoughts had conjured him up, he came walking into view in his yard. As earlier in the day, he led the pretty honey-colored mare and tied her to the post. But now she was saddled and bridled, and Antone had changed into clothes for traveling. With quick, light steps he hurried up onto the porch, gathered some items lying there, and then took them down to pack on the mare. Squinting, Flora could make out bulging saddlebags and a bedroll, so it looked like he might be gone some days. *Now, where is he off to?* she wondered. Just when she was trying to figure out a way to meet him, he up and left town!

The annoyance she felt disappeared when she saw him swing into the saddle. The sight of him took her breath—his easy grace, his shining black hair and wide shoulders and handsome face, now grinning as he waved toward his porch. Flora saw that Bruno had come out of the house and was waving a farewell. They exchanged some words in Italian, and then Antone nudged the mare into motion, and she stepped along out of the yard and into the road. As he turned to his right on Page Street—the direction that would take him south and perhaps over to the coast—he glanced across at her house. He looked right at her, but she was certain he couldn't actually see her behind the lace curtains. Still, she had the distinct impression he knew she was there—further proof, she told herself, of the bond that now existed between them.

Does he wish he could say good-bye to **me***?* she wondered. *Would he like to tell me where he's going . . . and when he will return?*

"Flora!"

She jumped like a startled rabbit at the sound of her mother's voice, calling from the kitchen. She had to take a deep breath before she could respond. "Yes, Mama?"

"Go fetch your father for me."

Flora gazed after the golden mare that was now trotting away, taking Antone with her. There was nothing to watch here now. Flora took another quick look around the parlor, straightening the corner of a Turkish carpet, and decided the wooden floors—which she'd swept only yesterday—would pass as they were. With a satisfied nod, she headed for the kitchen.

"What do you need?" she asked her mother as she entered the room.

Philomena Bogdonovich was a strong and handsome woman, aging gracefully despite a life of hard work. For all her fifty years, there was little grey in her auburn hair, and her brown eyes—a few shades lighter than Flora's—still needed no assistance for reading or needlework. At the moment, she was chopping onions on a wooden board. "Go tell your father I need more stovewood. Please."

"I can get some for you."

Philomena paused and looked at her daughter; she gripped the knife so tightly, the skin across her knuckles was stretched white, and there were tears in her eyes. Perhaps from the onions, but Flora thought not. "I want your father to do it."

They both knew where he would be. Flora nodded and went out the kitchen door into the yard on the south side of the house, where she'd fed the chickens earlier. Almost halfway down this side of the house was the opening to the cellar, and the doors were open wide. Flora could hear Papa singing inside.

When he wasn't tending his orchards, he spent most of his hours in this cellar, making wine as his father and uncles had before him. In the old country, they too had grown fruit—"mostly for eating, a little for wine" they would say— and here in the new world, Papa took the best recipes and experimented, making them better. The whole community agreed his plum wine was the best in the area. It made him a little bit famous and that was good. Even though he produced only modest amounts, his reputation spread. He was considered a master and was often asked for advice, which he freely gave.

He also made all his own tools and casks from woods he selected himself. It was the making and selling of tools and kegs—and the wine itself—that brought in some extra money, enabling him to continue his hobby without dipping into family household funds. And often there were trades of goods for the wine—fresh pork, kerosene, bolt cloth, harness leather. Flora knew how proud Papa was, carrying on the family tradition of winemaking, even on such a small scale. But he had learned to love his own plum wine too well. Still, it hadn't seemed yet to interfere with his craftsmanship or his winemaking.

Often, of an evening, his friends would congregate with him in the cellar, sampling his plum wine as they sang the old songs and talked of days gone by. Before he left Dubrovnik, Luka had been part of a *klapa*—a group of young men who walked through the city singing in harmony. The men visiting the cellar didn't sing as much as they used to, and the more Papa drank, the less he spent time with the concertina, but there were always the stories.

Through the years, Flora had spent long hours perched outside on the cellar doors, listening to these stories and waiting for them to get to the part she liked best. Flora could predict the shift in conversation by listening to the voices, for when they'd drunk enough wine to slur their speech, the conversation always turned to their coming to America. And Flora never tired of such tales: journeys, adventures, terrible hardships endured.

But not today. Papa was alone in the cellar, singing to himself some lusty ballad of lost love. Flora called down to him, and when he answered, told him, "Come on up, now. Mama needs your help."

He made some kind of answer, his voice muffled so Flora wasn't quite sure what he said, but a few moments later he came up the steps, clutching a cask of plum wine to his chest. "Just getting some refreshment for our guests," he told Flora, patting the keg affectionately. "This was an especially good batch."

"Mama needs more stovewood to cook a feast worthy of that wonderful piece of *morski pas* you brought." Flora reached out to steady her father as he swayed a tiny bit on the top step. "You take the wine in, and I'll close up the cellar."

"That's my girl! I'll go put this wine in the kitchen, and then I'll get more stovewood for my Philomena so she can make a wonderful feast for our new friends from the home country. Wait till they taste her baked shark!" He moved away, his steps becoming steadier as the fresh air revived him.

Closing and latching the cellar doors, Flora watched him go and shook her head tiredly. Though it was barely noticeable, she could tell he'd already had too much to drink, but he was nowhere close to the passing-out stage. She sighed, thinking the evening ahead might seem very long indeed.

In some ways, the evening was better than she had anticipated, but mostly it was worse. It was better because the "son about her age" turned out to be very nice. Karsten Tipanov was a plain-looking young man of twenty, serious and polite, but it was obvious to Flora that he had no intention of courting her. He was not at all like other young men her parents had contrived for her to meet. Those boys tried too hard to prove they were strong and smart, perhaps even witty and charming—which usually produced the opposite effect—and they all eyed her speculatively as if trying to judge her future performance in the kitchen, bedroom, and nursery. But not Karsten.

Both fathers, in high good spirits, seemed bent on making sure their children had some moments alone together. When the meal was finished but everyone was still seated around the kitchen table, something got Papa started talking about silver, and when Karsten expressed an interest, Papa said, "You must see the lamps Philomena's mother gave her in Dubrovnik. Flora, take Karsten in the parlor and show him." Both youngsters were dumbfounded at this, but obediently excused themselves and went to the parlor.

Alone there, Flora showed off the lamps and Karsten admired them, and then the two of them glanced at each other with apologetic smiles. Flora took the initiative. "Our parents seem to be trying to pair us up."

"I know," Karsten said, "but I must tell you something. You are a lovely girl and very nice, but I'm already in love with someone else."

"Ah-h-h," Flora said sagely, as if she knew much about these matters.

"Yes, a girl back home in Hvar. I want to bring her here and marry her; my parents want me to forget her. My family is quite wealthy. She is very poor and uneducated."

"I see," Flora answered. And then with great sincerity, she said, "I hope you make this dream come true."

He smiled at her. "Thank you. You are a very nice person." His voice took on a slightly teasing tone. "I hope you're not offended that I'm not trying to marry you."

Flora laughed. "No, no. Don't worry. I'm in love with someone too." There! she'd said it out loud. That must make it true.

"And your parents don't approve?"

"They don't even know!" And if they **did** know about Antone, it was hard to imagine them disapproving more.

Karsten smiled again, but before he could say anything else, Mama came hurrying into the room, glancing back over her shoulder toward the guests following her. Papa brought up the rear, carrying his precious cask and his glass. Flora got the impression there was more afoot than just moving the guests from the kitchen to a room more conducive to after-dinner conversation. It was as if Philomena wanted to prevent exactly what Papa had arranged: Flora and Karsten having time alone where an attachment might blossom.

This puzzled Flora since Mama had no reason to believe she should rescue her daughter from an unwelcome suitor—Karsten had proved to be just the kind of young man her parents should want her to marry. But as her parents and Karsten's settled into the comfortable parlor furniture, Flora realized Mama was probably horrified by the possibility her daughter might marry into the family of Sabina Tipanov.

The woman had been unbearable from the moment she arrived. Her husband Josko seemed a relaxed and good-natured fellow—especially as he quaffed glass after glass of Papa's plum wine—but his wife couldn't have been more different.

Sabina was very tall and very thin with a nose like a razor and a mouth so thin it looked like a slit made by that razor. In her drab-colored—but obviously expensive—dress, she moved as if she had a stick laced to her backbone. Even in a chair, she remained bolt upright, never leaning back or affording herself the comfort of the padded arms. Her piercing hard eyes seemed to view everything about her hosts and their home with distaste.

Though her husband had been effusive in his praises of Mama's fine meal (and he ate twice as much of the *morski pas* as Papa did), Sabina picked at her food and at one point, punctuated the compliments with a tight-voiced, "Yes, but there's nothing quite like a good piece of pork." Flora could see her mama was hurt—after all, the shark was perfectly done, smothered in onions and herbs with potatoes and cabbage to accompany it—but at that point, Philomena was still maintaining her façade of gracious hostess, and she hid her annoyance well.

After the gathering moved into the parlor, the evening deteriorated rapidly. Karsten did his best to observe the social graces and be a pleasant, appreciative guest, but—as his father got steadily drunker and louder, sharing his laughter and lewd stories with their equally boisterous host, and his mother outdid herself finding subtle ways to insult Philomena's home, cooking, and physical appearance—the young man began to sweat under the stress, and Flora thought she could see panic welling up in his eyes.

Mama made it very plain when she'd had enough: she simply withdrew. She fixed her eyes on one of the silver lamps across the parlor, and it was as if everyone else in the room had ceased to exist. Within herself, Philomena called it "going to Dubrovnik" because she could just immerse herself in her memories of her childhood home and forget about everything else. The men never noticed; Karsten and Flora both tried to include Philomena in the strained conversation, but when she remained unresponsive, they stopped addressing her; Sabina began to smirk, as if the happiest event of her day was making a generous hostess so hurt and angry she would abdicate that role.

But Flora was sure that her mother was even more furious at Papa. First, for inviting the Tipanovs (though Flora was convinced he must have extended that invitation before meeting Sabina), but above all for his inebriation and all the offensive behavior accompanying it.

Before long, and sooner than most nights, Papa simply passed out in his favorite chair with his mouth gaping open to accommodate his thunderous snores. Mama rose from her chair and without looking at anyone in the room, said, "I'm going to clean up the kitchen. Flora, please show our guests to the door." And she walked out of the room, toward the back of the house.

Flora glanced at Karsten, feeling the blush of her embarrassment at her parents' rudeness. How she wanted to apologize to him and say, "They haven't always been this way. It's just lately...." But she saw the understanding and sympathy in Karsten's eyes, and she knew he must often wish to apologize for his parents, just as he undoubtedly did in this moment. "We should be going," he said and began to help his father up from the sofa.

Josko looked around him, mumbling, "Where's my glass? Is it empty?"

"Yes, Father," Karsten murmured. "Very empty."

Sabina, still smirking, didn't try to assist. She followed them to the front door and then turned to Flora, who was right behind her. As Karsten was getting the door open and his father through it and out onto the porch, Sabina turned to Flora and said with thinly disguised sarcasm, "Thank you for a truly edifying evening. We must have you over when we've found a suitable house to buy." She gave Flora another smirk of a smile and added, "Of course, you'll probably have to come quite some distance. We wouldn't settle for a place where we had to put up with a bunch of those filthy Italians just across the street."

"Here, Mother," Karsten said quickly. He had his nearly unconscious father propped up against his left side, and he held his free hand out to help his mother down the steps. When she was safely at the bottom and heading for the front gate, Karsten glanced back at Flora and said, "Thank you. I'm very glad to meet you."

Flora found she couldn't speak, but she nodded and gave him a little wave to show she felt the same. She didn't watch them the rest of the way to their buggy waiting in the street but hurried inside the house and leaned against the door as soon as it was shut behind her.

Close to tears after the strain of the evening, she still felt the sting of Sabina's remark about her Italian neighbors. Flora comforted herself with an amusing thought: *If she knew how I feel about Antone, she'd probably faint . . . probably never have anything to do with me.* But her tired smile slipped from her face when she asked of herself, *But what of Karsten? Would he think so much of you if he knew who you loved?*

And what will Mama and Papa say when I tell them? The first impulse was not to tell them at all, but that was ridiculous. If she was going to love Antone— to marry him—then eventually, she'd **have** to tell them, wouldn't she? *And do you really think you will marry Antone?* a little voice seemed to ask inside her. *What makes you think he wants to marry* **you**? *You don't even know for sure that he cares for you. You could be totally wrong about what you saw in his eyes. He's Italian—different—how can you think you'd be able to know what he's thinking and feeling?*

Exhausted now with all the evening had contained, Flora tried to push away all thoughts of Antone and what the future might bring. She looked across the parlor at her father collapsed, still snoring, in his chair, and she shook her head sadly. She went about the room, blowing out all except one of the silver lamps. Then she went into the kitchen and silently helped her mother with the clean-up and dishes.

They didn't talk. Philomena's thoughts seemed miles away and an observer might have thought the woman was totally unaware of her daughter's presence, except that occasionally she would hand things to her to dry or put away.

When they were finished in the kitchen, still without speaking, they went back to the parlor, and Flora helped her mother put Papa to bed, where he continued his snoring uninterrupted and as if he hadn't a worry in the world. Then Mama went out on the porch and sat in one of the chairs. Flora followed her, but sat on the top step, leaning back against the post and gazing up at her mother. They sat listening to the echo of the crickets.

Flora watched Mama's face and tried to imagine what she was thinking. Definitely, it was about Papa. She recognized that certain wistfulness, an expression that often accompanied stories of her youth on the Dalmatian Coast. Was she remembering Papa in those early years? So handsome with his golden-brown hair and eyes the color of summer skies over the Adriatic. So full of life and dreams.

All her life Flora was aware of the love and passion her parents shared. It was hard to miss the smiles they gave each other or the way a touch on the cheek or hand or hair would linger. Through the years there were times when she had bad dreams, and awaking from them, she would pad next door to their room for comforting. More than once she found them awake, though oblivious to her standing in their doorway.

She had a vague notion of what they were doing —any child growing up on a farm will see animals coupling and need to have that explained, and if the child is lucky, there will be some kind of elaboration on how love can enhance that physical union for human beings. Thus it was with Flora, so when she saw the mysterious movements beneath the blankets and heard the loving tone of their voices and hushed laughter, she was not frightened or disturbed, but was able to return to her own bed feeling reassured about her world.

It occurred to Flora now that it might be a long time since her parents had made love. Every night Papa went to bed drunk, if not passed out entirely. And what of the changes in him? Beyond the childish behaviors, slurred speech, and unsteadiness, what of the way the wine was aging him: his eyes and nose were now mapped with tiny broken blood vessels, the once-fine lines of his face had slackened, and his belly protruded more and more over the restriction of his belt, as if a child were growing within him. If all this disturbed and saddened a daughter, what must it be like for a wife?

Flora thought it probably sickened Mama, and it must frighten her too. Men died from too much drinking; it could happen to Papa. Though Mama had never said a word about it, Flora knew her mother had never really been satisfied in America; she'd only come—and stayed—because she loved her husband so. Did she worry now what life would be like here without him . . . if drink were to take him or if she were to leave him? For a long time Flora had sensed the distance growing between her parents, but for the first time, she began to wonder if Mama might end the marriage. It was a frightening thought, and she realized—though her father was still a good and kind man and an excellent provider—he must do something about his drinking—and soon.

CHAPTER 3
SANTA CRUZ MOUNTAINS, CALIFORNIA — 1885

Dolce, the honey-colored mare, tossed her head and pulled at the bit, begging to run. Antone laughed and patted her neck but did not give in to her. "Are you as eager as I am to be home?" he asked. It had been a long nine days since he left Page Street, headed for the coast, but by tomorrow he would be home again, and he had good reason to feel elated. All his business matters had concluded well with very bright prospects for the future. The friendship between his family and that of Dante Fortunallo—whose Fortunallo Company was a considerable influence in the city of Monterey—had led to fruitful negotiations with some Greek glassmakers and the lumberman Sven Heglund on the San Lorenzo River. But beyond all that, he couldn't be more pleased with the new mare's performance. She'd taken well to the rough roads and mountainous terrain; her pace was quick but smooth to ride and sure-footed. She kept a watchful eye on all around her but wasn't given to spooking.

Not even when that peregrine falcon whooshed by them faster than any horse could run. Now, that had been a sight! He'd spotted such birds at other times, had heard their piercing, plaintive calls in the hills near the sea, had even seen one in its killing stoop plummet straight down the sky to snatch some hapless songbird for its supper. But never had he seen an aerial feat such as this. Topping a small ridge and enjoying the view below him, Antone had just noticed some birds off to his right, floating on an updraft of air. *Doves*, he thought. And then something streaked by him, larger than his head and fast as a bullet, straight toward those other birds. But what took Antone's breath was seeing the peregrine—as it shot beneath the birds—roll over on its back and strike a dove from below. Then it rolled upright and veered off, clutching its limp prey.

"*Dio!*" Antone whispered, watching it until it disappeared. A magical sight. But then, it was not the first on this trip. There was the usual magic of spring: the hills covered with lush green grasses and washed with bright fields of wildflowers. But at the edge of the Pacific over in Monterey, he'd seen his first glimpse of migrating whales: mottled grey backs that looked like mountains spouting steam as they rose from the sea. And he always felt in awe among the towering redwood trees, but this time, Sven—unable to convince Antone the legends were true—had taken him to find some white redwood, and he had learned it **was** true: some otherwise-normal trees **did** support living sprigs as white as any albino animal.

Magic surrounded him on this day, poised at the brink of vernal equinox, and he was filled with joy and hope, pride in what he had accomplished in his life and the longing for all that was yet to come. This was how he'd always imagined it would feel to be in love. Which, of course, he was, no matter how

23

he tried to deny it.

He'd done his best not to think of her. At times it was easier—when in spirited negotiations with the Greeks or drinking beer and swapping lies with Sven—but still it was as if she stood at the edge of his conscious thoughts, waiting to step in at the slightest invitation. And other times, when he was alone and lonely, it was impossible not to think of her. Huddled near his campfire in the mountains, he had pictured her lovely face and ripe body, which warmed him so much he had to throw off his blanket for awhile. In idle moments on the trail, he would think of her bold manner, the way it felt to have her eyes caressing him, that mysterious connection he had sensed as they stared into each other's eyes.

And every flower he saw made him think of her name. He uttered it now with a little groan: "Flora . . . " What was he to do? How could he hope to share his love with her? And marriage? Impossible! She was not Italian; she was not his kind. It would kill his parents. Mama had been close to death for years now; such an event was sure to push her over the edge, and then Papa—who wasn't well himself—would die of grief. All his life, Antone's parents had taken any opportunity to impress upon the boys how important it was to find good Italian wives, to marry their own kind. Yes, it was impossible.

But every time his thoughts got this far, some memory of her would overturn his logic and resolve, and his heart would cry out, *But what if this is the woman I've been hoping for—the one I am meant to spend my life with? Is there no way we can be together?*

Perhaps. For one thing, his parents wouldn't live forever. Antone did not think this coldly. They were very dear to him, but he had prepared himself for their passing, knowing that either of them could go at any time. Doctors hadn't thought Lucia Mellini would live to see 1880, much less '85, and the way Gian overworked his bad heart, it was a wonder he hadn't dropped dead long ago. Nothing Bruno or Antone said had ever made him ease up or take better care of himself; he was obsessed with making the farm and small vineyard profitable for his boys and with caring for his invalid wife.

And then there was Gregorio. Antone had only been five years old when his 12-year-old uncle—Papa's little brother—came to live with them. He remembered it was all very sudden and very mysterious; there was much whispering behind closed doors, and he got few satisfactory answers to questions he asked. He did know his Grandma Aguella had died and Baltassare Masuccio—the man she married after Papa's father died—had disappeared. At the time, and still today, Gregorio refused to speak about his stepfather and would leave the room if anyone ever spoke that name or talked about Aguella.

From the beginning, Antone feared the older boy. At first he had no reason and couldn't have said why, but that changed later, and Antone learned to keep as much distance as possible between them. Gregorio came to them bitter, cruel, and haunted-looking, full of suspicion and a rapacious desire to possess all he could, whether he needed it or not. And none of this ever changed, despite all the love and care the open-hearted Mellinis tried to give him. And as he grew older, he tried at every turn to usurp the leading role in the household. Bruno, only two years younger, was too easy-going to care about his status as elder son and rarely opposed his uncle; mostly he let Papa deal with Gregorio, though he would come to Antone's defense if needed.

For Antone seemed the focus of Gregorio's ill-will. The smartest and best-looking of the three and certainly well-liked in the community, he was more ambitious than his brother Bruno—he wanted to better himself and enjoy a more affluent life than his parents—but his personal integrity, his genial manner, and his honesty in business dealings set him far above Gregorio when it came to making deals and making money. And that made Gregorio hate Antone even more.

Returning now from such a successful business trip, Antone shifted in his saddle, easing his backside but not his mind. How would Gregorio respond when he heard the good news? He had opposed the idea from the beginning because it was Antone's, but Gian Mellini had seen the possibilities.

"We make good wine," Antone had said when he first made the proposal. "People like it and want to buy it, but the ten-gallon kegs are heavy and awkward, and many people can't afford to pay that much at one time. If we put the wine in smaller glass bottles, I think we could sell much more."

Thoughtfully, Papa Mellini stroked his chin, which rasped with heavy beard so late in the day. "How much smaller?"

"One liter, I think. Perfect for the table."

Papa nodded, but Gregorio snorted and said, "That's crazy! Bottles cost money and you have to get them here—without breaking—from . . . where? San Francisco?"

"Monterey," Antone answered. "On my last trip, I met these Greek brothers—twins—who make glass. They are truly gifted craftsmen—their product is much superior to what comes out of the glasshouses of San Francisco. Why, some of those bottles barely stand up properly! I trust the Lidakis brothers as businessmen, and they have a big freight wagon, so we might even be able to get them to deliver the bottles here themselves."

And it **had** worked out that way. In the contract he had just signed with the Lidakis brothers, they promised him a large initial shipment and then 100 bottles a month at a price that covered not only the bottles but safe delivery and was still cheaper than any San Francisco house had asked. Antone paid them cash for the first large order and another month in advance.

Riding home now, he could barely contain his excitement. In his mind, he saw bottles of Mellini wines on every table in Santa Clara County . . . and if that, why not in other counties . . . and beyond? And besides this family business, from which he would profit, the contacts he'd made in the redwood timber industry were pointing to some interesting new possibilities he could claim in his own right.

Best of all, the more prosperous he became, the more power he would have to decide his own future. And he'd need all the influence he could muster within his family if he had the faintest hope of courting Flora Bogdonovich.

Just thinking her name made his pulse quicken, and his eagerness must have communicated to the mare, for she pulled again at the bit. It had been nine long days since he'd seen that beautiful flower, Flora and he felt he couldn't bear to wait any longer than necessary to see her again, to find out if all he'd experienced was truth . . . or just some silly fantasy of an overactive mind and hot Latin blood. The thought of making another camp for the night and losing a whole night in sleep became suddenly unacceptable. He knew there'd be too little moonlight for traveling after dark, but Dolce seemed more than sound enough for a faster pace. Perhaps he could get much closer to home than he'd planned before making camp, and if he started out the next morning as soon as there was enough light, he'd be home well ahead of schedule. Perhaps he'd even see Flora as he rode into his yard, sitting tall on his fine new horse, the successful young businessman returning home.

He had to laugh at his own conceit and told himself, *Yes, she'd find you very attractive if she was close enough to see—and smell—the residue of your journey!* But still, the thought of seeing her again so soon was irresistible. They'd come down the last steep grade and the road stretching ahead looked invitingly easy to cover.

He leaned forward in the saddle, clapping his hand against Dolce's arched neck and asked, "What say you, my sweet one? Shall we get there a little sooner?" As if she understood him completely, the mare tossed her head and began to dance sideways, pulling as hard as she could on the reins. Antone laughed aloud and told her, "Very well, then, let's see how quickly **you'd** like to get home." He loosened his grip, trusting her to set her own pace.

Dolce leaped away with a burst of power that surprised Antone, but within a few strides, she settled into a gentle ground-eating lope that was a dream to ride. *Like rocking in a cradle,* Antone thought, and in his mind, he saw a vision, a little dream of the future. He saw Flora, beautiful as any Madonna in a gown of blue, gazing down into a wooden cradle as she rocked it. Antone couldn't see the babe sleeping within, but it made him wonder what a child born to the two of them would look like. Would the hair and skin and features resemble him . . . or her—or be some blending of the two? And could a child such as this help their families overcome their prejudices so that he and Flora might make a life together? In that moment, thinking of that child and of the future, Antone's heart felt sure that love could rise above all else, and filled with that hope, he smiled.

SANTA CLARA VALLEY—1885

When Dolce turned off Page Street into the Mellini yard that night, she was breathing heavily and her golden coat was flecked with lather, but she was nearly cooled out, because Antone had held her to a walk the last mile. He hadn't meant to come all the way home, but the mare was doing so well, he hated to stop and make camp.

In the last few hours, he'd come to realize he'd made a much better bargain than he'd even thought. Rarely had he heard of a horse that could cover such a distance with so little effort. She knew how to pace herself, and he had let her make the decisions about how fast to go for how long on which patches of road. And as the dusk deepened around them, he kept waiting for her to falter or let him know she was ready to call it a day. But that never happened with Dolce. She slowed her pace considerably, but she must have the night eyes of a cat, Antone decided, for she never misstepped on the trail, even though there was only a thin sliver of moon to light the way.

It was late and Antone was exhausted. He wanted nothing more than to get Dolce settled in the barn and to fall across his own bed, asleep before his head hit the pillow. He had no wish to even bother undressing or pulling off his boots.

But as he turned into the yard, he saw his brother Bruno emerge from the barn, a lantern swinging from his fingers.

"Antone, my brother! You're back early!"

"Yes," he answered tiredly, reining the mare to a halt in the yard. "What're you about at this hour?"

"The spotted cow just dropped her calf. A little bull calf to castrate and fatten for market."

Antone started to say "Good" but before he could get half the word out, Bruno had reached him. "What is the news? It is good?"

Antone, beginning to dismount, said proudly, "Better than that, it is wonderful news."

Bruno didn't even wait to hear specifics. He roared a sound of celebration and lifted his little brother—all six feet of him—and hugged him till the air whooshed out of Antone. "Let's tell Papa!" Bruno cried, sweeping his brother up into his arms like some girl needing to be carried over a mud puddle. "He's still awake, waiting for news of the calf. We have much to celebrate." He started toward the house, carrying Antone, who kept protesting, "Wait! Put me down! I need to put the horse away; I didn't even tie her."

"Just come tell Papa the news," Bruno insisted. "We'll have a drink to celebrate—then you can put your horse away. Don't worry. She won't go far, even if she does wander." There was no dissuading him, and Antone was much too weary to struggle, so he let his big brother carry him up the steps and into the house.

27

Dolce stood in the yard looking after them, and after a few moments, she shifted her feet restlessly. This was not the way the world worked. You did your work and then the one who cared for you took away the equipment and provided food and left you to sleep. There had been many new experiences in her last nine days, but she had come to trust that this new human knew the proper routines. He had, so far, been very aware of her comfort, and being left here tired, hungry, and thirsty was not what she had come to expect. More moments passed, and she began to move away, searching for some ease to her hunger and thirst.

One rein was still looped up over her neck, the left rein dragged along in the dirt; she moved carefully so that she didn't step on it and jerk her mouth. She was moving toward the edge of the road—where she could see a tangle of low, dusty grasses—when the breeze shifted and brought a fine green scent to her nostrils. She halted and turned to see what smelled so delicious. There, across the road, was a field of incredibly lush new grass, bursting with all the freshness of spring. It was irresistible.

Dolce headed for it, eager but still mindful of the trailing rein. She crossed the road and moved as close as she could to the wooden boards of the fence surrounding the field. She reached her head over as far as she could and snatched a huge mouthful of the precious green. It tore loose with a familiar, comforting sound, and as she chewed, she savored the taste and reached out for more. But before long, her teeth had taken all that grew within her range, so she had to reach farther. As she did so, she leaned her chest against the top fenceboard, using it to balance herself as she stretched farther and farther. Under the pressure, the board bowed . . . and creaked slightly . . . and then snapped with a sound like a muffled shot.

When the fence gave way, Dolce staggered forward, falling to her knees—cushioned by the deep grass—and then she picked herself right up and stepped over the undisturbed lower rail. Before her lay a chest-high sward of green grasses and her nose told her there was water in the trough against the far fence. The mare was thirsty, but she took her time getting to the water, stopping to munch great mouthfuls of the grass as she went. Paradise!

The snap of the fence brought Flora bolt upright out of a nightmare. She'd been dreaming that she was kissing Antone. But then some dark figure menaced him with a gun. And as she tried to warn him, a shot rang out—and Flora came awake, shaking and damp with sweat.

Thank God, it was only a dream. But there **had** been a sound, she felt sure. She held her breath and listened intently. Now she heard another sound, a rhythmic sort of soft ripping. She stared through her open bedroom door, across the parlor to the window on the north side of the house. Something was moving out there!

Flora flung back her covers and reached for the cotton robe across the foot of her bed. She padded barefoot from her room and across to the window, pushing aside the lace curtain to see better.

There! It moved again. A horse. It was too dark to distinguish its color, but she recognized the fine lines and grace of movement . . . Antone's horse! So he must be back at last. Her heart speeded up at this happy thought, but she was also spurred to action. There'd be hell to pay if a Mellini horse devastated the pasture they'd been saving for their own animals.

Without thinking much about what she was doing—still caught in the web of sleep and dreams—Flora slipped out the front door and made her way to the north yard. She soon came more fully awake. It might be spring, but the ground was still very cold and the tall grasses were wet with dew. As she moved across the field toward the horse, Flora pulled her clothing more tightly about her and shivered. The mare's rump was turned toward her as she approached, and she spoke to the animal so it wouldn't be startled.

"Hello there, pretty one." She spoke in English, as she often did with the chickens and other animals. The mare lifted her head from grazing and turned it to regard Flora with an unfrightened expression as she chewed. A long sheaf of grass dangled from one side of her mouth and was drawn steadily inward by the chewing motion.

"You're eating all our grass," Flora scolded, moving up beside the horse. "Your neighbors Dan and Bob and Ilka were to be turned in here tomorrow." She laid a hand on the still-sweaty shoulder. "What's this? You've traveled hard, haven't you? Didn't Antone take time to put you away? Or did you toss him off and come home on your own?" It was nonsense talk to soothe and reassure the horse as she took control of the reins and began to lead her back toward the road. But as she turned, she saw Antone standing there in the field, watching her. He must have come across Page Street shortly after she entered the field.

Suddenly aware of how improperly dressed she was: bare-legged with the dew-moistened cloth clinging to her body and her reddish hair tumbled loose around her shoulders, Flora crossed her arms across her chest to hide the way the chill made her nipples stand out. She felt her face flame red for the second time under Antone Mellini's gaze, but before she could decide on any action, he moved to meet her.

"I am sorry," he began in hesitant English. "My brother Bruno . . . rushed . . . me into the house before I could tie her." His voice was low, and Flora was glad her parents were heavy sleepers and that their bedroom was on the opposite side of the house. "I will repair the fence where she broke it." Antone stopped a few feet away from her, as if he were suddenly shy. Glancing down at his travel-stained clothing, he apologized, "I am not very . . . presentable, I think. I have been traveling many days and have not had time to bathe."

To prove she was not offended, Flora came closer to him, leading the mare. She caught his scent now, but it didn't bother her. She knew well the odors of sweat and body oils that gathered in the clothing of working men, but she also detected the woodsmoke sweetness of his campfires.

She shrugged and tried her own English. "Men work . . . men sweat . . . " She had intended to finish with "men bathe" but that conjured a sudden image of him waist-deep in a tub like her family's; it was a vivid picture of his bare brown skin wet and darkly furred and smelling of herb soap. Too vivid. She swallowed the last of her sentence and changed the subject. "She is a beautiful horse."

"Yes," he answered softly. "Beautiful." But he was not looking at the mare.

He never looked away from Flora, and she knew it was not only her face he was looking at. The darkness made it difficult to see expressions in his black eyes, but she could feel them touch her bare legs and the dampened gown stretched across her thigh and hip, and when she reached out to hand him the reins, she couldn't help revealing more of her bosom, which moved more than she wished with each quick breath. "What is her name?" Flora asked as she held out the reins.

"Dolce," he answered, reaching to take the leather straps. "It means . . . sweet."

"We would say *slatki* in my language," Flora told him.

When he started to take the reins from her, their hands touched, and the contact was electric. They both jumped—the reins fell to the ground, unnoticed—but neither drew back. On the contrary, when Flora made no move to break that contact, Antone took her hand in both of his, gazing deeply into her eyes for any sign of rejection. When he saw none, when he saw only his own feelings mirrored there, he raised the hand to his lips and kissed it, first on the back, then on the fingers, then he gently turned it over and kissed the palm.

Flora moved that palm, still cupped in his hands, so that it lay along his cheek, and with her thumb she gently traced the wonder of his full lower lip; how amazing that she had dreamed it so perfectly less than an hour ago. She had been dreaming that these lips were kissing her. Might that not happen now? As the thoughts moved through her, her tongue tip came out to moisten her own lips. That was when he drew her closer to him and closer to the house where they might be more sheltered from view. He drew her gently, giving her every opportunity to refuse him. Flora had no intention of doing that.

He did not pull her close against him, but leaned a little forward to taste her lips in a soft but unhasty kiss. As the kiss ended, Flora sighed as if some great question had been answered, and she moved fully into his embrace with her head resting beneath his chin. They held each other silently a long moment, both of them having found confirmation of all they had imagined and hoped was between them. Then Antone kissed her tumbled hair and whispered, "*Flora . . . bella, bella flora . . . .*"

She'd heard enough Italian words to know *bella* meant beautiful, and surely *flora* must still have something to do with flowers, but she really didn't care exactly what he was saying; she could hear all she needed to know in the huskiness of his voice. She pulled back enough to look up into his eyes. "Antone . . . "

Never had he heard his name pronounced with just that accent and in such a tone of love and longing. He kissed her upturned mouth, but less gently now, and her lips became as insistent as his own. She melted against him, and the firmness of her breasts and the warmth of her thighs pressed against him moved his body's responses more quickly than he could have imagined.

Flora felt herself lifted and carried on a tide of passion that was totally new and unexpected and entirely welcome. She drank in the scent of his maleness and did not resist when his hands cupped the sides of her breasts or when they slid around to her back and then slowly downward to her hips. Their kisses grew even more fervent, and Flora's hands wanted to do their own exploring. But in this she was still shy, and she kept them safely at his wide shoulders or above, caressing his hair where it curled at the nape of his neck. She felt his hands begin to move again, sliding lower down her hips and around to grip her buttocks, pulling her even tighter against him; she gasped against his mouth as she felt . . . something . . . hard between them, and then a voice called out like the voice of God.

Except it was in Italian: "Antone! Where the hell are you?!"

They sprang apart, panting and staring across the field toward the road and the Mellini house on the other side. "My uncle," Antone whispered, and Flora heard the touch of fear. "I must go before he comes looking."

Hastily they kissed again, a mere brushing of lips and a meeting of eyes which affirmed they both knew now for certain that they belonged to each other and to no one else. Then Flora shrank back against the house, and Antone hurried to grab up the mare's reins. Neglected and still untied, she'd moved several steps away as she continued her evening meal. He swung quickly into the saddle and rode across the field, past the piece of broken fence and out onto the road. "I'm here," he called to Gregorio in a low voice. "Don't wake the neighborhood. Bruno didn't let me tie the horse, and she was over devouring the Croats' pasture."

Gregorio snorted as if he only half-believed the story, but even in this dimness, one could see the proof of the broken fence, so he said nothing more. Antone rode past him, toward the barn. "I'll be in as soon as I've taken care of the horse." He didn't look back, even when he dismounted and led Dolce into the barn, but all the while, he felt Gregorio's hot, skeptical stare boring into his spine.

Panting, damp with dew and perspiration, Flora squeezed close against the house—crouching in the bushes below the parlor's bay window—until she was sure Gregorio's attention was all on Antone, back across the street. Then—mindful of her bare feet—she slipped to the rear of the house, between the rails of the fence, around the back to the kitchen door. She couldn't go back the way she'd come out; Gregorio was sure to see her if she went in the front door. But the kitchen door was unlocked, of course, and she knew just how to lift it so it wouldn't squeak. Once inside, with the door closed behind her again, she stole through the house, past her parents' open doorway (they were both snoring, blissfully unaware of Dolce's transgression—or hers) and into her own bedroom.

As she crawled into her bed, she found it had cooled while she was away. She pulled the covers over her head and huddled there in her damp clothes, shivering with delight. She thought once or twice of getting up and changing into something warm and dry, pulling some wooly socks onto the ice blocks that had once been her feet, but she didn't want to give up any part of the wondrous event she had just experienced. And lying all curled up with her head under the covers, she could still smell his aroma on her skin, blending with her own familiar scent as she remembered in vivid detail every word, gaze, and touch he'd given her tonight and all the wild feelings they had stirred in her.

It was a long time before she could get to sleep, and as she finally slipped away, she smiled and whispered, "Thank you, Dolce. You are the most wonderful horse in the world . . . ."

CHAPTER 4
SANTA CLARA VALLEY — 1885

Flora slept so deeply, even the crowing of roosters and the barking of the neighbors' dog did not awaken her the next morning. It was her mother shaking her by the shoulder that finally drew her from sleep.

"Wake up, Flora!" Mama's voice was very agitated. "That Mellini boy is here trying to tell your papa something. We need your English. Hurry up, get dressed!"

Antone! The thought jerked Flora fully awake, and she scrambled out of bed. Mama had left a pitcher of warm water and clean linens next to the rose-printed basin on Flora's dresser. She washed herself quickly and slipped on a clean dress. It was only an everyday workdress, but it was a pretty pale blue and it fit her well. What could Antone be trying to tell Papa? Surely not what they'd done last night! Her fingers flew as she deftly brushed her mane of auburn hair up into that familiar, demure bun and pinned it securely. She spared a moment for the briefest inspection of herself in the mirror to make sure she was presentable. Was it her imagination or did her face look somehow different—more womanly—this morning? Wasn't there a hint of something beyond her former innocence . . . something in the eyes? Had her lower lip always looked that full and lush?

"Flora!" Mama stood in her bedroom doorway. "Hurry, child—don't keep them waiting!"

Flora followed her mother out the front door and down the porch steps, around toward the north yard. Ahead of her, at the broken fence, she could see Papa and Antone standing, awkwardly avoiding each other's eyes in that way of people unable to communicate. They both looked toward her with relief when she arrived.

Her eyes met Antone's briefly, but she had to look away. She hoped her parents would think her quick breathing and sudden blush were the result of an awkward situation with a virtual stranger. She focused her full attention on Papa, who said with some exasperation, "At last you're here! I can't understand a thing this boy is saying...."

Flora half-turned toward Antone, but couldn't get her eyes to lift above the middle button of his brown shirt. She could see all his clothing was fresh and spotless, and she had noticed in that first quick glance that his face was scrubbed and his hair still damp, as if he'd just come from bathing. She pulled the correct English words into her mind. "How can we help you, Gospodin Mellini—ah, I mean . . . **Mr.**...Mellini?"

Antone was having some trouble himself. He hadn't anticipated having to meet with Flora like this so soon and under the careful eye of her father. But this **had** to be done. If only she didn't look so radiant this morning! It was the only time he'd been so close to her in the daylight, and it was all he could do to ignore her appeal—and put the images of their last contact out of his mind. He thought she was wise to avoid looking directly at him, but—unable to comfortably look at any part of her—he was forced to pin his eyes on a fencepost just beyond her shoulder to keep his thoughts undistracted by her beauty and her nearness.

He, too, struggled with his English. "Please tell your father I am very sorry." He paused, perhaps thinking of what else he might apologize for, then he dashed on. "My horse broke your fence and came into the field and ate much grass."

Flora remembered what Antone had told her last night, and turning to her father, she elaborated as she translated into Croatian. "He came home last night from a long trip and his brother rushed him into the house and didn't let him tie his horse. It wandered over here and broke the fence and got in and feasted on our grass."

Papa grunted his understanding. If he wondered why her explanation used more words than Antone's, he didn't question her. He trusted her.

Antone, too, was aware she'd given more details than he had. "Will your parents understand what we say in English?"

Flora swallowed, staring again at that shirt button. "No."

"Tell your father I will repair this fence today, if he will . . . allow . . . me to."

This Flora translated faithfully. Papa considered and then said, "Tell him yes, if he can do a careful, competent job."

"Papa says, thank you, he would appreciate that."

Antone nodded at Papa, who nodded back.

Riding high on the success of this encounter, Antone grew bolder. "Tell your father he has the most beautiful daughter in the world."

Startled speechless, Flora couldn't help looking up into those black eyes and saw them laughing at her now, though the lips remained solemn. "What did he say?" demanded Papa; he was standing closer to her than she remembered.

Flora dragged her eyes away. "He says he's fortunate to have such an agreeable neighbor." Papa seemed satisfied and ready to end the encounter, but Antone had more to say.

"Perhaps I should apologize now for some . . . disturbance . . . I may cause him in the next few weeks."

Whatever could he mean? Flora wondered. *He can't mean to tell Papa about . . . us . . .?* Since Antone was waiting for her to convey this part of the message before he continued, she went ahead with the translation, and she thought it wisest to say exactly what he was saying, since she had no idea what he was up to. When she finished, Papa looked as baffled and curious as she felt.

"We," Antone gestured to his house across the street, "will build a new barn. A **big** one. For making our wines better. Our business is becoming very successful." It was as if Antone were saying this part for her benefit, indicating his bright prospects for the future. "I fear there will be much noise and . . . wagon traffic . . . and dust."

When Papa had heard Flora translate this, he nodded. Ignoring the reference to the success of the Italians' business, he merely nodded to acknowledge the apology and explanation.

Antone could see Flora's father was ready to end the conversation, so he nodded back and said, "Thank you for your understanding. Good day." He looked then at Flora, who stood uneasily before him, her eyes still downcast, and her hands clenching each other at her waist. "Thank you for translating, Miss Bogdonovich. I hope you weren't too . . . inconvenienced . . . last night."

Flora's eyes leaped from his shirt button, up to his face and back again. *How can he do that?* she wondered. *How can he laugh at me with his eyes and never let it show on his lips?* Dare she be as bold in this conversation? She might have been speaking to that shirt button, for she managed not to look up at his eyes. If he was going to tease her, he must be prepared to be teased in return. "No inconvenience. I quite enjoyed . . . meeting . . . you." She could tell he was surprised at her response . . . her admission, and there was a tense moment as she sensed his sudden urge to take her in his arms and kiss her then and there.

But in the end, he only said, "Yes, perhaps we can . . . meet . . . again sometime . . . ?"

Before she could answer—could boldly suggest a time and place—her father interrupted impatiently, "What's he saying now?"

"He's bidding us a courteous farewell and says he hopes we were not overly inconvenienced." And then in English, "Good day, Mr. Mellini."

Antone knew his welcome had worn thin, and he had no wish to alienate this girl's father. "Good day." He turned and made his way back across to his side of the road.

Flora and her papa watched him go. A soft voice spoke up behind them. "He seems a nice, polite young man," Mama said. Flora had forgotten her mother was there all along, and she felt her heart lift at the favorable impression Antone had made.

"Yes, he does," Papa agreed after a moment of consideration. "Nice and polite . . . for a guinea."

Within the hour Antone was back, and he made quick work of the fence repair—replacing the broken board and painting it white to match the rest. Flora had hoped she might be able to talk to him again . . . perhaps take him a cool mug of cider? But Mama kept her busy with laundry, and by the time she was free to suggest the cider, Antone was already finished and gone.

As it turned out, two whole weeks passed before she could speak to him again. Just as the honey-colored mare had proved a friend in bringing them together, the new barn seemed an enemy bent on keeping them apart.

The men across the road worked at a furious pace on it. Before dawn, Flora would see their kerosene lanterns moving about as they organized their work for the day, and long after dusk had settled, she heard their saws and hammers. No laziness there. As she went about her own chores during the day, she often saw Antone at work. He seemed to be everywhere, involved in every aspect, pointing out directions to the others—though frequently his Uncle Gregorio appeared to dispute this, and there was more than one heated debate which needed Papa Mellini or Bruno—or both—to resolve. Antone seemed to work tirelessly, and it was always his lithe form she saw attending to the high work. He moved like a cat up on the framework for the loft and the beams of the peaked roof. She imagined at night he must fall totally exhausted into his bed and probably had no thought of her.

She was correct about the exhaustion. Antone was up every morning at four and spent each evening studying his drawings of the evolving structure and planning the next day's work. But when he fell each night into his bed at midnight—or even later—it was Flora who filled his thoughts in those few moments before sleep claimed him. He yearned to talk to her again, to hold her close and feel her heart racing like his own, but for the present, meeting with her was impossible. If he was to have a future with her, he must ensure the success of the family business, so the barn had to come first. All the dedicated work paid off. Thanks to a Saturday when many of their Italian friends pitched in, the barn was finished just two weeks later.

And just when Flora thought she'd never get close to Antone again, a pair of unusual gentlemen appeared and gave love a hand.

When Flora heard the knocking at the front door, she was back in the kitchen, baking bread. She wondered who it could be. Most of their family friends would come to the kitchen door. Papa, of course, was out among his trees, caring for their springtime needs; Mama had gone to tend her good friend Gospodja Tesla, who still suffered bouts of fever from the malaria she'd contracted crossing the Isthmus of Panama on her way to California.

Flora had just pulled two plump loaves of rye bread from the oven when someone's fist thundered on the front door. She quickly turned the loaves out on a cooling rack and wiped her hands on her apron as she hurried toward the continuing noise.

Opening the door, Flora was at first alarmed at the sight she beheld: two stocky, round-faced foreigners, almost identical in appearance. They stared at her with their mouths dropping open—as if they were not only surprised to see her, but awestruck as well—and then they gazed at each other wordlessly. Who could these fellows be? Flora wondered. And what were they doing here?

It was not until one of them spoke that the initial alarm left Flora. The one on the left said, "Hey, me Demetri. And here," he pointed to the likeness beside him, "me brother Theodore. We here to see Antone—deliver bottles to hold the wine." He gestured behind him toward the road, and looking past him, Flora saw a large freight wagon standing in front of her gate. The team of horses looked very travel-weary, as if they'd come a long way.

Flora relaxed and smiled at the men—which caused them to duck their heads shyly and then glance at each other again. Flora guessed they were in their early twenties and their accent was not any she recognized. It had an Italian lilt to it, but they didn't look Italian at all to her. At first she'd thought they were bald, but she could see now their blond hair was just cropped very close to their heads—as if they couldn't spare time for unnecessary personal grooming—and judging from the irregularity of the cuts, it looked as if they probably barbered each other.

"Oh, I see," she said in English. "But you have the wrong house." She started to point out the Mellini house, and as she looked that way, she saw Antone coming from across the road toward them. His long strides and wide, white grin were eager and happy as his eyes moved from Flora to Theodore and Demetri and back to Flora again.

The brothers turned to follow Flora's gaze and when they saw Antone, they leaped down from the porch into the yard, and pandemonium erupted. At the same moment, all three men started waving their arms and yelling, though they were barely five paces apart, "*Buon giorno, amico mio!*"

They appeared to have forgotten Flora entirely, and like a child at a dog-and-pony show, she watched in delight what must be a familiar ritual for the three. Each brother took turns gathering Antone into a bearlike hug which lifted him totally off the ground. Antone, in turn, patted the tops of their shorn heads and laughed loudly the entire time he wasn't having the breath squeezed out of him.

At the end of this bizarre, but beautifully comic display, they once again became aware of Flora. As Theo set him on his feet the final time, Antone suddenly blushed, sensing Flora's gaze on him in this undignified situation. But when he looked toward her, she was smiling happily as a child at a fair. As if drawn by a magnet, he left his companions and went up onto the porch closer to Flora. How could he have forgotten how good she looked? The pale brown of her dress made the color of her eyes seem even deeper, and since—for once—she wasn't blushing, he could appreciate the true creamy tones of her skin and discover a hint of apricot in her coloring.

He thought, *She must have been baking bread.* She had the look of one who'd been working in a hot kitchen: the top two buttons of her dress were undone, her sleeves were rolled up, and her russet hair was doing its best to escape the pins and curl around her face. There were traces of flour on her dress and around her wrists where they'd pushed into the dough as it was kneaded, and the smell of baking was all about her. The sight and odor made him remember the wonderful days when his mama was well and happy and loved no household task more than baking bread. This girl did not look the same or smell the same—the scent of some unfamiliar spice permeated the aroma of freshly baked yeast bread—but it was enough to bring a lump to his throat.

She was staring at him, waiting. He had to say **something**. "I see you have met my Greek friends Demetri and Theo Lidakis...?"

If they were Greek why were they speaking Italian? "Yes." Flora could hardly believe it was true, but here, indeed, was Antone—on her porch in broad daylight, and with a good excuse. It was such a temptation to have him so close. How she longed to take his hand in hers and hold it, but that would be much too dangerous. Even with Mama half a mile away and Papa out among the trees, it was not safe for any public display of affection—or even friendship with an Italian boy. Who could tell who might ride by and see them? And Vlach Stanich often sat in the window so he could keep an eye on everyone's business as he drank his daily wine.

For the long moments that Flora and Antone stared at each other and resisted reaching out to touch, the Greek brothers studied them with interest and then looked again to each other and after a silent communication, nodded and smiled their agreement. It was plain to anyone with eyes that these two were deeply in love, and who knows how long the couple would have stood staring at each other had not the twins' amusement turned to chuckling.

The sound brought the two back into the moment, and Antone glanced at them and announced in English, "My friends, this is Bella Flora." She blushed at having Antone address her so in front of others—especially strangers. But then Flora had the most peculiar feeling these Greeks would not be strangers for long. The men came up onto the porch, and as each took her hand and bowed over it in what Mama would call "old world courtesy," Antone continued his introduction. "She is my neighbor. I live..." he pointed "across the road."

The Greeks looked where he indicated and then at each other, obviously embarrassed at their mistake. Flora, noticing their discomfort, reached out to first one, then the other, gripping a hand and looking squarely in the eyes of each. "It is all right, Demetri. It is all right, Theo. I enjoyed watching you and Antone greet one another. I see that you are friends." This direct, but warm, response put the Greeks back at ease, and those boyish smiles crossed their faces once again—smiles that seemed not only similar, but identical.

Demetri rose to the social occasion and told Flora, "Theo and I first meet Antone a few months ago—in Monterey, where we live."

Theo, obviously the shyer of the two, spoke up as if he worried his brother would get all Flora's notice. "Hey, you know Monterey? Pacific Ocean?"

"No," Flora told him with a sad shake of her head. "I've never seen Monterey or the ocean. I've never been out of the valley."

Theo beamed. "Then you come visit us!"

"Yes, yes!" Demetri agreed, but he was intent on regaining Flora's attention. "Antone is smart one. He sees our glass is best—wants our bottles for his wine. Orders whole wagonload!"

As he watched the twins vying in conversation, Antone chided himself for feeling left out, but before he could stop himself, he was speaking too: "Yes, these fellows make the finest California glass I have seen. And, my friends, you are so...efficient...you are two days early! Our barn is barely ready, but already the Mellinis have their bottles!"

Now the twins really beamed, proud of their skill and reliability—and to have these qualities recognized by someone whose opinion mattered to them.

"Bottles for wine?" Flora asked curiously. When Antone explained briefly his idea of people buying more wine in smaller containers suitable for the table, Flora got very excited. "My papa makes wonderful plum wine. Perhaps he would be interested in such bottles too."

Hearing this, Theo immediately leaped down off the porch and ran to the wagon. He lifted the tarp and rummaged in one of the wooden crates, pushing aside the straw packing until he could grab the neck of a bottle and haul it out. He held it high, like a trophy, and then rushed back up onto the porch. He started to hand it to Flora but paused—at which moment Demetri also grasped the bottle so he could share in the presentation—and looked at Antone, asking, "You do not mind, do you, my friend, if your first bottle goes to your Bella Flora?"

Antone smiled warmly at the twins. "No, no," he assured them. "It is fitting she have our first bottle. It will be a symbol of a new beginning." But he, too, took hold of the glass container. After all, wasn't it **his** to give to her?

A little embarrassed by all the attention and having near-strangers casually refer to her as **Antone's** Bella Flora—in public—Flora reached out to receive the gift. But as she touched the cool glass, time seemed to stop for a moment, and the four of them stood transfixed, the bottle held by four pairs of hands, four pairs of eyes. It was beautifully crafted of pale green glass, rather squat in shape with rounded shoulders and an elongated neck stoppered with a cork. A simple, utilitarian item, but somehow much more.

And in that breathless moment—though none of them could ever explain what happened or why they felt such certainty—these four young people from three very distinct cultures felt the forging of a lifelong bond and knew that they were forever linked in some mysterious fashion. They exchanged glances, each affirming that the others felt it just as strongly, and then the bottle's full weight sank into Flora's hands, the men relinquished it, and the moment was past.

41

But then, to Flora's great amazement, Theo grabbed her by the shoulders and kissed each cheek. Then it was Demetri's turn. Antone kept his distance and Flora thought that wise. They were all laughing now and no one had to talk about what had happened or try to figure it out.

"Hey, me hungry," Demetri said suddenly. "Let's go your house, Antone. Feed horses. Feed us." Everyone laughed again. "Hey, we brought *oúzo.*"

Antone clapped Demetri on the shoulder. "Sorry. I am a better winemaker than a host."

The Greek returned the gesture and joked, "I hope so!"

In turn, the brothers took Flora's hand again and bowed over it as they said their good-byes. Teasing them a bit, she dropped into a curtsy. But when Antone decided it was safe to try the same ritual and took her hand, bowing as the others had, it did not feel the same. She squeezed his hand, wishing there was a way to arrange another meeting—seeing the same wish mirrored in his eyes—but they must still protect their secret, even from Antone's friends—her friends. So with great reluctance, she released his hand, and he turned to his Greek friends, putting an arm around each, and asked, "When you lived in Napoli, did you ever eat cold *polenta* toasted on the grill? Papa's is *squisito!*"

Antone forced himself to act as if he had forgotten Flora standing on her porch, watching them go down the walk and out the front gate. Theo swung up on the wagon seat and stirred the horses into motion. Antone and Demetri walked together toward the barn with Theo maneuvering the wagon behind them.

But they'd only gone a few steps into the Mellini yard when Demetri slapped Antone across the back and asked in his more fluent Italian, "My friend, why did you not embrace your Bella Flora before leaving? A creature as lovely as that deserves more than a handshake." Antone stopped short, looking embarrassed and a little apprehensive.

Sensing some intrigue, Theo hopped down from the wagon seat and joined his brother. Any sign of merriment had vanished from Antone, and he spoke gravely, in a low voice that would not carry far from their ears. "My friends, I must trust you. I am not able to speak with my family about the way I feel."

The brothers looked alarmed; they had never seen Antone this somber, and they couldn't guess why. "Yes," Antone continued, "she is my beautiful flower, and I love her so much that I can think of little else, but we must keep it secret. I have no one here I can talk to about my feelings."

Looking puzzled, Demetri asked, "Why secret?"

Antone sighed deeply, from the center of his sad heart. "She is not my kind—Italian—and if my family finds out, they will make me choose between her and them. That I could not bear."

The twins nodded. They knew the strong ties of all the ethnic groups transplanted in America—the drive to maintain cultural identity. But they themselves had experience in four nations and with many ethnic groups in America. They did not see the problem as insurmountable. "Some things just take time," Demetri said consolingly. "You could get your family used to the idea slowly...."

"Perhaps," Antone said miserably. "But I burn for her now, and I have no way to meet with her . . . spend time with her . . . get to know her better." He was flooded with the sensations of the passion they had shared that night in the field, the feel of her eager body as he'd pulled her tight against him just before Gregorio interrupted them. A small groan escaped him at the memory.

The Greeks' expressions now changed as they both smiled at Antone. Each put a hand on one of Antone's shoulders. Gently, Demetri asked, "Antone, are we the only ones who know the way you feel?"

"Yes." Antone's voice was very soft, almost too quiet to hear.

Theo probed further, "And what about Flora?"

"Yes, she must know how I feel, and I **think** she feels the same for me, though we have never spoken the words."

At this, the two Greeks broke into laughter, unable to contain their amusement in finding their friend so smitten—and their sense of hope that all would work out well. They could see this angered Antone, that he must think they were laughing at him. Still with hands on his shoulders, they patted him gently. Demetri's voice was full of love for his friend. "Dear Antone, your secret is safe with us, but you might want to let your Bella Flora know before too long. She is so lovely, why do you hesitate to tell her?"

The twins' lightheartedness had lifted Antone's spirits. He shrugged and countered with his own question: "Is love always so frightening?"

"Like jumping off a cliff," Theo said with a grin.

"Like rushing into a burning building," the smiling Demetri offered.

Antone had to laugh. "You, my friends, are a great comfort to me...."

They all laughed then and headed for the barn, leading the team that pulled the freight wagon full of new bottles for a new beginning.

"Hey, now," Antone said, still in a low voice. "You both must promise to keep my secret—at least until it's time to tell. What do you say?"

They teased him a moment, pretending they wouldn't make the pledge, but then they both—in unison and without any cue—said, "I promise!" as they laughed and slapped him on the back. Grinning with new hope, Antone reached for each of their near-bald heads and rubbed them, as if making a wish.

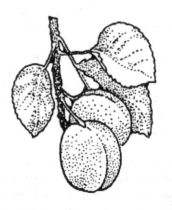

CHAPTER 5
SANTA CLARA VALLEY — 1885

It was the Monday after Easter, but there was still a riot of huge lavender irises blooming along the front fence, and Flora decided to pick a mass of them to brighten the kitchen and chase the chill of this foggy morning. From the corner of her eye, she could watch the activity over in the Mellini yard, though the fog made it difficult to see very far.

The Greek brothers, who had stayed the whole weekend with Antone's family, were hitching up their team to the freight wagon, which now held only crates of packing straw. All the precious bottles had been unloaded into the new barn designed for winemaking. All except one.

Flora had shown the bottle to Papa the very day it was given to her. She told him about how the Mellinis were going to bottle their wine and sell it for the table and that the very nice men who made the bottles would be glad to supply Luka Bogdonovich as well. Papa held the bottle a long time, scrutinizing it against the light, as if looking for any possible flaws. He found none, but still he rolled the bottle in his hands and didn't speak. Flora grew impatient. "It's a good idea, isn't it, Papa? Smaller amounts in smaller containers at a smaller price?"

He didn't answer immediately, but held the pale green glass up to the light and studied it yet another time. "It's a good idea," he conceded at last. "But so small? Why, everyone would have to have his **own** bottle, so what's the point?"

Flora wanted to say *Not everyone drinks as much as you and your friends,* but instead, she pointed out, "Some people might like that. Maybe one person wants grape wine and another your plum wine. Or maybe they'll try a small bottle of your plum wine and find how good it is and want a whole keg."

"Well, I'll think about it," Papa said at last to end the discussion, and he gave the bottle back to her. "Here, you keep this somewhere safe. It might get broken in the cellar."

Thinking he probably didn't want it in his cellar because it would be a constant reminder of the decision he was avoiding, Flora wondered if he found the thought of change too threatening. She'd always seen him as eager to learn anything that would improve business, more than willing to try new equipment and methods. Perhaps his reluctance in this instance had more to do with a feeling he might be seen as "copying" the Italians or "riding their coattails" as some might say. Naturally he would resist that. But would he continue even if it meant losing a considerable income? That was yet to be seen.

In the yard, watching the Greeks prepare to leave, Flora knew she must let her father come to his own decision. It was **his** wine. His hobby.

She had not yet seen Antone across the road; certainly he would show up to bid his friends farewell? Flora lingered, hoping for even a brief glimpse, but when he did finally come into view, her heart sank. He was leading Dolce and both of them were outfitted for travel. Theo climbed up on the wagon seat and picked up the reins. Antone swung gracefully atop his mare and turned to make sure the flaps of his saddlebags were secured. Flora squinted to see better against the fog. **Now** where was he off to? And for how long?

With a start, Flora realized Demetri was coming across the road toward her, carrying something in his hands. He came right up to the gate, grinning broadly. "Hey, we go now."

"It was very nice to meet you," Flora said sincerely as she approached the gate on her side. "Would you like some irises? I cut more than I need."

"Que bella floras," he said, and she knew he was teasing her, but it seemed harmless enough. There was no one near enough to overhear them. "Ah, thank you," he continued in unsteady English, "but no. They die before we are home. But look, I have a thing for you." Curious, she shifted the irises in her arms and reached for what he offered. "Antone wants you have one this color too."

Flora saw the gift was another bottle, exactly like the first only formed of a rich amber-colored glass. "Well, thank you, but we have the one, and Papa hasn't decided yet if he wants to try bottles or not." She was trying to hand the bottle back to Demetri, but he kept pushing it into her hands, insisting, "**Antone** wants you have it," and he turned the bottle on its side a little so that she could see that there—between the lip of the bottle and the cork—was a scrap of white paper.

"Oh!" Flora said. A note from A*ntone?*

Demetri began to speak quickly and quietly, yet with an intensity which urged her close attention. "Our friend Antone also travels now. To Sacramento with papers for new business. He will be . . . gone . . . a whole week."

Flora could hardly believe what was happening. This new friend was giving her messages from Antone! She hoped her eyes and voice conveyed how truly grateful she was in her simple "Thank you, Demetri." His face opened in that wonderful smile, as if he was pleased she could distinguish him from his brother—which was not yet the case. She merely assumed if one twin was talking, it would be Demetri.

"We go now," the Greek said. "See you next time . . . or if you come to Monterey . . . ?"

"Perhaps," Flora said to the question in his voice. "Someday."

An impish expression flickered across his face. "Maybe you come with Antone?"

What does he know? she wondered desperately. *Has he guessed . . . or did Antone tell him—and if so, **what** did he tell?* Surely he wasn't the kind of man to brag to his friends about how willing she'd been in his arms? She knew she was blushing, and she looked shyly away from Demetri's scrutiny, unsure what to say.

But the young Greek took pity on her. He reached up to pat her hand, and both his touch and voice were very gentle and reassuring. "No worry, friend. It will . . . how you say?…work out…."

Voices called from across the street, and Demetri quickly took his leave with a little bow and hurried over to swing up beside Theo on the seat of the freight wagon. There were boisterous good-byes. Flora could see Bruno and Papa Mellini joining in, shaking hands one more time with the Greeks and slapping Antone's saddlebags for luck. And there was Gregorio, hanging back on the porch, leaning against one post with his arms folded across his chest, silent and sullen-looking.

Then they were all on their way, and as they turned in the street, the Greeks' wagon went to the south and Antone on Dolce went in the opposite direction. If he looked her way, she couldn't tell. It was like so many times in the past when the two of them had ignored the comings and goings of the family across Page Street, because those neighbors were of another culture and their lives held no meaning on this side of the street. But all that had changed . . . and in her hands she held a secret message from the man she loved.

Flora started to turn the bottle so she could better see the note, but a familiar voice—speaking in Croatian—made her freeze like a startled doe. "Who was **that**?"

Glancing down from the porch, Flora saw Mattiza Stanich standing nearby with a paper-wrapped parcel in his hands, gazing after the wagon as it disappeared into the fog.

"Some Greek glass blowers from Monterey," Flora answered. "The Mellinis are going to start selling their wine in bottles. Papa may too, and Demetri . . . Gospodin Lidakis . . . was leaving another sample." She hoped she'd made the whole matter sound businesslike and matter-of-fact.

Mattiza's gaze turned to her; his grey eyes were wide and observant, and he knew her better than anyone . . . even her parents. He always seemed to have an uncanny kind of intuition about her and what she was feeling. If anyone could see through her, it would be this neighbor boy, her childhood friend. If he guessed her secrecy, he didn't say so. He regarded her a long moment and then changed the subject, hefting the package he held, "I brought the pork for your mama."

The Staniches made their living as pig farmers. They had some fruit trees and a small garden, but their income came from selling pork or pigs on the hoof, and all the work of the farm fell on Mattiza, for these days his father's drinking—and the constant related illnesses and injuries—kept him from any significant contribution.

"Oh, good. I know Mama was looking forward to some fresh pork. I'll take that, and you can go down in the cellar and get a keg." Neither of them felt very pleased that their fathers' trade was pork-for-wine—there were so many things the Stanich household needed more, and his father's drunkenness put Mattiza more at risk for beatings—but it was their fathers' decision to make, and Vlach Stanich still controlled his household, no matter who did the work.

Flora tried to take the parcel from him, but her arms and hands were crowded with cut irises and the amber bottle with its precious cargo. Mattiza said, "No, no, let **me** help **you**" as he reached to relieve her of the bottle. But she moved deftly, dumping the irises into his arms and slipping the package out of his hands while hanging onto the bottle. "There," she said brightly. "Thanks for your help."

Looking a little bewildered at what he'd ended up carrying, Mattiza came up onto the porch and followed her through the door into the parlor. Flora's bedroom was to the right, and she ducked in there to leave the amber bottle beside the green one on her dresser, calling over her shoulder, "Papa's having **me** take care of the bottles so they don't get broken."

Trying not to agonize about having to leave Antone's note unread and vulnerable to discovery, she gave Mattiza a big smile as she rejoined him and led the way back to the kitchen.

There they found Mama at the table, polishing her precious silver lamps. Flora's heart sank a little in her at the sight. This was a task her mother always chose when she was feeling especially homesick for Dubrovnik, and at those times, she preferred to be alone. But Flora tried a cheery smile and said, "Look, Mama—Matty has brought the pork."

The boy nodded to Flora's mother—he'd been around this family long enough to know what tending those lamps meant too—and crossed quickly to the sink counter, where he deposited the irises. He headed straight for the door, saying, "I'll just get Papa's keg and be on my way...."

Mama didn't respond at all, so Flora called after him, "Thanks again. Good-bye!"

Fretting to get to Antone's note, she hurried to put the irises in water. Mama spoke behind her: "What are you doing right now?"

"I'm putting these beautiful irises in vases to chase away the fog."

"Ah, well, why don't you leave that for now. Just put them in a pail and finish them later. Then what are your plans?"

Flora could think of little beyond the mysterious note waiting for her in the neck of an amber bottle. What excuse could she give for spending some time in that end of the house? "I thought I'd tidy the parlor a bit."

"I did that when I gathered the lamps. But I could use some stovewood and kindling." She looked then at her daughter, and her face softened. "You know sometimes I like to be alone, *janje.*"

"Yes, Mama, I know." After using the hand-pump at the sink to fill a bucket, she recut the iris stems before sticking them into the water. Then she went to the coat rack by the back door, donned one of the jackets hanging there, and tied a scarf around her head and neck. She knew it wasn't necessary to say anything more to her mother, so she went out into the yard and over to where the axe stood ready with its blade sunk into the chopping block. Nearby a treetrunk had been cut into a tumble of chunks still too large for the kitchen woodstove.

A sudden frenzied barking greeted her, and she said sternly, "Hush, Vučak!" But the Staniches' big black brute of a dog—who had known her all his life—only continued to bark. It was a maddening sound, but no one got close to Stanich property without hearing from Vučak, who suited well his name meaning "wolf." Unfortunately, their barn was near the Stanich property line, and it was almost impossible to go anywhere near it without having Vučak alert the whole neighborhood. Flora gritted her teeth now against the sound— knowing only two people could make the dog quit—and was relieved when Mattiza shouted from the window of his house and the dog fell silent.

Shivering a bit as the chill seeped through the layers of her clothing, Flora gathered several of the pieces of treetrunk and dumped them by the chopping block. Expertly, she worked the axe blade free, set the first section on the block and split it with one exact stroke. Four strokes later, she felt her muscles settle into the task for the day, but her mind was full of only one thing: what was in that note and when would she get to read it?

Philomena Bogdonovich cleaned and polished each lamp as tenderly as if she were caring for a child. How well she remembered the day her own papa brought them home, a gift to his wife—Philomena's mother Neda—to celebrate their imminent departure for America. Philomena herself was twenty years old and had been married to Luka barely a year. She was the only one who didn't really want to go to America. She loved her beautiful home in Dubrovnik and was satisfied to live her whole life there. But her parents thought they would be happier elsewhere—they were weary of the political, religious, and ethnic stresses in that port city which had seen its fill of history—and her Luka was a daring would-be adventurer who complained to her frequently, "I'm a quarter of a century old, and I've never been farther away from home than the island of Hvar!"

What could she do? Everyone had heard of the beauty and wonder and riches to be found in America. Her parents were going, that was certain, and if she said "no" and stayed behind, she would be separated from them; and if she made Luka stay, how could he help being resentful? She could see herself spending the rest of her life married to a bitter old man who turned more and more to the pleasures of drink.

So she hid her true feelings and said "yes"; plans were made, packing began; they started to gather a few treasures—not only household items and heirlooms but also iris bulbs and other seeds—to take with them to the new world so they would not forget their roots in Dalmatia. When Papa brought home the lamps, he expected his Neda to go ahead and use them, but she refused, saying they could wait until she was in her new home in a new life in a new land.

Then in the excitement of the last days before their departure, a stroke ravaged Neda's body, leaving her paralyzed on the left side and unable to make the journey. Philomena wanted to stay behind and help her parents, but they insisted she go. "Your passage is already paid," her father pointed out. "You don't want to lose all that money. And you don't want to disappoint your husband. He wishes to give you a better life than you would have here."

"Go, *janje*," said her mother. "And you must take these lamps with you so part of me goes to America as I have always dreamed."

What else could she do but go and make her parents happy . . . make her husband happy? It was not until after she arrived in America that she learned of her parents' deaths. Her mother died first, following another stroke. Three weeks later, her father—alone and separated from all his loved ones—succumbed to his grief.

She had hoped she would come to love her new home as much as her old, but that had not happened. California was beautiful in its own way, and the weather agreeable enough, but she missed the blue Adriatic and everyone speaking her own language. She wanted to dance the *kolo* and join family and friends in the evening stroll through the city, talking together until the whole city hummed like a hive of bees and this *korzo* ended when dusk turned to night.

It was not that life in America had been bad, but she shared some of Luka's disappointment. He had a good farm which fed them well, but he had promised her more: vast orchards and plentiful livestock, a large home full of rich furnishings, many children, perhaps servants so they could have more leisure time together.

She didn't fault him that he had not fulfilled the promise; he had always done his best in the early days. It was just harder here than they had expected. And what did they have? Ten acres of orchard, three animals besides the chickens, and a four-room house across the street from Italians.

And they had Flora. Cvijetanka, they would have named her back in Dubrovnik. But here they gave her the American form: Flora. She was the flower of Philomena's life. She had been worth the wait . . . not that either she or Luka minded the trying.... But they had worried a child would never come . . . and there were the two small graves at the far side of the orchard, overlooking the creek....

Philomena sighed as she filled the last of the lamps with kerosene. It was not the life she'd thought she would have when she married the handsome Luka Bogdonovich. But it had been, all-in-all, a good life—until the last few years when the pain of those unfulfilled dreams pushed him further and further into his cellar.

Staring at the six gleaming lamps, Philomena wondered, *What am I to do?* She carried the lamps—one by one, for they were heavy and she would take no risk of dropping them—back to their usual resting places. First the four to the parlor, then one to the bedroom she shared with her husband and his snoring. The last lamp she carried to the room of her dear Flora, setting it carefully on the table beside the bed, beneath the sketch of apricot trees. It was the last sketch Philomena ever did, finished the day before her daughter was born. She leaned down to smooth Flora's bedspread, crocheted by Mama Neda when she was first married. It was an understated cream color and much plainer-looking than most of the decorative covers in the house, but closer inspection revealed a wealth of subtle detail in the stitchery itself.

Flora's mother straightened up and gazed about the room, pleased with its tidiness and warmth. Her daughter would make a good wife, a good homemaker, a good mother. It was imperative that she find a suitable husband to support and cherish her. Someone like that young Karsten Tipanov—if only he didn't have that witch of a mother! But somewhere inside herself, Philomena felt convinced Flora would find the right man to love, and she was filled with the hope that her daughter would have a life even happier than her own. She would do everything within her power to make it so.

As always when Philomena thought of her daughter's future, she felt cheered, able to slip free from her earlier melancholy thoughts like a snake shedding its skin. That's why she always left Flora's lamp to the last.

Philomena's eyes came to rest on the two bottles on Flora's dresser. The green one she remembered clearly, but the amber took her by surprise. She started toward the dresser to inspect it more closely. Now, where had **that** come from? Flora hadn't mentioned it when she came in with Mattiza. "Oh!" she said aloud—and halted midstep with her hand reaching for the bottle—remembering that she had wanted to be alone and had sent the girl away to cut firewood. A glance at the window showed the day was even foggier and colder than before. Why, Flora must be freezing out there! She was always too ready to inconvenience herself for her mother's comfort and privacy.

The amber bottle was forgotten, and Philomena hurried back to the kitchen door, opening it to call, "Flora! Come in, child!" She saw her daughter had cut quite a lot of wood, and apparently Mattiza had returned, because he was helping stack the lengths in the woodshed, "Come in, both of you, and have something warm to drink!"

Mattiza was just finishing, but he declined and said he had to get the pigs in because he thought it was going to rain that night. Flora carried in a sizable store of kindling and was glad that even when her mother drifted in memories, she remembered to stoke the fire, "M-m-m," Flora commented. "It's toasty in here." She stripped off the now-damp jacket and scarf and pressed nearer the stove to warm herself. There was a big pot of *pileća čorba*—a savory chicken stew—simmering on the cast iron surface, and when Flora wondered how long it would be till supper, she realized she'd never stopped for a midday meal.

Philomena said guiltily, "I'm sorry you were out so long. It would have been all right for you to come in."

"Oh, it didn't bother me," Flora answered truthfully. "As long as I was working, I was perfectly warm. It's when you stop that you start to feel the cold coming through—especially if you're sweating." Though she was trying to reassure her mother, she couldn't help shivering again.

Her mama reached high up in the cupboard—above and behind the remaining bottles of fruit from last year's crop—and removed a small bottle of brandy. This she brought down rarely and only to share with Luka when toasting very special occasions, such as birthdays, record crops, and additions to their orchard property.

Mama worked the cork from the bottle, poured some of its contents into a tin and placed it on the stove. When she had replaced the cork and carefully put the brandy bottle back where it belonged, she brought two of her wedding cups from the glass cabinet Papa had made for her when they purchased the house. Setting the cups on the table, Mama looked right at Flora and said, "Sit."

Flora had warmed a bit standing next to the stove—at least on the outside—though her hands and feet were still uncomfortably cold, but she moved to the table and obediently sat. She had never tasted brandy before, though she had been allowed modest amounts of wine on various social occasions. (And as a child, she'd been given tiny sips of Papa's plum wine. He'd laugh with joy at the expression she would make from the taste, which she both liked and didn't. Then he would pour himself a large cup and drink it in one gulp.) Mama retrieved the now-sizzling tin from the stove and divided its contents equally into the two cups. She then sat next to Flora, lifted her glass as if toasting Flora, and said, "Drink."

The brandy barely filled the bottom of the cup. Flora brought it to her lips. The heady aroma penetrated her nostrils, and the sweet, strong taste warmed her inside as it slid down her throat. She could instantly feel her cheeks flush. Her hands and feet warmed as the sensation passed throughout her body. She liked the brandy and the effect it had on her. Flora looked at her mother, who had been staring at her the whole time.

"My dearest Flora," she said with wonder and pride in her voice. "You are a beautiful woman. No longer a child, and soon to be in need of a companion."

Flora felt a little intoxicated and suddenly very happy, listening to her mother; perhaps this was a good omen, though she was not silly enough to dare mention Antone yet. She thought it was probably wiser to say nothing at all until she could see where all this was going.

"You know, Flora," Mama continued, "I love your Papa very much. When we were young and so full of dreams, he would say the sweetest things to me. He called me his soul, his life, and loved to sit for hours and let me sketch him. He brought me flowers—wild irises from the hills near the city. Often we would climb above the city and sit together overlooking the Adriatic, the most beautiful sea in the world. Below us was the town of Dubrovnik—all those white marble buildings with their pink tiled roofs. Covered with roses. So pretty— and safe-looking with the old medieval fortress walls and towers and all the churches. I do miss my home."

She had been staring into space, seeing that old place and time, but now she focused again on Flora. "I was content there, but your papa was a dreamer, as was my own. I remember them talking of not providing enough for their families, but we were never in need. This was just a mask covering their true desires. The dream of the new world, they said, was for us—the women. So unselfish they did seem, they convinced my mama and got her so excited, she died for that dream. But I always knew it was not so unselfish. Your papa longed to journey to a new world. I went along because I loved him and would have gone anywhere with him. And because my parents wanted me to have a better life than they did."

Philomena looked down into her empty cup and told her daughter, "I had my own dreams. Simpler dreams. I wanted nothing more than to live my life there and raise my children as I had been raised. And then I dreamed that maybe I could make my own Dubrovnik in America and still raise my children in the old ways, keep all our own customs so we would never forget who we are and where we came from."

Flora had never heard her mother speak like this before. Some of it she had guessed or figured out on her own, but never had Mama spoken of it. Continuing, her mother said, "The first years after arriving in America were filled with newness and excitement and hard work to get to California and get our farm started, and I didn't have much time to think of myself and it has been a very long time since—"

Just then they both heard the sound of *Vučak's* barking and Papa's voice as he came from the orchards and paused to call hello to Vlach Stanich. Philomena startled Flora by grabbing her hand and holding it tightly. Their faces were very close, and Mama looked straight into her eyes, and said with great intensity, "Never forget who you are and what you want in life—no matter how much you love a man." With that said, as if sharing a secret, she scooped up the cups and tucked them in the sink behind the bucket of irises. Then she grabbed some wood from the box and stoked the fire.

Flora sat in silence, staring at her mother as her papa noisily entered the kitchen. He filled the room with his presence and size and his fine good humor. "What a crop we will have this year, eh? Twice as many apricots as last year and the plums? Superb!"

All the love she felt for her papa welled up in Flora, and she went quickly to him as she had as a child: clasping her arms tightly around his huge torso and kissing his chest which was as high as she could reach unless he bent down. And Papa responded as he always had, rubbing the back of her head, his huge hand encompassing half her skull. His familiar odor was everywhere, and it made her feel safe. She snuggled more tightly against him before letting go.

Papa smiled then at his wife and moved to kiss her softly on the cheek and slap her backside as he always did. And Philomena always made as if this embarrassed her when Flora was present, but it was clear that she cherished the ritual. Looking at her father and mother, now behaving like young lovers, Flora could see the love her parents shared was still alive. But within an hour or so, the mood would change as usual—a result of Papa's drinking. Flora knew once again Mama would turn silently inward, taking herself to Dubrovnik, dreaming of days gone by.

Standing back now, at the edge of the room, watching Papa pour what was supposed to be his first glass of wine for the day, Flora almost wished her mother hadn't opened up so much this afternoon. Hearing confirmation of her mother's desperate unhappiness only made her feel heartsick and helpless and afraid of the future.

And what **of** that future? What would life with Antone be like? Would he also, with the realities of providing for a family, let his boyhood dreams slip away? Would he let life and aging grind him down until he fell into the trap of wine and all its waste? It was a horrifying thought, for she knew one day Antone would be hers.

But not if they couldn't find a way to meet and spend some time together! That's when she realized with Mama's startling confidences, Flora had forgotten about Antone's note for nearly an hour now. She watched her parents talking together and laughing as Papa told a story about how he'd surprised a skunk under one of the trees and almost paid the price for it.

It was not unusual for her to quietly slip away at such times and afford them a little privacy. She did so now, her steps carrying her quickly and silently toward the amber bottle in her room.

She felt breathless and lightheaded as she picked up the bottle, her ears attuned for a parent's step in the next room. It was true she'd only had a little brandy, but that—combined with the missed midday meal—was catching up to her now. As she fumbled with the cork, trying to remove it without damaging the note or shoving it farther into the bottle, Flora's senses filled with memories of being touched and kissed by Antone. What would it be like the next time they were alone together?

The note was printed in pencil. The words were English, and she remembered how he used to struggle making the letters on his slate in school. There were only eight words:

"Meet me. Same place. Next Monday, midnight. Please."

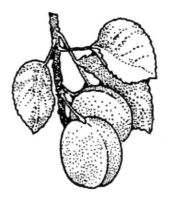

CHAPTER 6
Monterey, California — 1885

The incoming tide combined with high winds pushed a constant flow of sea against the pier, washing over the walkways and threatening the nearby warehouses. Most were darkened at this late hour, but the one which bore a sign reading "Lidakis Glass" had several lamps lit within. Small fishing boats tied firmly at the pier rocked helplessly atop each new surge, and the twisting and crackling of the boards echoed above the wind.

At first glance, the area appeared deserted—as it should be at such an hour and in such an increasing storm. Cold spring rain lashed the boats, the wooden buildings, the dimly lit street, and the almost-empty field across that street. For, on closer inspection, an observer—had there been anyone around to observe—would have seen two stoutly built characters wrestling in the mud of that field. Both had close-cropped hair and wore loose-fitting clothes that were soaked to the skin with thick reddish-brown mud. Even without the mud, it would have been hard to distinguish one from the other, they were so alike.

For over a hundred years, Monterey had served as a frontier outpost, and it was no stranger to fighting. But this was not the usual kind of fight. Both men were so evenly matched their vying resembled dance more than combat. Sometimes it even seemed that they moved to music, though their only orchestra was the wind and the sound of the sea pounding against the wooden pier. And there was no animosity in the wide white grins that split the red mud masks of their faces.

They circled and lunged, feinted and parried, grappled and crouched and rolled again in the mud. With open hands, they slapped at each other's heads and necks as distraction; they intently watched each other's waists as a focal point that would signal the next shift of body weight; often one or the other would dive at his opponent's knees, trying to push him off balance, but it never gave him the upper hand for long; every loss of ground was regained within moments. Meanwhile, the rain came down in torrents, temporarily blinding the men until they could swipe the mud and water from their eyes.

Hours passed, but neither seemed to notice. The grins faded and disappeared so that only the eyes showed white in the muddy faces, but there was still no rancor, only the purity of muscle and bone pitted against its equal match. And all without words. Just the labored breathing—the grunts and groans and gasps of exertion—escaped those two bodies, small sounds lost immediately in the wind.

Only one thing could end this match: the impending daybreak, which would bring other workmen to the pier. For the Lidakis brothers had long ago decided it would be safer for them if no one knew that they were wrestlers. So they prepared now for the final round: the tempo dropped, and the men came up from their crouches, standing more upright but still hunched in the shoulders. Mirroring each other, they let their arms drop to their sides with outstretched fingers, shaking their hands to increase the blood flow. Then again, as one, they took the position of attack. Slowly they circled, and the slapping at each other's heads became only a motion of hands with no contact intended or accomplished. All energy was being conserved.

One of the men suddenly lunged with full force at the other's waist. Charging, head down, he came like a cannonball, only to veer away in midair, an ultimate fake as the other leapt and captured only that air. They ceased to circle but stood with feet spread and firmly planted. Only their upper bodies swayed, and eyes remained riveted on the opponent's waist.

All around them, the night was softening into dawn. Sea gulls began to appear in increasing numbers—crying as they circled, searching for breakfast and jostling each other for possession of any tempting morsels exposed by the retreating storm. In one hushed moment, the rain stopped, and then the wind sighed its last breath over the choppy waters. And it seemed in that moment, the wrestlers would stop and call it a draw, which it certainly had been all along.

But then, at the same instant—as if the two minds and bodies were still the single organism they had been at their creation—the twins lunged together, heads down, with the force of two rams colliding. With a sudden dulling thud, they collapsed to the earth, limp and exhausted. Both bodies lay face down in the mud, completely unmoving until they were forced to raise their heads to breathe again.

Slowly and painfully, both men struggled to their knees, still wobbly and trying to gain balance with their hands, their heads down like beaten dogs. Still head-to-head, they crawled close enough to touch and, using each other for balance, made it to their feet, all the while uncertain if they would lose balance and fall. They stood now fully erect except hunched at the shoulders, with their heads snugged firmly against each other's chests. It was a few moments before they could back away and stand alone. Still a bit unsteady, but starting to regain balance, each looked into the mirror of his brother's face, and the broad smiles once again appeared on their faces as they burst out in laughter so loud it sent the nearest gulls squawking into flight.

Laughing and staggering like two drunks, they helped each other to the dock and climbed down the ladder into the bay waters frothing around the pilings. They yelped and gasped with the cold, but they dunked themselves until all the mud was gone and they felt thoroughly bathed. Then they scampered up the ladder and raced toward the warehouse where they knew their glassmaking ovens would provide a welcome warmth.

An hour later, they sat warm and dry beside that roaring fire, sipping hot soup laced with brandy and lost in thought. Completely unaware, the two were relaxed into their chairs at just the same angle, feet propped up on the same packing crate footstool, and all of their movements were completely concurrent: mugs lifted to lips at exactly the same rate, each taking a long noisy sip—and then another—before closing the eyes to savor the taste and then lowering the mug to rest on one thigh. But beyond the synchronicity of their bodies, it might have surprised even Theo and Demetri to find their thoughts so closely paralleled as they both dreamed of their youth in Greece and the events that forced them to leave their homeland—and another—before they came to America and finally to Monterey.

GREECE AND ITALY —1863–1878

Theo and Demetri were born aboard the Greek ship *Xanthe* in the year 1863. No one planned it that way. When the ship left its home port on Ithaki, its owners—Nikolaos and Alexi Kalidas—had no idea they were about to become parents at last. They had almost given up hope, since Alexi was nearing forty and had never become pregnant. Niko, by the age of forty-one, had taken the ships of his prosperous merchant father and parlayed that success into even greater wealth. But this demanded long absences on sailing journeys, and he desperately missed his Alexi. Through the years she had resisted accompanying him—admitting to irrational fears of the sea—but finally, she agreed to join him on a long voyage up along the western coast of the Italian peninsula, with a visit to family lands near Napoli.

At first all was well. Alexi was surprised to find herself so comfortable aboard ship, and sharing that time was bliss for a couple whose love had borne so many long separations. By the time Alexi realized she was pregnant, it was too late to turn back, and —since she seemed to be doing quite well—she decided to remain on board with her husband until near the time of delivery. But the labor came early and without warning, and no one had expected there to be two babies or that they would be so large.

There were no other women on the *Xanthe,* so Niko held his wife through the long hours of torturous labor and delivered the babes himself with only the assistance of his ship's captain Hylas Sedakia—who had helped his own wife on several occasions. The twin boys were surprisingly robust considering the circumstances, but Alexi slipped away only an hour after she held them and gave them their names. She died in Niko's arms, and he was forced to bury her at sea off Italy's Ligurian Coast, west of Genoa.

Another man might have blamed those sons and resented them all their lives. Nikolaos blamed himself: It was he who had pressured Alexi to accompany him, and he was sure she would have survived if she'd been in a proper location with a skilled midwife. His heart broke with the grief and the guilt, and he might have followed his wife under the waves had it not been for those two strapping sons crying for food and the comfort of a mother they would never know. He and Hylas made do with what they had on hand, feeding the babes with clear soups strained from boiled meats and cereal until they could reach port and find more suitable fare.

Nikolaos put his ships and fortunes in the able hands of his friend Hylas and spent the next few years at home on Ithaki, pining for Alexi and trying to raise two boisterous sons with the aid of his widowed sister. By the time she died just after the boys' fifth birthday, Niko had had his fill of Ithaki. He had no loved ones left there, and the home he'd shared with Alexi was a constant reminder of her absence.

Meanwhile, the last of his relatives in Napoli had died, and those lands passed to him. Since he was certain by now he would never return to his life as a seafaring merchant, he sold out all those business holdings to Hylas Sedakia and moved the boys to the five-acre farm near Napoli. Its small vineyard was already well-established and producing a very decent wine, and he was getting many ideas from Paul Geraud, his childhood friend in Provence, France.

Nikolaos had a way of making friends for life. Many years earlier—when Niko was only ten and beginning to accompany his father Andreas on short commercial trips between Ithaki and nearby Greek ports, they had come upon a sinking boat and rescued a family on holiday from France. And since the Gerauds had lost all they had with them, Andreas Kalidas took them along back to Ithaki and opened his home to them until they could contact their relatives back in France. The father, Raimond Geraud, credited Niko with saving their lives, since he'd been the one to spot the craft in heavy seas and get his father to bring their ship about. Though the Kalidas family saw the rescue and hospitality as a matter of course, Raimond insisted a great debt was owed that must someday be repaid. His son Paul was just Niko's age and in the few weeks they spent together, they became fast friends, and Paul was as adamant as his father about repaying the debt. Parting was difficult, but the boys vowed they would never lose touch, and Paul made Niko promise he would visit him someday in France.

But as the course of their lives unfolded, the boys were never able to meet again. They did keep part of the vow, however, and stayed in contact by correspondence. Niko was very glad his merchant father had insisted he learn to speak and write French and Italian as well as his native Greek (and as Demetri and Theo grew, he demanded the same of them).

At least once a year, around the anniversary of the Geraud family's rescue, Paul would write to bring Niko up to date on his life and to extend again the invitation. Niko would write back, with his own news and thanks for the invitation, which he had to decline. Thus the boys grew into men. Paul inherited the Geraud Vineyards and married and was blessed with one son— Remi Nicol Geraud; later they took in a young orphan girl and raised her as a daughter. When his wife died, he never remarried. Meanwhile, Niko married

Alexi, but the years went by without children, and by the time the twins were born, Remi was already ten.

When Paul first learned of Alexi's death, he urged Niko to bring the twins and come share the Geraud home. "We can raise our sons together," he wrote. But at that time, Niko was not prepared for such a change, and later, when he was, he decided he'd rather have the autonomy of his family's land near Napoli.

Paul was clearly disappointed, but eager to help his old friend Niko improve his Italian vineyard. He wrote long letters—volumes—of advice and sent slips of his most successful grapevines to Niko—a crateful of cuttings, packed expertly in canvas so they arrived still moist and fresh.

And so Nikolaos Kalidas and his twin sons made a new life on the coast of Italy and found some happiness there. But Niko never fully recovered from the loss of his wife; he never even considered remarriage. Truth be told, he longed for the day when he would see his Alexi again, for he held an unwavering conviction that would happen. He also dreamed of sailing north and visiting the spot where he had had to leave her.

And there was another, older, dream he had. From as far back in his childhood as he could remember, he'd wanted to excel as a wrestler and win some competition like those he'd read about in the Olympic valley when he studied Greek history. He tried his best. He learned the moves; he practiced for long hours; he got his friends involved so he had partners to vie against. But by the time he was fifteen, it was clear he would never be more than mediocre. His build wasn't right for it, and he simply hadn't the innate skill. As a man, he relinquished the dream of competing himself, but he maintained his interest, and from a very early age he saw in his sons the potential he had always lacked.

Their bodies were built for the sport—stocky and low to the ground with thick necks and stout shoulders. And the boys loved it. They learned quickly under the expert tutelage of their father—who could teach well what he could not perform himself—never complaining about the rigorous regimen of exercise, including rowboat races to develop the upper body strength they needed. As Theo and Demetri approached their fifteenth birthday, they had been wrestling with each other for nine years.

The boys worked hard in their family vineyard, and they took their studies seriously, but any free moment was an opportunity for them to try new maneuvers on each other, practicing until each was perfected. They were many years beyond the basics and over the last three or four years had developed their own unique style and moves. Every evening before supper—no matter what the weather—they held a match on the knoll overlooking the sea and about a hundred yards from the house. From there, Nikolaos could watch his sons. As the sun sank red into the sea, making black silhouettes of the boys, Niko could fancy he was back in ancient Greece, watching the games of old, so skilled were these sons of his.

A fantasy began to play itself out inside his head. He'd learned that—on the Ligurian Coast west of Genoa—in a village called Aurelia, which still maintained its Roman amphitheater, athletes had begun gathering for wrestling competitions, open to all ages and all nationalities. He was sure he could coordinate with Hylas Sedakia to journey up to Aurelia on one of his voyages. They could spend some time at the competitions, and he could rent a boat and visit the resting place of his dear Alexi. And as he considered all this, his thoughts got bolder: it was not that far west to Provence . . . why not go on and make that long-postponed visit to Paul Geraud, let his sons meet Paul's son Remi? It would be good to see that old friend again, to walk in his vineyards and talk about the grapes and wine and how their lives had gone.

Theo and Demetri were ecstatic when they heard the proposal—and so was Paul Geraud, who wrote back immediately, saying he would come to meet their ship at the harbor in Fréjus and escort them back to his home. Plans were made, the Kalidas holdings would be tended by a trusted farm manager, and they only awaited the arrival of the *Xanthe*. Another letter came then from Provence, written by the son Remi, apologizing that his father had fallen ill and would be unable to meet them, and he himself could not leave his father and the vineyards. But, he assured them, "We are most eager to have you come. In fact, that's the only topic of conversation that distracts my father's mind from dwelling on his discomfort, so please do not think of changing your plans!" He had enclosed detailed maps showing how to get to their home from the coast.

The *Xanthe* arrived the next day, so the journey progressed as planned. It'd been a long time since Nikolaos had been out to sea, and for the boys, it was the first since their birth. Their rowboat races and frequent fishing forays never took them much past the reefs in their small boat. The journey to Aurelia was thrilling for the boys but relatively uneventful.

Every evening, stuck below decks and too excited to sleep, Theo and Demetri practiced their French as they pored over the maps Remi had sent and made games of testing each other on the information. On one of these occasions, Niko watched them, smiling affectionately. To look at their stout bodies and round faces and their quiet demeanor around strangers, one might make the mistake of thinking they were a bit slow mentally. But any such person would be in for a surprise. Both boys had good minds and good common sense, an ability to learn quickly and master most things they attempted. They were fluent in Greek and Italian and could communicate well enough in French. Beyond that, they were kind and gentle, with a good sense of humor and all the social graces he knew to teach them. He sighed in satisfaction, realizing he had done well raising these boys. Alexi would be proud. If only she were here to see them now! If only she were here to share the rest of his life. . . .

Nikolaos Kalidas set aside his wistfulness and smiled more broadly at his sons as they traced the route to the Geraud Vineyards with their stout fingers.

"No, no," Demetri was saying. "We have to go across this bridge . . . see?"

"I swear, Demetri," Niko said. "I believe you could get there blindfolded in the dark."

Demetri looked up at his father solemnly and said, "Probably." And then they all laughed together, warm in the belly of the *Xanthe.*

CHAPTER 7
Ligurian Coast and Côte d'Azur — 1878

Hylas Sedakia and the *Xanthe* left Nikolaos and the twins in the port of Aurelia and turned back for Greece. Niko had never regretted passing the family business on to his friend Hylas, who had proved, if anything, **too** conscientious in business matters and unable to bend a schedule to take a few days of leisure with an old friend.

"No, no," Hylas had said when Niko extended the invitation. "I have a cargo waiting." But then he studied Niko a long moment and said, "It must be sad to return here after all these years."

"Yes," Niko admitted. "I've long dreamed of this ... visiting where I had to let my Alexi go. She is still so much with me. I wonder if I will sense her presence there. Do you think she might haunt that spot as well as my heart?"

Hylas reached out and squeezed the other man's shoulder, shaking his head sadly, as if saying, "I don't know." But when he spoke, it was of more practical matters: "You have made arrangements to get to Fréjus in Provence?"

"Yes. A fellow named Ursetti will take us there in his sailing boat, and then from there, we will make our way to the Geraud Estate."

Hylas nodded. "My next trip up to Genoa, I will check with our friend Sebastiani to see if you are there and wish transport back to Napoli."

"We appreciate that. But we may already be home in Napoli by then. Who knows what will happen on this trip and how long we will be in France ...?"

The two men gazed at each other a moment, and they both felt a chill flicker over them, accompanied by the thought that they might not ever see each other again. Then they both shrugged it away and embraced with gruff back-pounding as if to dispel any vestige of anxiety. One at a time, Hylas grabbed the boys—whom he'd helped to deliver all those years ago—and gave them each a hearty farewell, and then went on his way, leaving the Kalidas men to find accommodations.

Even though the town was crowded, they had no trouble locating a comfortable room, where they collapsed into sleep, the boys a bit disoriented being on solid land after so long aboard a rolling ship.

In the few days before the tournament, they explored the village, sampled the local cuisine, and flirted with the girls. Why was it, Theo and Demetri wondered, they were always attracted to exactly the same ones? The twins went to survey the old amphitheater, sizing up their future competition as wrestlers practiced in the arena. They gave themselves a good workout there too, but they didn't show off the moves they had created themselves. They would be among the youngest participants, and they wanted to maintain any element of surprise.

The day before the competition, Papa confirmed all his arrangements with Ursetti, the man who would take them to France the next week. That same evening, as they were checking over all parts of their plans for the rest of the trip, they discovered they did not have the portfolio of maps and letters Remi Geraud had sent. "They must still be on the *Xanthe*," Niko said resignedly. "And she's on her way back to Greece."

Demetri and Theo looked at each other and said the same words at the same moment: "I thought **you** had them!"

Both boys started to defend themselves, but Niko cut it short with a dismissive gesture. "Never mind. It's done. It's just a good thing Demetri memorized those maps. Now let's get some sleep."

The twins looked at each other questioningly, both sensing that difference they'd noticed in their father since their arrival in Aurelia. More than once it had occurred to them that he was unusually pensive, but there was always so much excitement around them, they were easily distracted, and the times they asked him about it, he only said, "I'm just tired" or "It's nothing really." And now he did the same, saying, "You have a very big day ahead tomorrow, and we all need to be well-rested." Thinking about the tournament on the morrow was all the boys needed to shift their attention away from their father. They were very excited, of course, but they were only just beginning to feel nervous.

The next morning, the three of them walked from the hotel to the amphitheater. The street was packed with people—all laughing and eager for the day's events—and lined with bright banners from participating countries. The closer they got to the arena, the more tense they felt, and their steps began to slow. Their father walked between them with an arm around each, and he, too, seemed subdued. When they walked through the long, cavernous corridors, and stood at the edge of the big, open arena and saw the thousands of faces looking down on them, the boys felt suddenly awestruck, as if for the first time they really understood the difficulty of the challenge before them and the magnitude of this experience compared to anything else in their lives.

A total of sixty-four men were competing, paired against each other in a series of single-elimination matches that would narrow the contest down to the last two contenders, and the victor in that would be the winner of the entire tournament. At the beginning, there were eight matches going on at the same time.

As Theo and Demetri stood waiting for their turns, they could feel the anxiety rising in them. Watching the other men talking or warming up together, it seemed that most of them knew one another—even those from other lands, and most had probably competed here before. Though no one was rude to them, the twins felt more like outsiders than ever. And people stared at them, for their impressive builds and identical faces drew many curious gazes.

Their father took them to the side for some last-minute instructions and encouragement. He looked at each for a long, appreciative moment ... touching first Theo's blond hair, then the little nick Demetri had gotten shaving that morning. "My dear sons ... " he said wistfully. "When I was a child, I dreamed of being a wrestler ... of competing in just such a tournament. But by the time I was your age, I knew I didn't have the build or the power I needed to make that dream come true."

He smiled sadly. "For years I grieved that loss of my dream. But then I fell in love with the most wonderful woman in the world, and I was lucky enough to marry her and share her life for more than twenty years. I found new dreams ... of a happy life ... and sons I would be proud of."

The boys looked away from the pain in their father's eyes, but they listened carefully to his words. "Alexi and I had that happy life ... for a while. And I couldn't be prouder of any other sons than I am of you. But when she died, I couldn't bear the loss of that dream. I wanted to die. I wanted to throw myself overboard. I wanted to hate the two of you, but I couldn't. I certainly couldn't imagine how I would manage to raise two babies when I could barely take care of myself. I thought about joining Alexi under the waves. I even thought of taking you with me so that you would not have to suffer in life as I had."

He paused, lost in memory, but the boys waited until he went on. "Now this I have never told anyone before—not even Hylas, who was asleep in the adjoining cabin when it happened. I had been lying awake—I hadn't slept since I lost her—but my eyes were closed so I could better picture her in my mind. And then I heard her speak my name—softly but very clearly, so there was no possibility it was part of a dream or fantasy. Imagine how quickly I opened my eyes! And there she was—standing beside the cradle where you two were sleeping. The room was dim and it was hard to see her clearly. It was like a misty glowing light that formed her figure, and she was bending over the cradle, looking down at you."

The boys couldn't look away from their father now as they waited breathlessly for the rest of the story. "I was not alarmed, but I was afraid to move or speak ... that it might break the spell or cause her to leave. Then after a moment, she turned and looked at me and reached out an arm to me, as if inviting me to join her at the side of the cradle. She didn't speak again, but in my mind, I could hear exactly what she would say: *These are our sons, Niko. I gave my life for them, but you must **keep** your life for them. They need you.* She started to fade away, but I could still hear her voice inside my head, saying, *One day you and I will be reunited. I promise. But now is not the time. You must give our sons the love they deserve and the dreams that will make all their struggles worthwhile.*"

Nikolaos sighed. "And then she just disappeared. Before I could try to go to her or even to speak—to tell her one last time how much I loved her ...." He was silent for a full minute, but still the twins did not speak. "I never saw her again—though I have felt her presence several times through the years. Almost always when I was watching you two at some important point in your life. Your first birthday ... when you started your studies ... when you first rode horses and handled a sailboat around the reefs. And I feel sure she is watching over you today."

He smiled. "You two are the living proof of our love and our dreams. When you enter the circles this day, no one will be able to match the spirit within you. You will wrestle as never before, and you will be victorious."

Nikolaos gently kissed his sons and then went to take his place with the other coaches, leaving the boys still enraptured and puzzling what to make of their father's story.

They stood reading each other's eyes and grasped each other's forearms, experiencing a sense of united strength beyond anything they had ever felt before. And all the nervousness was gone. They turned toward the arena, aware now of the sound of the crowd—a deafening roar like being under water—knowing it would soon be time for their first matches.

Theo was paired with a local champion and Demetri pitted against a wrestler from France. When Theo heard his name called, he touched his brother's arm and said, "I will fight today with all the power love lends those who believe in it."

Demetri nodded. "And I for the man who brings his dreams to life."

They both won their first match—and the second. By the end of their third victories, some of the onlookers were chanting the boys' names. Their youth and physical beauty—and the way they so easily defeated their opponents with moves never seen in this area—had taken the fancy of the crowd, and there was much anticipation that the final match might come down to these two boys. The chant became "Demetri, Theo, Demetri, Theo." And as the boys vanquished their fourth and fifth adversaries, the voices and anticipation of the crowd swelled and crested.

Then, as Theo and Demetri approached the circle for the final challenge, the arena fell suddenly and completely silent. And this, too, seemed deafening. The two faced each other, remembering all those evenings on the knoll and how that training had led them to this moment. Peripherally, they were aware of their father looking on with great pride. Perhaps they were even aware of Alexi's spirit watching over them. Then they each put full concentration on the other.

The flag dropped, signaling the beginning of the match. Slowly, they circled, as if sizing each other up, though each knew the other's capabilities well. The crowd took up its chanting again and seemed fairly equally split with half the people rooting and chanting for Demetri and the other half for Theo.

Neither thinking about victory or defeat, the brothers began to thrill the spectators by pitting their common style against each other. Just as it appeared one would overcome the other, the tide would shift. Ironically, it was the wrestlers who kept their audience off-balance, but the crowd seemed to love it.

The first two three-minute rounds ended with no clear victor, and as they entered the final round, it was clear to all a draw was in the making, and the crowd was less than pleased. They had come to see a smashing victory, not a draw—especially if they'd placed wagers on the outcome. They began to make rude noises and shake their fists.

Both boys knew they would have to make a real battle of it if they were to satisfy their audience. Crowds could turn ugly; it might even be dangerous for them to underestimate the need for a clear victor.

So Theo, the warrior of love, and Demetri, the warrior of dreams, clashed now in earnest, trying to win the match. They fought not as brothers, but as enemies, and the crowd roared its approval. It was no longer a wrestling match, but a battle of strength and will. But try as they might, neither could get the upper hand; they were more equally matched than even they had imagined, and perhaps they could even read each other's thoughts too well. It seemed an impossible situation. What were they to do? The circles tightened until they stood at arm's length, time ticking down to the final seconds. Then, at the same instant they lunged—one mind, one flesh, and with nothing held back. They smashed together, their heads colliding with a sickening crack. Stunned, they stumbled but remained upright for a long moment, and then both fell unconscious to the ground, one upon the other.

The judges proclaimed a draw, and pandemonium ruled as the crowd wildly screamed the two names. The anger was gone; the ruling was approved, for it was evident to everyone that the twins had given all they had and were just too evenly matched. People rushed to the arena floor and hoisted the semiconscious wrestlers up onto their shoulders and paraded them all around the amphitheater. Among the loudest voices of approval were those of the competitors vanquished earlier, for they could truly appreciate the uniqueness of the contest. Never before had the tournament ended in a draw, and everyone present knew they had just witnessed history being made—and the privilege of being present during such a spectacle far outweighed any other considerations.

Once again fully conscious, Theo and Demetri took in all the glory that was being bestowed upon them, and as the crowd carried them back to their starting point, they could see their father beaming at them as if his own dream had come true.

Later that afternoon, Nikolaos sat alone in the hotel room. The boys were still out being wined and dined by the populace. He knew they had never been as adored as they were in this moment—nor had they ever been as drunk. And judging from the number of hot-eyed girls hanging around them, they were probably about to experience some other delights for the first time. Niko begrudged them none of it. But seeing them as grown men at the age of fifteen made him feel not only happy and proud, but also melancholy and alone. "I wish you were here, Alexi," he whispered with tears coming to his eyes, "so we could share this fulfillment of our love and our dreams."

Suddenly the loss became overwhelming. Soon the boys would leave him to live their own lives and what would he do then? With whom would he spend the remaining days of his life? Grief cut through him more sharply than it had since the first days following Alexi's death. Nikolaos could stand it no more.

He rose and put on his jacket, then wrote a note and tucked it under a vase on the dresser where the boys would see it if they came in before he returned. Then he hurried out of the hotel and down to the harbor.

It took some talking to convince Ursetti. Their arrangement had been that **tomorrow**—the day before they sailed for France—he would take Niko to visit the spot where he had left Alexi. He was not enthusiastic about going out that late in the day, but Nikolaos seemed so distraught and assured him the mission would not take long. Ursetti was an accomplished sailor and could calculate that the night would be clear and still with plenty of moonlight, so there was no worry about getting back after dusk. And when Nikolaos offered to pay double the price, Ursetti found himself agreeing.

Awakening the next morning with the worst hangovers they had ever experienced, the boys noticed their father was not in the room. At first, they thought he had gone to the privy. Sitting on the edges of their beds, staring at each other, they mirrored slack-faced misery mixed with the recollections of the tournament and the pleasures that had followed. Thinking these thoughts, they both started to grin, but then winced at the sharp pains stabbing through their skulls—which after all, had suffered some the day before.

Groaning, they held their heads in their hands—trying to enjoy the memories of the day before without causing themselves pain—while they waited for their father to come back from the privy. They could recall a good deal of what they'd experienced, but neither of them could remember returning to the room. Some of their adoring followers must have carried them back and deposited them safely in their beds. Had their father been here then?

As time dragged out and there was no sign of him, they began to worry. Finally, they rose to look around the room, and that's when they found the note beneath the vase on the dresser:

My dearest sons, If I am not here when you return, I should be back before midnight. I really must go visit the place I left your mother. I hope I can convince Ursetti to go out so late in the day. Take care. I will join you shortly.   Your loving father, Nikolaos

The boys stared at each other with growing apprehension. The way the shadows fell across the floor proved it was well past midday, which meant he was more than twelve hours overdue. Theo and Demetri didn't have to speak. As one, they hurried from the room, left the hotel, and headed for Ursetti's dock.

They saw the gathered crowd well before they reached their destination. Excusing themselves between and among the people, they were soon able to see Ursetti himself, seated on a wooden crate next to his dock neighbor, a squid salesman. Ursetti was drinking from a glass of wine, and his hand was very unsteady. When he lowered the glass and saw the boys, his face twisted with regret and he said, "I am so sorry."

Theo and Demetri stood before him, speechless and uncomprehending. Someone who had just arrived asked the question the boys could not voice: "What happened?"

"I warned him it wasn't wise to go out so late," Ursetti said, taking another shaky drink of wine. Then he looked directly at Theo and Demetri and continued his story. "But he insisted, so I took him to the spot where he had left his wife's body years ago. He was so sad, it touched my heart. I gave him what privacy I could, and he went to stand in the front of the boat with his back to me, but I could hear him talking to his dead wife—your mother. Not the words, just the loving tone he used. It was sunset by then, and he stood silhouetted black against the red sky. It was all so beautiful, it brought tears to my eyes."

Ursetti paused, reviewing his memories. "I don't know exactly what happened. I heard him gasp and saw him stagger a little and I rushed to help him, but before I could reach him, he had tumbled over the side. I don't know whether it was his heart or something else, but he had passed out. I could see him floating face-down in the water, but I had trouble reaching him. I couldn't get him up into the boat. I was all alone and not as strong as when I was young. And he was a very large man. Before I could get some line to secure him to the boat at least, the currents caught him and drifted him out of my reach. I'm afraid they took him farther out to sea. Or maybe he just sank. I lost sight of him. I searched all night, but I found nothing."

He had finished, but still the boys said nothing. "Do you understand what I am saying?" Ursetti asked softly and with sincere compassion. "Your father is dead."

Theo's voice came out in an anguished bellow: "No-o-o!" And like a wounded animal writhing in pain, he lashed out at the nearest object, which happened to be the squid-seller's stand. The wooden framework shattered like toothpicks, and pieces of prime octopus and squid went flying in all directions, falling down into the puddles of stagnant water—or worse yet, off the dock into the sea.

"Hey!" The squid-seller roared, punching Theo's arm. He was a small, frail man, anger-fortified by the loss of his livelihood. "You can't just—"

Barely feeling the blow, Theo was more angry at being disturbed as he tried to comprehend what had just happened. He grabbed the little squid-seller by the shoulders and lifted him completely off the ground. "Don't you understand?" he cried, shaking the man violently. "My **father** is dead!" The man's head flailed wildly with the shaking, and everyone heard that terrible snap, like a pistol shot.

Theo felt the man go limp in his grasp. His hands opened and the squid-seller fell like a discarded rag at his feet.

All this time, Demetri had stood as a sleep-walker, transfixed by disbelief. Now he moved toward his brother, crying, "My God, Theo!" but he was met by a violent shove which pushed him to the ground.

The crowd stood petrified. Even those who hadn't witnessed the tournament had heard all about it and knew of these boys' strength. Not a person there would lift a hand against them.

With a terrible noise, Theo turned and raced away like a wild dog. Demetri was up immediately, running after him. No one else followed. No one dared. Demetri chased after his brother, pounding down the narrow streets and out of town, along the shoreline until dusk closed in around them. Just when Demetri thought he could not go another step, he saw his brother stagger and fall to the ground. Wheezing and shaky, Demetri stumbled the last steps and fell beside his brother, who was gasping painfully as his body tried to breathe and cry at the same time. The boys held each other and tried to get control of themselves.

When they were breathing normally again, Theo seemed to have gone into some kind of trance and was barely responsive. Demetri put aside his fear and grief and set his mind to escape. The death of the squid-seller had been an accident, but he was sure the citizens of the village would consider it murder, and all the acclaim they had received from winning the tournament would be forgotten in the people's lust for vengeance.

Night had settled around them, but Demetri could see a few lights ahead of him on the shore. He coaxed Theo to his feet and walked him down the beach toward those lights. He found a small jetty with several boats tied to it, bobbing peacefully. The lights came from a nearby building, but there was no one in sight. Demetri stopped, listening intently in the direction from which they'd come. As yet, there were no sounds of pursuit. The darkness was now their security.

He picked the finest vessel—a full-rigged sailboat about twenty feet in length with the name *Stella* painted on her bow—and helped Theo down into it. Then he cast off, got himself aboard, and quietly rowed out to sea. The outgoing tide made passing the breakers an easy chore. Setting sail and heading west along the coast, Demetri allowed himself a moment to grieve for his father. The shock of the death had just begun to set in when, looking back over his shoulder, he saw something that chilled him. At this distance from shore, he could see all the way back to Aurelia, and there, at the edge of town, was a mass of bobbing lights, what he knew must be the torches of hundreds of villagers searching for the murderers.

Demetri knew they were heroes no more. By daybreak, if not before, the stolen boat would be missed, and their pursuers would know for sure which way the fugitives had gone. Looking at his sleeping brother, Demetri realized he had never felt so ... apart ... from his twin ... so different. And he knew that their survival—for the present at least—depended entirely upon him. He vowed he would use his every ounce of wit and strength to keep them safe and free. They were far from home and going the wrong direction to get back there, but perhaps his flight had been guided, for he realized their only hope lay now with the Gerauds. Instead of spending time in grief for his losses, Demetri set his full concentration upon the maps he had scrutinized, and as he guided the boat along the coast in the moonlight, he reviewed those documents in his mind.

When Demetri was sure they had passed the port of Fréjus, he found a rocky cove—cut off from the rest of the shoreline—and intentionally ran the boat aground on the reef. When the wooden planks scraped and splintered against the rocks, Demetri felt the tearing in his soul, but he knew what he had to do.

Theo was difficult to awaken. Demetri managed to get him to his knees and then pushed him overboard. Jumping in after him, he found the cold water was reviving Theo, but he still needed help swimming ashore. Demetri urged Theo up above the tide line to the base of the cliffs and got him settled in a little area sheltered by large boulders. Theo curled himself into a ball and fell immediately asleep, despite his wet clothing.

Demetri swam back to the *Stella*, and calling up his reserves of strength, he pushed her free from the rocks, boarding her as she slipped away. There was a hole where the reef had ripped her, but she was a strong, well-built craft, and it might be days before she sank. Demetri looked around him and picked up the leather bags he'd found in one of the cabinets, once again thankful to whoever had equipped the *Stella* for her next voyage. The wineskin of drinking water and the bag of cheese, hardtack, and dried meat had sustained the twins during their voyage, though Theo could be coaxed to eat very little. Demetri tied the bags to his belt and began maneuvering the *Stella* well out away from the rocks and reefs.

Then, with great sorrow and self-loathing, Demetri picked up the heaviest metal object he could find and began bashing at the bottom of the boat where the boards were already broken and letting in the water. More and more began to pour in, but he kept at it until the *Stella* began to sink. He swam quickly for shore. When he stood panting on the sand and looked back, the boat was no longer visible. Exhausted, he dragged himself up to the sheltering boulders and collapsed beside his sleeping brother. He never even felt his cheek touch the sand.

It was crying that woke him. Demetri rolled over and saw his brother sitting, huddled miserably and sobbing as if he'd never stop. It was dusk again, though Demetri couldn't have said of what day. His clothes were completely dry and he could feel the heat of sunburn wherever his skin was bare. He reached out and touched Theo's arm.

The other boy turned to look at him. The shock was gone from Theo's face, followed by horror and grief and fear. "Demetri, tell me it was a nightmare ... it isn't true that our father is dead. Tell me I didn't ... kill ... someone!"

Gripping Theo's arm to strengthen him, Demetri said gently, "It is all true."

"Oh God, dear brother, I wish I were dead. Where in God's name are we? And what are we to do?"

"We are in France, near where we were to land on our way to the Geraud Estate. We must find our way there and ask Paul and Remi Geraud for help. I can think of no other plan."

"But, brother, you killed no one. There is no need for you to be a fugitive too."

"No one will care which of us killed that man," Demetri answered. "We look so much alike, they won't know which of us was to blame. If we are caught, they'll probably hang us both."

Theo hung his head in shame at the devastation he had brought to both their young lives, but his brother squeezed his arm again and said. "We must put our regrets aside and think only of how to reach our destination safely. I think the more we keep our guilt from our thoughts, the more innocent we will appear. Now, let us eat and try to sleep some more. I don't think I can find the way at night, so we must travel fast during the day. It will take some time for news of our crime to reach this area, so no one should be watching for us around here yet. But I think it's wisest if we try to avoid being seen together."

And so it was that they traveled the two days' walk to the Geraud Estate. They moved as fast as they could during the day, skirting populated areas, and slept exhausted each night underneath a hedgerow or in an open barn. If they saw someone approaching on the road, they would hide themselves if they could or one would turn his head or hide his face in a such a way that passersby would not notice they were twins.

And as they walked, they made more decisions and plans. They would tell the Gerauds as little as possible and try to avoid meeting or talking to anyone else. Planning never to be seen together, they would pretend to be one person named Alexios Nikolaos, honoring both departed parents. If any talking or explanations were needed, Demetri would handle them, and they would never let anyone know they were wrestlers.

The maps had been very exact and the boys' memories served them well, so they never had to ask directions. There was even a sign at the turnoff from the main road. "Geraud Vineyards" it said, surrounded by a painted border of grapevines.

Theo and Demetri walked a long time down that road, past acres of grapevines—a sight that brought them close to tears, it looked so much like their home near Napoli. The house itself—a mansion in the boys' eyes—was nestled on the edge of a hardwood forest.

They tugged and brushed at each other's clothes and hair, trying to make themselves as presentable as possible. Then Theo slipped off to hide in the woods while Demetri steeled himself to walk alone up all those stone steps to the enormous mahogany door. He cleared his throat and then knocked, but the door was so thick, his knock was like a whisper. He tried again, louder, and listened intently. He could hear quick, light steps coming toward him. He swallowed again as the big brass doorknob began to turn. And then the door swung open.

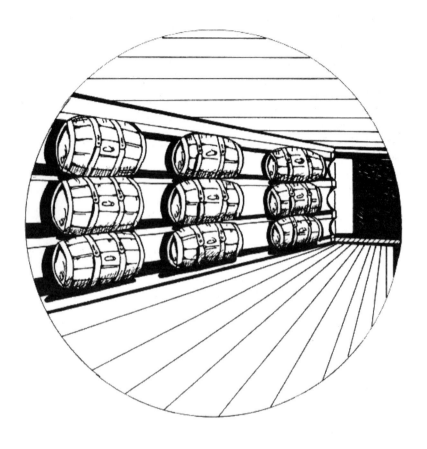

T. Robertson

CHAPTER 8
Santa Clara Valley — 1885

Flora Bogdonovich sighed and slid lower in the tub so that the hot, soapy water came up to her chin. Eyes closed, she rolled her head back so all her auburn hair was immersed. The kitchen was very warm—just the way she liked it. How could anyone stand to bathe in a cold room? Steam from the hot water covered her with the scent of Mama's homemade lavender soap. It was wonderful to feel so relaxed, to feel there was no need to hurry. All her chores for the day were completed; she couldn't remember a time she'd worked more quickly and efficiently. Papa was out in the orchard dusting with lime powder to discourage insects. Mama had gone to town with Gospodja Tesla and wouldn't return for at least another hour, so Flora was assured her privacy. She settled herself in a more comfortable position, eyes still closed, and let her thoughts drift.

She was thinking of Antone. Today he was to return from Sacramento, and tonight ... tonight she would meet him in the north yard at midnight. And what would that be like? All this week of waiting, she'd been thinking about his kiss and hoping to experience more of those sensations, but she also wanted to talk. They'd never really had a chance to do that. She wanted to learn more about who he was as a person, and they should certainly discuss plans for the future. Were they both contemplating the possibility of marriage—despite the opposition they would face from both their families? It would be good to have these things clearly spoken and understood. Then there might be time for a few sweet kisses.

She couldn't help thinking about her last kiss from Antone. How many times had she reviewed that meeting in her mind? And each time, she felt again the fever that had touched her body along with Antone's hands. Remembering now, she let her own hands travel the route Antone's had taken: cupping the sides of her breasts, then sliding down to her hips and buttocks. It felt so good, so exciting, but not quite as exciting as it had been then. She imagined it was Antone's hands now, sliding over her soapy skin, and she was surprised at just how effective that could be. She whispered his name and let her imagination wonder, where they might have gone if there had been time ... if she had let him ....

At 11:30 that night, Flora rose from her bed and dressed again. She didn't dare light a lamp, and it was very dark. She had taken down her hair for the night, but now she went to her dresser and picked up her brush. It was so dark she couldn't see herself in the mirror, but she faced it anyway out of habit and gave her long, thick hair a thorough brushing. Then she pinned it up into its customary bun. After arranging her pillow and bedclothes so it would look as if she were still there, she fumbled in the dark until she found her shoes and slipped them on. Wrapping herself in her warmest shawl, she left her room and moved silently toward the kitchen. It was safer to pass her parents' room and go out the back door than to go out the front where someone might see her from the road.

She paused outside the other bedroom. It was too dark to see anything, but she could hear Papa snoring away, and she knew her mother had taken to sleeping with little pieces of soft wax stuffed in her ears to block out that very sound. Flora moved on. She'd lived her whole life in this house, and it wasn't difficult to get to the back door in the dark. Remembering to lift the door past the place that would make a squeak, she managed to get outside and close it behind her without a sound.

Outside, it was just as dark—only two days before the new moon—and even chillier than she'd expected. But this time she was dressed more warmly and was wearing shoes. Also, when she ducked between the rails of the north yard fence, there was no tall grass to soak her with dew. Bob and Dan and Ilka had dispatched that bounty with ease when they finally got their turn at the field. The horses were still there (Flora thought she could see their shapes against the white of the fence), but Ilka was in the barn where it was more sheltered.

Flora moved slowly to the spot where she and Antone had stood ... had kissed ... over three weeks ago. She hoped this was where he meant by "same place" in his note, and knowing she must be early, she also hoped that wouldn't seem too eager. *When will he come?* she wondered, pulling the shawl more tightly around her and squinting her eyes against the darkness, peering in the direction of Antone's house. She knew he was home. She'd been sitting on the cellar doors, drying her hair after her bath, when she saw him ride into the yard looking very tired and dusty.

Perhaps he'd been so tired, he'd gone to bed and wouldn't even remember to wake for their rendezvous. A thousand doubts suddenly flew up in Flora like a flock of startled birds. *Maybe he won't even come!*

And then a shadow moved against all the other shadows, and Antone appeared before her. Startled, Flora wondered if he would just grab her and kiss her, but he stood a long moment simply gazing at her, and then he murmured, "Bella Flora...." He reached out his hand and waited for her to take it. As she did, she wondered if he would draw her into an embrace, but he merely stood that way, holding her hand and gazing at her.

At last he spoke. "Would you go somewhere we can talk?" When she nodded, he asked, "Would you like to see our new winemaking barn?"

"Is it safe?"

"Yes, I think so. Papa stays close to Mama at night in case she has ... " he fumbled for the English, " ... bad breathing. Bruno is with a girl who will keep him busy all night." Realizing what he'd said, Antone paused, embarrassed.

Remembering last time, Flora asked, "And your Uncle Gregorio?"

Antone smiled suddenly, a flash of white in his dark face. "I brought him a very big bottle of whiskey from Sacramento, and I made sure he was passed out before I left. He won't wake until morning ... and when he does, I think he will have a very bad headache."

Flora laughed softly and let Antone lead her across the field. Slipping between the rails of the fence where Antone had repaired it, Flora had some trouble with her skirts tangling, and he helped her. He seemed unaffected by his accidental contact with the back of her knee, but she was very aware of his touch.

Hand-in-hand, they went quickly and silently across the road. Flora had never been on the other side of Page Street before, and in some ways, it felt as alien and dangerous as stepping onto the moon.

Inside the new barn with the doors closed, Antone lit a lantern. Flora looked surprised and apprehensive, so he assured her. "No windows facing the house." He took her hand and led her around the building, holding the lantern as high aloft as possible so she could see better in the dimness. First he opened the doors to the great underground cellar they'd dug, now walled with barrels of aging wine; but they didn't venture into that cold and earthy-smelling room. He showed her the redwood vats they were building and the shelves full of the Lidakis brothers' bottles, and an array of artifacts and implements that would be needed for the winemaking process. As he told her about the things he was showing her, all his shyness vanished, and Flora was impressed with how enthusiastic and knowledgeable he was.

Here was a man who knew what he wanted to do and how to do it to benefit his life. It was clear Antone Mellini was going to make something of himself. That might give him the power to marry outside his own culture, and it certainly should hold some weight with her parents, who wanted her to marry someone who could provide a life even better than their own.

When the tour was finished, Antone seemed a little awkward again. Both very aware of the hands they held, they stood at the rear of the building in a little alcove with a desk and one rickety chair. Gazing away from Antone, Flora stared at the surface of the desk, hardly aware of the cartons and ledgers and other items there. Antone must have been looking there too, for he suddenly asked, "Want to taste some?" When he reached toward the desk, Flora saw there was also a tray there holding one of the familiar green bottles and several clean glasses, turned bottom up.

Flora nodded and Antone released her hand to take up the bottle, work free the cork, and fill the two glasses. "We always keep this ready here," he explained with a little laugh. "Whenever we start feeling ... discouraged ... we take a taste to remind us what we're working for."

He handed her one of the glasses and waited tensely while she took a sip. It wasn't sweet like Papa's plum wine, and—full-bodied and rich as its deep red color—it was much tastier then most grape wines she'd had in other people's homes. "Oh," she said, "that's very good!"

His relieved smile broke like dawn across his face. "I'm glad you like it," he said, "because ... " he reached into a carton on the desk and handed her the piece of paper he pulled out "...this is the label we'll be putting on our wine."

Flora could hardly believe her eyes. The printed paper label had a border of intertwining grapes and roses and above the words "Mellini Vineyards / Santa Clara, California" she saw in flowery script the name of the wine: "Bella Flora."

"Oh!" she said again and then fell mute, unable to voice even one of the questions in her mind or her heart.

Antone answered one of them. "None of my family knows I call you that. In fact, I ... planted the seeds ... so carefully, everyone thinks it was my mama's idea." He grinned. "If I can just keep those Greeks from giving me away with their teasing ...."

Flora smiled back and whispered, "I'm honored ...."

Clearly pleased, Antone asked, "Would you like to sit down? I don't think you should trust that chair, but we could sit over there." He gestured toward some bales of straw along the far wall. They went and sat and sipped their wine while Antone told Flora about their grapes—how his papa'd been given slips brought from Europe and had originally raised them as table grapes for the lucrative San Francisco market. But much like Luka Bogdonovich, the Mellinis had made their own wine, which gathered a local following and now, when many California wineries were being devastated by phylloxera, the Mellini vines were healthy and bearing as never before. Flora talked some, too, about the wine her Papa made, and the minutes ticked by.

When they had finished their wine, they held on to the glasses for a long time so they would have something to do with their hands. But finally, Antone took her glass from her and set them both on the floor, then took her hands in his. "I have so much I want to say to you ... but it's difficult in English."

Flora didn't look away from his eyes. "I know."

"I want to kiss you, Flora. Ever since the last time, it's been hard for me to keep my mind on anything else in my life. I just keep thinking of what it's like to kiss you."

Flora did look away now and said again, "I know." She hesitated and began to blush. "I want you to kiss me too, but I worry ...." She faltered and fell silent.

"About my intentions?" he asked, and when she nodded, he assured her fervently, "I want to marry you, Flora. I want to be with you for the rest of my life ... to have children with you, and never think about another woman as long as I live. I only hope you feel the same way about me ...?"

It **was** a question, and Flora was so filled with joy at his declaration, she could think of only one way to answer him. She leaned across the distance between them and kissed his mouth. He gripped her hands more tightly and kissed her back with all the love and yearning he had tried to express. It was not a kiss like last time. The way they were seated prevented that kind of body contact and neither of them made any move to change positions, as if they knew how dangerous that would be.

But the kiss did deepen and become more passionate and they released each other's hands and let them go elsewhere. Antone's went to her face and hers went up around his neck so she could pull his mouth even tighter against her own. Their breathing quickened still further, and after a few moments, Antone's hands began to move again, caressing down from her cheeks along her neck to the tops of her shoulders and down her chest until they cupped her breasts.

She gasped and pulled away from the kiss, but when he started to remove his hands, she held them there with her own. She saw the surprise in his eyes and told him, "This, too, I worry about. We ... want each other ... so much, but I want to be a virgin when we marry."

"Of course," Antone agreed. "That is only right. I want that too." His hands on her breasts lifted and squeezed slightly, and he saw the response in her eyes. "But there are ways that we can pleasure each other and still have that be so. If you will trust me."

Relieved to hear that he was of a like mind, she smiled. "And if I can trust myself?" He returned the smile and nodded. Feeling his hands hot on her breasts, Flora lost her smile and whispered, "Show me ...."

She'd worn a dress that buttoned up the front and Antone's fingers moved to undo those buttons to her waist. She wore no corset—she needed none—but instead a soft white cotton camisole with a bit of lacing down the front. Despite the urgency he felt, Antone made himself proceed slowly, and he first caressed her body outside the camisole. Concetta Podesta had led him this far the second time she kissed him, but this did not feel the same.

Eyes closed, Flora whispered, "Oh, Antone ...." and pulled his face down to hers. The kiss went on a long time, and somewhere in the middle, he began to unlace the camisole so his hands could move inside. The touch of his fingers on her bare skin electrified them both, and intensified the kiss until they both had to pull away. They stared at each other, eyes wide with the awe of what they were feeling.

Then Antone pushed open her camisole and gazed at her bared breasts. Perhaps a little smaller than those of the overly endowed Concetta, these were pale as cream, and the areoles were golden-pink in the lantern light, very different from Concetta's. "Beautiful," he whispered and touched them gently with his thumbs.

Flora sucked in her breath and suddenly found herself braver than before. She reached over and began to unbutton Antone's shirt. It wasn't easy. The cloth was stiff and unyielding. She wondered if he'd bought the shirt in Sacramento so he'd have something new to wear for her. His chest was bare beneath, and the opened shirt revealed a mat of dark hair, just as she'd imagined. Like a child whose feet can't resist a lush lawn of grass, her fingers were drawn to it, found the hair surprisingly soft and silky. She stroked the wonder of it, and her own thumbs came to rest on his nipples where they hid in that dark forest.

They stared at each other a long time, both wanting to kiss and feel their bare skin touch, but they fought the impulse, knowing perhaps that they were entering more dangerous ground. At last, Antone spoke, and his voice was deep and breathless. "I don't want to say this, but I think we'd better go. It must be very late ... early."

Flora glanced toward one of the windows in the wall beside them, and she could see the sky was lightening. "Yes," she said regretfully. "Papa is a very early riser."

They moved apart and began to fasten their clothes. Blushing at her boldness, Flora asked, "When can we meet again?"

Antone gave her a joyful smile, but then it fell from his face. "I must leave again in three days." Seeing the disappointment on her face, he was both sad and elated. "I need to go to the coast again. And between now and then, I had better get a few nights' rest or I may fall asleep aboard Dolce and tumble into some mountain canyon and never be seen again." That made Flora smile, as he had hoped, but it did nothing to ease the disappointment in either of them. Antone, struggling with the last stiff button, pondered the future. "It's difficult to plan when I might get away again ...." Then his face lit up with a plan. "My bedroom window is at the front of the house, facing your house. I could put something in the window to signal I will meet you that night at midnight."

"Yes!" Flora said, amazed to find that all these years, their bedroom windows had faced each other from opposite sides of Page Street. "My window is across from yours. If I see your signal and can meet with you, I will put something in **my** window. I know! I'll put the bottle you sent the note in!"

Antone laughed. "Good! I could use one of the Greeks' bottles too. I share the room with Bruno but he never notices things like that."

"Should I come here to the barn?"

"No. We'd better meet the same way for now, and if it's safe to be here, I'll bring you across."

They smiled at each other, pleased with the plan—even though it would be a long time before they could meet again—and then they hurried to get home to their beds. Antone put their empty glasses in a washbucket that already held several others. Then he escorted her quickly to the street, glancing about to see if anyone might be around. A cool mist had settled in, but even through it, one could see the sky was streaked with pink in the east. It was lighter than they thought, and they both realized with disappointment that it would be very unwise to share a parting kiss, even though they felt sure no one would see them.

In the middle of the street, Flora said, "I'd better go the rest of the way alone. Just in case .... There's enough light now."

Grudgingly Antone agreed. They both wanted to speak of love in parting but felt suddenly shy, so they only whispered, "Good night" and Flora hurried across the street and made her way to the kitchen door.

No sooner had she undressed, undone her hair, and slipped into her bed, than she heard Papa rising in the next room. She heard his cavernous yawn and his sleepy shuffle toward the back door on his way to the privy.

That was *close!* Flora thought drowsily. She'd have to be more careful in the future. *The future!* Smiling to herself, Flora gazed across the room to where she knew the amber bottle rested on her dressing table, and she fell asleep dreaming of that future.

Head pounding and body aching, Luka Bogdonovich leaned against the tree next to the privy and urinated, noticing there was more blood in the flow than last time. He looked away toward the hills where pink was painting the sky. The morning mist which settled on his head and face felt refreshing, but the sudden twisting in his stomach and bowels dropped him to his knees, and he vomited violently in the dirt of the yard. He continued to retch until he brought up only phlegm. Groaning and shaky, he sat back on his heels and considered his situation. Though no one else was aware these attacks had become a morning ritual, he was feeling truly alarmed. He'd been drinking—and getting drunk—all his life, it seemed. It had never felt like this. There was something wrong now. Inside him. Something bad.

With the vomiting finished he felt a tiny bit better. He got to his feet, shaky as a new colt, and made his way to the nearby watertrough. He dunked his head and took in great mouthfuls of water to rinse and spit the foulness from his mouth. He sat then on the edge of the trough and thought about what he must do.

He was in many ways a strong-willed man, always capable of doing whatever he set his mind to. Looking up to the sky, as if to seek guidance from the heavens, he made a vow to himself. The drinking he loved so much had to end. He thought of Flora and Philomena and felt ashamed. He neglected, embarrassed and enraged his beautiful wife. He had seen sorrow and pity in the eyes of his daughter, who had once treated him like a god.

He knew it would be difficult to stop drinking ... it would be agony—for weeks, perhaps. The drink was a devil inside him, trying to take over his spirit and—like a weakling—he had succumbed to it. This thought above all, re-pulsed him, and he swore to God and the heavens above that he would stop ... now ... today. Still looking upward, he blessed himself and prayed silently to his God and to the saint for whom he had been named. *Please give me strength! Let me live. Let me earn the respect of my wife and daughter again. If you will only help me overcome this devil inside me, I promise I will be your most devout and humble* servant. *Please, please hear my prayer and help me through this day ... and the next .... Amen.*"

Firm now in his resolve, he went to the shed and got a hammer and a tin can full of nails. Then he made his way to the cellar. The doors were closed. Inside, he knew, were his family's recipes and his own variations; there were wooden casks both empty and full. In there, too, was his release from the disappointments and regrets of his life, his camaraderie with other men of his culture, and a means for supplementing his family's income and larder.

Well, he decided, he would have to find other ways to fill those needs. Despite his shakiness, he made quick work of nailing the cellar doors closed. "There!" he said, both sadly and triumphantly. "Thank you, God." And he crossed himself again and felt renewed. He went to kick dirt and leaves over the evidence of his sickness, then walked a little more steadily to the back door and entered the kitchen.

Flora wasn't up yet, but his dear wife was there in the kitchen, and she had the woodstove roaring beneath the black iron coffeepot.

"What was all that hammering?" Philomena asked irritably. She was breaking eggs into a skillet, and she didn't look up at her husband.

He went to stand directly in front of her, but still she didn't look up. "I nailed the cellar shut," he said and waited.

It took a few long moments for her to realize what he meant. She looked up hopefully. "You did?" Then, cynical again, "For how long?"

"Forever!" he vowed.

Philomena was still afraid to trust what she was hearing. "Why?"

"I want my life back," he answered. "I want my health back and my appetite and my daughter." He touched her face gently. "Most of all, I want my wife back."

Tears welled up in Philomena's eyes, and she left the skillet, moved into his arms. They held each other tenderly for long moments, then Philomena brushed the tears from her eyes and told him, "Sit, Luka."

He sat at the table and she poured coffee for them both. Then she sat with him at the table and they talked and laughed together as they had not done in many years. And that was where Flora found them still when she padded in, yawning, several hours later.

CHAPTER 9
PROVENCE, FRANCE — 1878

The great mahogany door swung open, and Demetri saw a startled-looking girl about his own age. He thought she was the loveliest creature he'd ever seen: tiny in stature but exuding a sense of self that would make people forget how small she was. Where Demetri came from, it was not unusual to see hair that black and shiny, but he was used to darker-complected Greek and Italian girls, so the porcelain-white of this girl's skin seemed especially exotic, and it made her eyes glow like bright emeralds in her heart-shaped face. She was neatly dressed, but neither as a servant nor a lady of leisure, so Demetri was a little unsure how to address her.

Meanwhile, she stared at him with open curiosity and caution but no fear. He knew—despite those efforts to make himself presentable—he must look a sight: travel-stained, rumpled, unshaven, his blond hair sticking out in all directions and with little bits of leaves stuck in it from sleeping on the ground. And he knew he smelled even worse. Fearing she would take him for a beggar— or something even more unsavory—he hurried to speak, but the words came out clumsily.

"Mademoiselle, please forgive my inexpert French. I wish to see Paul Geraud."

Something flickered across the girl's face. "That's not possible."

"Then, perhaps Remi Geraud?"

"Is he expecting you?" the girl asked.

"Actually," Demetri said with a touch of irony, "he **is** ...."

She studied him a long moment as if she didn't quite believe what he was saying, but then she just opened the door wide and gestured for him to enter. She said, "I'll go get Remi," and she left him there in the foyer and disappeared through another door. The foyer opened into a huge and elegant room on the right, but he hadn't been invited to sit, so he stood admiring it as he waited.

Polished wood pillars supported a high ceiling with a gigantic chandelier hanging from its center. At the far end, facing a garden, was a window big enough to sail the *Stella* through. The mahogany-trimmed walls were papered in a rich blue, printed with tiny white flowers. All the overstuffed furniture—in shades of blue and grey—looked very comfortable and inviting, especially to someone who had traveled so hard. Just inside the room was an imposing rolltop desk, its open cover revealing a tidy clutter of papers and writing implements—the desk of a man handling numerous important matters in an organized manner.

At the sound of footsteps approaching, Demetri turned to see a tall, handsomely dressed man of twenty-five or twenty-six approaching. He had dark hair and eyes of bluish-grey that looked warm and open, even now when they were somewhat reserved as they surveyed this unexpected and disheveled visitor.

"Do I know you, Monsieur?"

"I am Demetri Kalidas, son of Nikolaos."

Surprise and delight lit the man's face. "My dear boy! You're here!" He sprang forward to embrace Demetri as if he were a long-lost brother. "Oh, if only Father had lived long enough to see you!"

Thunderstruck, Demetri stammered, "Paul Geraud is ... **dead**?"

The smile left Remi's face. "Yes. Barely a month ago. Just days after I sent the maps. Did you get those?"

Still stunned, Demetri only nodded. What would happen to them now?

Stepping back, Remi looked around. "You're not traveling alone? Where are the others?"

"There was ... an accident ...." Demetri began. "**Our** father is dead also— lost at sea where our mother died." Remi exclaimed in dismay; then Demetri said, "My brother Theodore is outside."

"Outside?"

"We have had some trouble, and it is better that we are not seen together ... that no one knows there are two of us—except of course, **you**."

"What has happened, Demetri?"

"Monsieur Geraud, we desperately need your help. We have nowhere else to go. But we are both exhausted. Could we please rest here tonight and discuss this more tomorrow?"

"Yes, of course! Where are my manners? Let me go call your brother in. You are both welcome here, and you are safe now. But you must be starving too, am I right?" After Demetri's nod, he continued, "There's one thing I must insist upon, however: you must never call me Monsieur Geraud again. Promise you will call me Remi."

Demetri smiled tiredly and gratefully and nodded again.

"Go through that way to the dining room, and I will have Michele set places for the two of you."

"It's already done," a voice said behind them, and when they turned, there was the beautiful green-eyed girl. "And Remi, if you'll send them both through to the kitchen, I'll show them where they can wash up first." He thanked her, and she added, "Oh, I'd better go put out some guest towels." With a swish of skirts, she turned and disappeared into the next room.

Remi started for the door to find Theo, but Demetri clutched his arm and asked anxiously, "But, Remi ... what of the girl? Will she keep our secret?"

The man gave a short laugh and said, "Nothing goes on in this house that Michele doesn't know—she's been running it since she was twelve—and there's no safer person to keep your secret."

"Is she your sister?" Demetri thought he remembered a reference to her in a letter Niko had received from Paul Geraud, but it was vague in his mind now.

"Her mother died when she was very small—no one knows what became of her father—and my parents took her in. I was eleven then, and I'd always wanted a sister, so that is how she was brought up. Now let me go get your brother."

Demetri waited nervously until Remi returned, one arm around the shoulders of the equally exhausted and unkempt Theo. The twins went off in the direction Remi pointed, and Theo whispered under his breath, "I hope there's enough to eat ...."

Remi Geraud wanted a few moments alone to think things through. He had, at various moments during his conversation with Demetri, felt confused, alarmed, dismayed, and heartsore. What had happened to the boys? What had they done? Having only recently lost his own father, he knew how devastated a son could feel—and he was a grown man, not a boy of fifteen in a foreign land. But there was more here, some dark secret that had sent the twins into hiding. He could tell that Demetri feared for his life. Surely they hadn't been the **cause** of their father's death?

Remi shook his head. There was no use speculating. Either the boys would tell him or they wouldn't. The important question to contemplate now was: What to do about it? The wisest thing would be to send the boys on their way—and perhaps notify the local authorities. Why embroil his life and possibly risk his future in the problems of two half-grown foreigners?

The question was easily answered: He owed a debt to them. If not for their father, Nikolaos Kalidas, he himself would not exist. His father and grandparents would have drowned off the coast of Greece decades ago. All Remi's life, his father had spoken of the debt he owed Nikolaos, and on his deathbed, knowing the Kalidas family would be coming to visit, Paul Geraud had been more concerned about this matter than about any of the holdings he was bequeathing to Remi. Gripping his son's arm very tightly, he'd said, "Now, Remi, when Nikolaos and his boys arrive, you must open our home completely to them. Anything they need, as long as they live, you must provide it. Now promise me!" And of course, Remi had. What son could deny a dying father's request?

But he hadn't bargained on it being so complicated and potentially dangerous. It was frightening enough to be suddenly the heir to a vast fortune and responsible for the future of a successful family business that dated back centuries.

What other choices did he have if he helped the boys? He could certainly arrange safe passage if they wanted to go home to Napoli, where their own family wealth would sustain them. But if they were in real trouble of some kind, they might have to abandon that heritage. It would be more prudent, then, to ship them off somewhere else—the Gerauds had many friends and business associates around the world who would employ the brothers—and let them establish a new life in another part of France ... or Austria ... or their native Greece ... or even America!

But it seemed so heartless to cast away these mere boys who had been so touched by misfortune. Surely he could think of a way to help them here, where he could watch over them as his father would want. And with that thought, an idea came to him, and he began to smile.

He went into the dining room and found the boys just sitting down. They'd tidied up a bit, and their hands and faces had been scrubbed until they were bright pink. He knew that Michele had planned a simple meal of braised rabbit and vegetables that could hardly stretch to feed these obviously ravenous visitors. But, looking at the table, Remi could see the girl—ever a genius with any domestic emergency—had added rice, bread, cheeses, and fresh fruit. Remi chose an appropriate wine from the tall glass-fronted case, and when the four of them were seated, the meal began.

Silence prevailed. The exhausted boys had no energy beyond what it took to shovel food into their mouths; they kept their eyes on their plates, as if already choosing the next forkful.

Remi and Michele faced each other across the table, eating at a more leisurely pace. When she gazed over the boys' bent heads and lifted an amused eyebrow at him, he couldn't help smiling back at her. How good it was to have his little Michele—his almost-sister—to enliven the house. Since Father died, Remi'd had many dark moments, and without her, his grief and depressions would surely have been more painful and prolonged. Sharing the sorrow had brought them closer together in the last month. For a mere child of fifteen, she radiated an uncanny sense of inner peace and acceptance in the face of such a loss—Paul Geraud was, for all intents and purposes, her father too—and Remi had drawn much strength from her example.

Remi knew his father considered the girl a daughter, though there was no blood tie at all, and in those days when he lay dying and made Remi promise to attend to many specific matters, the most important were his debt to the Greeks and making sure Michele's future was secure. Legal constraints on the estate made it impossible for him to bequeath any part of those holdings to someone outside the Geraud bloodline, but he'd arranged a handsome annuity. Still, he worried, and in his final moments, made Remi swear to him that he would protect and care for the girl, no matter what.

When the meal was finished, the boys sat looking self-conscious about the quantity they'd eaten and at what speed. When Demetri started to put together a stumbling apology, Michele smiled at him warmly and patted his hand. "Hush, now. You were hungry. No need to apologize for that."

Remi looked at the boys and said, "I know you must be eager for bed. We can talk about the future tomorrow, but in the meantime, know you are welcome to stay here as long as you want—or if you wish to return to Napoli, I will make sure you get there safely. Now, I'll show you your room, and perhaps you'd both like to bathe."

Michele said, "I have gallons and gallons of water heated." She gave them an impish smile and declared, "Thank goodness we have two tubs!"

A few minutes later, the four of them—each toting two buckets of steaming water—climbed the great, curving staircase and went to a guest room with two beds and a fire burning cheerily in the fireplace. The boys exclaimed over the luxury of their room, and then Michele took them where the tubs were kept, and they carried them almost effortlessly back to their room. Michele brought towels and soap and told them to help themselves to the personal grooming items on the dresser. Remi found two nightshirts and dressing gowns he thought might fit them.

Michele told them, "Just leave your old clothes outside the door. I'll take them and burn them."

"Yes, that will be safest," Remi said. "Put on these dressing gowns in the morning, and we'll find you some new clothes. Though I don't expect to see you until afternoon. I want you both to sleep as late as possible and we'll have a midday meal when you waken." He glanced at Michele, who nodded to confirm she'd be glad to provide that. "Sleep well."

Remi and Michele, leaving them to their bath and bed, went downstairs to the kitchen, where Michele began to put together a tray of food. "I cooked three rabbits," Michele said, "but these are the only two pieces left. Tell François I'm sorry."

"I'm sure he'll understand," Remi assured her, adding a demijohn of wine to the tray and covering everything with a white linen cloth. "I don't think I'll need a lantern; there's a moon out. I'll stay awhile with François and talk to him about having the boys take Philippe's place, so I probably won't see you again before morning."

"That's a good idea," she said, already elbows-deep in dishwater, cleaning up after their meal. "François needs the help."

"Sleep well, little sister." Leaving Michele, Remi carried the tray outside and made his way along a well-beaten path lit by the moon. François Avelin lived and worked a short distance away in a large barn converted into a small-scale bottle factory. It was François—a long-time friend of Paul Geraud—who had brought Michele to the estate some fourteen years ago. Remi, eleven years old at the time, remembered it well (intrigued by the sudden visit of a man and a baby, he'd eavesdropped on his parents to find out what was really going on): François, a family friend of the widow Charlotte Devereaux, had been the only person willing to take her young child when she died. But François was a bachelor and quite unprepared to rear a young girl. Remi's parents had taken them both in, giving François his own living quarters and a livelihood making bottles for the specialty wines of the Geraud Vineyards. It was an unusual arrangement, but he was a master at the art of glass blowing, and talent such as this could not be wasted. And they took the beautiful little Michele Devereaux into their hearts as their daughter, so from that time, Remi had a new sister and a new uncle.

Arriving at what they all called the glasshouse (it was a wry joke to compare it with the gigantic glassmaking factories where François had worked), Remi bumped the door with his boot toe and called, "Dinner!" Almost immediately, the door swung inward, and there stood François—his wild white hair looking like a halo around his head, illuminated as it was by the glowing fires behind him.

"Thought you and Michele were trying to starve me," he teased, ushering Remi in with a grand sweep of his arm.

"Sorry, François. We had guests ...." Remi didn't elaborate at this point; he knew François would not be the least bit curious. He mostly preferred a solitary life, and though he had always been welcome at the Geraud table, he rarely supped there, but was content to wait for a tray when the household had finished its meal. In earlier days, when he was younger and stronger, he often was still working the glass when the tray arrived.

Remi suddenly noticed how much smaller and thinner the old man was looking, his wiry frame almost lost within the baggy clothing. *Strange*, he thought, *how one can see a person every day and not be aware of how that person is changing.* He carried the tray toward the back of the building, behind a partition to the area that now served as François's living quarters, and set it on the table. Then he sat in one of the chairs and watched the old man sit down and uncover the dinner with an appreciative sound. There were three glasses on the table, and Remi filled two of them from the demijohn. As he took his first sips, he glanced around the alcove, asking, "How is this working out?"

"Fine, fine," François mumbled around a mouthful of food. Until recently he had lived up above the glassworking area in a huge loft, which was spacious enough to also accommodate a helper or apprentice. Over the years there had been a series of young men; the most recent—Philippe—had left only a few weeks ago, headed to Paris with the girl who'd helped Michele with the housekeeping.) François had always been so independent—he would have done his work without an assistant if he could—but negotiating the steep ladder was becoming more difficult with the advance of the years, and worse yet, cataracts were stealing his sight. "This rabbit is splendid," François declared. "Our Michele becomes a better cook every day, does she not?"

Remi had lost himself in thought, and it took him a moment to concentrate on the old man's words. "H-m-m? Oh, yes, she does." He realized

François had stopped eating, and when he glanced over, he saw his friend staring at him. In the lamplight it was easy to see the cloudiness of those old eyes. "What, François?"

"I have a gift for you. Over there, on the second shelf, wrapped in the grey silk." He pointed across the room with his fork. Curious, Remi rose and went to retrieve it. Whatever the cloth covered was heavy and rather round but not smooth all over; he didn't look inside until he returned to the table and François insisted, "Open it."

Remi knew it would be one of François's beautiful blown glass figurines, but even so, when he pulled aside the silk, he was stunned. The two doves, embraced at the neck, were so perfectly formed, Remi fancied they had once been real birds, and by some wizard's magic had been turned to pale-blue ice. He half expected the warmth of his hands to break the spell and send them fluttering up into the rafters. Awed, Remi exclaimed, "Oh, François, this is exquisite! I don't know **how** you do it—especially now—but this is your best piece yet. I don't think I've ever seen a sculpture more beautiful."

The old man took a drink from his wineglass and then gave a satisfied nod. "It is my last. I can continue with bottles, using the molds, but my eyes just aren't enough for free-blown work anymore. Truth be told, this piece was more God's work than my own." He smiled. "I can't expect He will keep doing them for me and let me take the credit, now can I?" Then he became serious again. "It is for you, Remi. I was thinking of you as I made it. You and Michele. Somehow it reminds me of the two of you."

Startled, Remi stammered, "But ... she's my little sister ... a child."

"**Is** she?" François asked, and something in his tone created an image of Michele in Remi's mind: He saw her again as she had looked moving about the kitchen. Had he been blind? When had her body filled out like that? When had her face lost its pudginess and become so perfectly heart-shaped? When had her eyes taken on that smoky green hint of mystery, and when, pray tell, had her hips learned to move that way just to get her from one part of the room to another?

As disconcerting as Remi found these thoughts, his mind's eye was not finished with him yet. Unexpected—and certainly unbidden—an image of her flashed before him: how she might look standing naked at the foot of his bed with her raven hair flowing down and her arms reaching out to him ....

"No!" he declared, his voice half a gasp. "I mean, maybe she's not a child anymore ... maybe she's not really my sister, but what could be between us? What would people say?"

François finished the last of his bread and washed it down with more wine. He refilled Remi's glass. "When a thing is right ... when two people love each other, there are ways to—"

"But," Remi interrupted, "I'm not in love with Michele!"

"You're not?" François asked dryly.

Remi took his glass and gulped down half the wine to avoid having to answer. *Besides*, he thought, *she can't be in love with me. She's never given any indication she sees me as anything but her brother.* He looked across at François regarding him with a knowing amusement and decided it was time to change the subject.

"Of course I'm not." Then, trying to sound the assertive young business-man, he told the old man, "This is no time to lose ourselves in fantasies. I have an important matter to discuss with you. Remember Father and I were expecting the Kalidas family? Well, events have taken a tragic turn ...." He focused his attention entirely upon explaining the situation to François. He described the boys' arrival, their news of their father's death, their mysterious—and perhaps criminal—secrets, and how Remi thought he might be able to resolve several sets of problems converging at the Geraud Estate. In conclusion, Remi said, "So if you insist on continuing to work—even though I've encouraged you to retire and move to the house where life will be easier—then this seems the best solution. Though it remains to be seen whether such hands as theirs will be able to handle the glass with enough delicacy. If not, they can still do the heavier work for until we decide on another plan. What do you think?"

François had been nodding for some time. "I can use the help now. Not just with the glass but with everyday things. I keep setting items down, and then I have to shuffle all over to find them. I practically have to be standing on top of something to see it. But, Remi, are you sure you want to do this—not knowing what trouble they might be in?"

"It may sound strange," Remi answered, "but I trust them. I'm convinced they would never harm any of us, and if we can conceal their presence by pretending there is only one of them, we shouldn't find any trouble ourselves. Here's how I thought we'd ensure that ...."

They talked for several hours more and drank all the wine. Remi had most of it, and on top of what he'd already consumed, it made his walk back to the house quite unsteady. He had to admit to himself that he was reluctant to return to the house, to be closer to Michele, who had suddenly become a different person in his eyes. It was like a young child with a pet caterpillar, one day finding that well-loved companion had transformed itself into something quite spectacular.

Despite all the wine, he felt too restless to sleep. He took another bottle upstairs and drank and worried and paced the floor for hours before he finally fell across his bed without ever undressing. And when he did sleep, he dreamed of Michele.

Michele Devereaux was the only one up early the next morning, filled with the excitement of having guests—and moreover, people her own age from another land! She was eager to get started on the day's tasks, but as she left her room, she noticed the door to Remi's room was standing open. She went to close it so he could sleep as late as the twins, if he wanted. But when she glanced shyly inside, there lay Remi, on top of the bed, fully clothed and with his boots still on. The long, audible breaths through his open mouth proved the depth of his slumber, providing temptation to Michele, who had never had such an opportunity to view him so intimately and secretly.

Without a sound, she slipped into the room and stood beside his bed, looking down at him, but ready to flee the instant she saw any indication of his waking. Despite the slack mouth and black stubble covering the lower part of his face, Michele asked herself, *Was there ever a more beautiful face than this?*

She had been in love with Remi Geraud as long as she could remember. He was the dearest brother and protector one could hope for, but her thoughts of him as brother had changed long ago, and as her body matured, those feelings intensified until she wondered how he could not notice—how he couldn't see the pain it caused when he still called her "little sister." She'd been mooning after him for over a year, but he was always so busy and distracted—especially as his father failed in health and passed away. She was sure Remi had no idea Paul had spoken to her of this matter shortly before he died. As Remi left the room one day, Paul noticed her longing gaze follow him. Caught, she blushed, for wasn't this her brother? Paul smiled tenderly and told her, "You know he's not really your relative, so nothing stands between you except his own blindness. Perhaps soon he will discover your love and the love I know he has for you. Nothing would please me more, and such a union has my blessing."

Michele gazed down at the sleeping Remi, wanting to touch that ruffled black hair as she memorized the lines of his face, his lean and muscular neck, the way his shirt pulled taut against his powerful chest and forearms. Boldly, she let her eyes travel to his finely tailored breeches, which revealed well-developed thighs and that intriguing bulge below his belt-line, now appearing larger than she'd ever noticed before. Her impulse was to reach out and touch it, to learn more, but as she struggled with these feelings, he stirred slightly in his sleep, and *it* moved too! Her eyes flew up to his face to see if he was waking and were caught by the movement of his full lips as he whispered a word in his dream. *I wish it were my name!* she thought wistfully. And how many times had she dreamed of kissing that mouth?

Too many to resist temptation now! She bent and kissed him softly, imagining he was kissing her back, but then he began to stir again, and she fled for the door like a startled fawn. Out in the hall with it shut behind her, she pressed her hands against her chest to slow her breathing. A long minute went by, but there was no sound or movement from the room behind her, so she assured herself her secret was safe and headed for the kitchen.

By noon she had a feast arranged on the table—enough to feed twenty: thinly sliced ham, several kinds of cheeses, and two loaves of bread, accompanied by pots of spicy mustard and her best homemade marmalades. A huge blown-glass bowl overflowed with peaches, bright-colored oranges, and some early grapes.

Remi appeared first, freshly shaven as usual, but much more casually dressed than was his habit. He surveyed the table with appreciation and then turned his gaze to Michele. Her heart speeded up. Was it possible she saw something new in his eyes? He started toward her, his lips parting to speak, but another voice interrupted.

"Are we too early?" Demetri asked shyly. He stood in the doorway, looking very self-conscious in the dressing gown. His brother Theo hung back even more and never met their eyes.

"No, no!" exclaimed Remi, coming to escort them to the table. "Come in. Sit down. See what Michele has done for us?"

The boys ate more politely than the evening before, and Demetri even managed a bit of light conversation. Theo spoke only when addressed directly and rarely more than "Yes" or "No." At meal's end, Michele excused herself to clear the table, but Remi asked her to stay while he and the boys discussed the future. After learning from them that they preferred **not** to return to their home in Italy, he offered them meals and lodgings at the glasshouse, and they were eager to repay this by any work they could do to help François. Remi agreed with their decision to maintain a single public identity as Alexios Nikolaos, and as far as they all were concerned, the name Kalidas was washed from their memories. The boys were so excited, they were ready to go immediately to the glasshouse, but Remi reminded them they must not both be seen and suggested they wait until after dark when it would be safer.

When all this was settled, Michele withdrew to the kitchen, and Remi took the twins upstairs to a room with armoires and steamer trunks full of clothing and told them, "These belonged to an uncle of mine, and I think they should fit you once Michele can do a little hemming. Help yourself to any and all items you can use. Now, I must attend to some matters about the estate. I'll see you at dinner."

Theo and Demetri spent several hours choosing suitable garments. Feeling rested, well-fed, and safe, they were even able—for a little while—to avoid thinking about their recent ordeal. They laughed and jostled each other, posing dramatically before the mirrors as they tried on different articles and occasionally mocking items that were foreign to them. Once they had what they needed and the room was put back in order, they returned to their room to wait for their evening meal with Remi and Michele.

They lay on their beds, looking out the windows and across the vineyard hills striped with the green rows of vines growing heavy with fruit. Had Demetri not been lost in thoughts about the lovely Michele, he might have been reminded of home by the peaceful beauty of the vineyards.

So it was for Theo, and he was suddenly overwhelmed by the inescapable truth that he would never see his father or his home in Napoli again. Lost was all he held dear—except this brother who had protected him—and any heritage they might have gained from father's wealth. All gone—even their good name—and worst of all, an innocent man was dead. *All because of my stupidity!* thought Theo. It was too much to bear. He began to sob uncontrollably, great wrenching gasps, and he made no attempt to restrain them.

At first startled, Demetri left Theo alone, sensing it was not a time to interfere. *Why don't I have any tears?* Demetri wondered. *Is it because the guilt is truly his? And is his grief simply for the lost lives of our father and that poor squid-seller—or for the helplessness of not being able to control his actions? I must be strong enough for both of us and not allow anyone or anything to cloud my thoughts. We are still in great danger; if anyone finds the boat, we could be caught. I must be strong, I must be strong ....*

Demetri rose and moved to comfort his still-sobbing brother, but a knock at the door made him stop short. Theo seemed oblivious to all about him, so Demetri went to the door and opened it. Surprised to see Michele and instantly awkward in her radiant presence, he slipped out into the hall and closed the door on the sounds of Theo's grief.

To her concerned and curious gaze, he said quickly, "I'm sorry. Did we disturb you?"

"No, no! I was only worried. Is something wrong?"

"My brother grieves for our father ...."

"Of course. There are still nights I cry myself to sleep thinking of my father, Paul Geraud. I still cannot believe he is gone."

Moved by her beauty and the sudden sorrow in her eyes, Demetri reached out to pat her shoulder gently as he soothed, "It is hard for all of us, but it will get better, I think."

Her eyes dampened at this kind consolation, and she smiled at Demetri. As he was basking in this glow, she suddenly stood on tiptoe, threw her arms around his neck, and pulled his head down so she could kiss his cheek. "Oh, Demetri, you are very kind. It is so wonderful to have you here—someone my own age that I can talk to—especially about this painful time in our lives. Now, I must get back or the roast will burn. I came to tell you dinner will be served in one hour." She spun around and hurried toward the stairs.

Demetri stood staring after her, touching his cheek where her kiss still burned, and thought fiercely, *She's mine! When—if—Theo comes to himself again, he'll fall in love with her too. Who could not? But she likes me, and this time I'm putting myself before my brother.*

Feeling more happy than he had in days, Demetri turned and went back into their bedroom.

Theo, no longer crying, was sitting upright on the edge of his bed, staring out the window. Demetri wasn't sure what to do or say—or even if his brother knew he was there, but as soon as the door clicked shut, Theo turned and looked directly into his brother's eyes and said, "This is a beautiful place, is it not? I think we are where we belong."

It took Demetri off-guard. It seemed he hardly knew his brother any more. Only moments ago, he was weeping as if he'd never stop, as if nothing around him mattered. And now it was as if those bitter tears had washed out all that was hurting inside him. *If only that would work for me!* Demetri thought enviously. For he found hidden behind his own pain, a good deal of anger and also fear that his brother might do something else that would make matters worse or lead to their capture.

"I want to thank you for what you did," Theo said quietly. "If you hadn't been so strong and level-headed, both of us would have been killed back there, and it would have been my fault." He rose and came to stand before his brother, put his hands on the other's shoulders. "That old life is over. We will never see home again. Mother and Father are together, and that is God's will. I can never bring back the life of that poor man or ease the sorrow of his family. You have saved my life and have sacrificed your own for me. You are the best brother in the world, Demetri, and I love you." Then he pulled him close, and the two hugged each other so tightly it squeezed the breath from them both, and they laughed.

Then Demetri said, "I love you too, Theo, and I know you would have done the same for me. Now, let us straighten up this room and ready our new clothes to take to the glasshouse. Dinner will soon be served." The thought of food—of Michele's cooking—made them both smile blissfully.

When they came to the table, Theo and Demetri were startled to see it covered with the finest linen, china, silver, and crystal, and they stood awkwardly in the casual clothing they wore. When she saw their discomfort, Michele smiled reassuringly. "Sit down, sit down! You are very welcome here." Demetri was positive she was looking directly into **his** eyes as she said that.

Remi, pouring wine, explained, "I'm afraid this will have to be your last meal in the big house—unless we smuggle you in one-at-a-time on some future occasion—because it will be safer for you to take your meals at the glasshouse with François. So we decided to make this meal special—the way we'd originally planned to entertain you when you visited."

The boys soon relaxed, and both were more talkative than during the last meals, though—as usual—Demetri did most of the talking. Though Michele was polite enough to share her attention around the table, Demetri thrilled at how often her green eyes favored him, proving her love for him. The roast lamb was the best they'd ever eaten, the potatoes perfectly browned, and they were quite surprised to find something as ugly as a snail could taste so delicious smothered in garlic sauce. And after all that—and a caramel custard—Remi said, "Let's all go into the drawing room and have a brandy."

The twins found a cozy fire going when they got there, and four glasses were set out by the brandy bottle. Remi filled them and handed one to each. He raised his high, motioning for the others to do the same. "To family!" he declared, and the others repeated the words, smiling. "To new beginnings!" Again the echo. "And to the future!" The chorus of this last seemed to echo throughout the house, and the foursome tossed their heads back to drain the glasses and ended up coughing and laughing together as the brandy burned its way down inside them. Remi was the first to turn and throw his empty glass into the fireplace. As it shattered against the stone, the others followed, consummating the ritual.

Demetri felt such joy and love and a sense of belonging that he thought it would go on forever. But at this very peak of his elation and hope, something terrible happened, and he watched the whole thing with a horror and disbelief similar to what he'd felt as he watched Theo kill the squid-seller.

Remi and Michele turned and gazed into each other's eyes. Slowly, as if entranced, Remi took her hand and lifted it to his lips. "To love," he said and kissed it. Time stopped in that room as the two spoke to each other with their eyes. It was obvious they had forgotten the others in the room, and the twins stood frozen. Then Remi and Michele moved into each other's arms and shared a kiss that was so clearly pure and passionate and perfect that it brought Demetri's entire world crashing down around his ears.

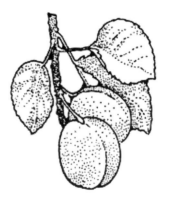

CHAPTER 10
PROVENCE, FRANCE — 1878-1879

When the kiss ended, Michele and Remi drew apart and smiled at each other, then they turned to the boys, less self-conscious than rapt with the wonder of having discovered such a powerful mutual love. Michele said, "I must go fix François's tray before we go. I could use a strong fellow to carry it. Theo?"

He followed her eagerly back toward the kitchen, leaving his brother and Remi in the drawing room. Demetri stood, still crushed by what he'd seen and the realization he had misinterpreted Michele's interest and affection. She really did care for him as a friend, but nothing more. Her love for Remi was unmistakable. And the irony of it! He'd been ready to oppose his brother for the love of the girl, but the one man in the world he could not challenge was Remi Geraud, who was giving them the sustenance and protection they needed for life itself.

In one part of himself, Demetri realized the situation would not feel so devastating if it weren't for all the other unresolved troubles in his life. His father's death, Theo's terrible crime, the harrowing flight by sea and on foot, concealing the truth from Remi, who had been so unconditional in his aid. Suddenly Demetri felt like one of those silk balloons, filled with heated air to rise into the sky, but over-filled until it swelled and stretched and at any moment might burst apart.

"My dear boy," Remi exclaimed, grasping Demetri's arm to steady him. "Are you all right?" The sincere concern in the man's eyes only intensified the misery Demetri felt. There was no way Remi could know what was wrong, but he made his own guess. "Are you still worried about the arrangement here? I assure you it will be safe if we are as careful as we planned, but I must tell you, it would be better if I knew exactly what your trouble was." He grasped Demetri's other arm as well, holding him at arm's length as if he wished to give some of his own strength to the boy. "I have sworn to support and shelter you— no matter what happened—whether you tell me or not. But if I knew, I could better protect you should anyone come asking questions. The choice is yours."

This kindness was too much, and Demetri burst like the over-filled silk balloon, sobs wrenching from him, so that at first his words were nearly unintelligible: "Papa ... fell out of a boat ... they never even found the body. When we ... found out, we were so ... upset, we grabbed someone who yelled ... shook him ... his neck broke. He died." The sentences were so broken by the gasping sobs, they were hard to follow, and the use of "we" was confusing to Remi. Was it merely a struggle with French pronouns or some result of their bond as twins? Which one of them **had** killed the man?

"We ran," Demetri continued, "hid ... stole a boat ... followed maps ... came here."

"Where's the boat?"

"Sank it. Deep water." Demetri stared intensely into Remi's eyes, trying to make the truth understood. "We're sorry. It was ... an accident."

The boy's eyes were full of such abject pain and fear—even now—that Remi might turn against them. The man pulled the boy into his arms and held him as he sobbed. "Of course it was an accident. I know you boys would never intend to harm anyone."

This opened the floodgate entirely, and the boy wept so heartbrokenly that it tapped the spring of Remi's own grief for his father, and he, too, began to cry.

When Michele and Theo returned a few minutes later, they were astounded by the tableau they found. And moved to tears themselves. François's tray was set aside, and the two went to embrace Remi and Demetri, the four of them in one embrace where each touched all, and there was a bond formed then, in a moment lost to grief on the brink of new hope and adventure.

They did not end the embrace until all had finished crying, and then they moved apart, looking at each other's red and swollen eyes, and they laughed softly together and shared the handkerchiefs that Remi and Michele had.

Demetri was surprised to find how good he felt: the tears seemed to have washed away much of the grief and fear, anger and disappointment and guilt. He still hurt; he knew it might take a long time for the pain of these last weeks to disappear—if it ever did—but it was different now, more manageable. He didn't even feel so bad about Michele. Disappointed, yes—and a little foolish—but he could handle that too. Above all, he felt part of a family again.

When tears were dried and noses blown and everyone felt ready to move on, Theo picked up the linen-covered tray, and the foursome left for François's glasshouse.

"There's plenty of room for both of you in the loft," François said, gesturing up the ladder. "It'll give you some privacy and a splendid view of the pond—one I've enjoyed for many years." He sighed. "These failing eyes have taken that joy, I'm afraid, and it's only prudent for me to move down here to the ground floor where it's safer."

Theo and Demetri stood listening attentively, touched by the words of this strange and wild-looking old man, whose warmth and generosity seemed a natural extension of the treatment they'd already received from Remi and Michele.

"And I can assure you plenty of work!" François continued. He tilted his head toward Remi, who stood nearby with his arm around Michele. "With Remi's fine wines in such demand throughout France, I'd have a hard time producing enough bottles—even with perfect eyesight. I must admit I've never been as enthusiastic about the bottle-making as I am about creating glass sculptures. We'll start you out with bottles and see how you do and how much you like the work. Perhaps you'll even want to make figurines too. Are you good with your hands?"

It took the boys a moment to realize François had finished speaking and was waiting for a response. Then it was Demetri who answered, "Yes, Monsieur Avelin, Theo and I do very well with our hands. And we are quick learners."

"Good," François said with a satisfied nod. "But please call me François. I know we will be great friends."

"Yes, all of us!" said Michele, giving the boys one of her sweet smiles, and Remi laughed aloud, looking pleased at how everything was working out. Theo and Demetri, having just spent themselves in tears, could think of no way to express the gratitude they felt to these people who were caring for them.

Theo turned abruptly and scrambled up the ladder to the loft. "Demetri!" he called back joyfully. "It's huge up here! And come see this view—so beautiful in the moonlight!" Giving a little nod to excuse himself, Demetri was quick to follow his brother, leaving the other three below.

They smiled at one another, savoring the perfection of the moment, where each of them had found something precious. Theo and Demetri had a safe temporary home and François, the opportunity to pass on his craft to youths who could help him with his work while providing welcome companionship.

And, it was clear even to François's dim eyes, Remi and Michele had found each other.

The following months were filled with the eagerness and excitement new beginnings bring.

Remi and Michele decided it would be wiser to wait a year to marry. It would be a suitable period after the death of Paul Geraud, and Michele would be sixteen by then. Meanwhile, Remi courted Michele in the most gentlemanly fashion.

Though he was tempted to hire a new housekeeper to relieve Michele of those chores, she convinced him it would be safer for the Greek brothers if he didn't. "I don't mind so much," she told him. "A woman likes to keep house for the man she loves. Even such a big house."

Though he had quite enough to do running his business—especially as the bottle-making crew increased production—Remi found ways to help Michele with some tasks like the heavy cleaning, and he found surprising benefits in this. He loved it when there were floors to scrub, so the two of them had to work together on their hands and knees. Michele was not afraid of hard work, and the energy of her scrubbing dampened her skin, bringing her subtle perfume alive all around him. Wisps of her black hair would escape their pins and curl about her face, which wore such an endearingly determined expression. And the movement of her arm and shoulder would make her young breasts sway inside the bodice of her dress—which often had several buttons undone to keep her cooler, allowing Remi delicious new vistas.

On one such occasion, as he feasted on the sight of her, she suddenly sat back on her heels, using the side of one hand to brush damp hair from her eyes, and stared speculatively at him. Wondering if she guessed what he'd been watching—and thinking!—he felt himself begin to blush and tried to sound genuinely innocent as he asked, "What?"

A smile lit her face as she said, "I was just thinking that you've gotten very good at these cleaning chores. If only your friends and the other wine barons of France could see you now...."

"Lord!" he said, laughing with relief. "Just don't tell them—I'd never hear the end of it!"

During those months, they also shared the preparation of the evening meals, and he found he had quite an innate talent with food, leading Michele to tease him that if she wasn't careful, he'd run away to Paris to become a Master Chef. Each night after they'd eaten, they took supper to the workshop and lingered awhile as François and the twins ate, talking about the day's work and inspecting the results. Then Remi and Michele would go back to the house and spend the next few hours together before retiring to their separate rooms. Often they read plays together, acting out the various roles with different voices, laughing and getting to know each other as never before.

More and more often as the days progressed, Remi left the work of the winery to his manager and stole time alone with Michele. They took long walks away from the vineyards, around the pond and through the woods to the wide meadows on the other side. There Remi liked to sit in one spot and just watch Michele roam about, gathering wildflowers or spying on the tiny creatures that lived in the grasses. So full of joy and youthful exuberance was she that sometimes she just raced herself down a hillside with bare feet flying, skirts billowing above her knees, black hair flowing back from the wind against her face. On such occasions, Remi found himself so aroused it took all his will to keep from running after her, pulling her down into the tall grass and making her his at last. How he wanted her! And he didn't know how much longer he could resist that temptation. What had started out as a few chaste kisses had grown steadily into more passionate sessions, now ending each time with ever-hungrier exploratory touches. It was always Remi who drew the line; Michele seemed as eager as he for more, but dare he ask it? How could he think of tarnishing the reputation of this girl who had been placed in his care...even though she was also the woman he loved?

Meanwhile, François had found Demetri's assessment more than true. To say the brothers were quick learners and good with their hands was like saying Michelangelo could paint churches.

Before they began the actual training, François made sure they understood the honor being bestowed upon them. They were about to learn secrets of a craft reserved for only noble families in France; secrets so precious, Italian glassmakers had been held virtual prisoners on the island of Murano under penalty of death for divulging them; secrets of creation which seemed so magical they were in many ages associated with the black arts.

Suitably impressed, the boys then learned to tend the furnace and prepare the mixtures of sand and soda and lime, how to get the right temperatures and consistency of melted glass in the big clay pots and how to minimize the number of tiny air bubbles in the finished product. Soon—scarcely before François could believe it—Demetri and Theo were forming bottles without his help. So they both would be equally skilled, they took turns assisting each other.

Seemingly oblivious to the heat, one would dip the heated end of a five-foot blow-pipe into the molten glass and gather up a mass of it, a great orange fireball which—when held aloft on the end of the iron pipe—quickly cooled to rose-red and then went back into the pot for a second coating. With the ball once again orange-red at the end of the pipe, the glassworker would blow a small puff of air into it so it expanded, becoming a thick bubble which could be rolled on an oiled slab of smooth stone to make it the same thickness all over. Then more blowing to expand the bubble while working it in a scoop-shaped block of wetted wood, twirling the pipe until the bubble began to take on the approximate shape of a bottle. Still more blowing would expand it further as it cooled to crimson and then to deep red. The assisting brother would ready a hinged metal mold and—when the cherry-red glass was lowered into it—close the mold around it. Breath through the still-attached blow-pipe forced the bubble into every crevice of the mold and when that was opened, one would find—instead of the bright red bubble—a sparkling glass bottle. It was still much too hot to touch, but it could be carefully cracked from the end of the pipe and placed in the annealing kiln to cool down slowly over a number of hours. The brothers also learned the less dramatic methods for smoothing and finishing the still-warm bottles when they came from the kiln.

François marveled at their power of concentration, at the way they appeared to communicate by reading each other's thoughts. It seemed that once their minds and hands had grasped a concept or method, no repetition was ever needed. They worked with such unrelenting dedication—rarely speaking and even more rarely smiling—and with such astounding precision that having the boys making bottles was almost like having a machine to turn them out. *And wouldn't that be a lovely thing? François mused. Imagine a machine to make glass bottles!*

Yet still, in the evenings, when there wasn't enough molten glass left to make another good bottle, they were eager for more. They cherished the last puddles of workable material in the pot, adding to it from another pot (where they'd melted down the scraps of broken or defective glass from the day's work) until there was enough to learn from François how to create objects offhand—without molds. As their skill and interest flourished, he began to allow them to mix batches of colored glass other than the basic bottle green. He shared his own recipes—what minerals and temperatures and techniques to get deep blue and rose pink, amber and amethyst—and that most miraculous of all: crystal clear, like sparkling ice, with only the softest whisper of its natural green.

And at these times, the brothers' manner changed too. Gone were the solemn faces and brows furrowed in concentration. Demetri and Theo let their youthful spirits soar, guiding their hands and breaths to create whimsical forms in continual contests to see who could make the other laugh the hardest. François often watched them dumbfounded. Who could believe such sturdy hands could be so nimble twirling the pipe to keep the shape balanced? Or that these boys who seemed so practical could produce such exquisite, whimsical images? And more than that, how could they manage such steady rhythms breathing life into the glass when they were doing so much laughing?

François was not proud to discover he was a bit envious of their quick skill. It hadn't come so easily to him—in that year after his Charlotte died and he found he no longer had the will to paint. Forced to return to the craft of his family—a heritage he had once rejected—he'd struggled with the familiar discomfort and tedium of glasshouse work and was only able to endure by channeling his artistic nature into freeform creations such as his loving doves.

But François made himself put away those sad memories and his envy and focused on giving his best to these exceptionally talented young men—who themselves had suffered great tragedy and deserved to find happiness and fulfillment in their lives.

As for Demetri and Theo, they thrived in this atmosphere and at finding work which moved them to art. Revering François as an accomplished teacher, they were likewise awed by the old man's stamina. He worked the same 18-hour schedule they did, every day, for none of them felt moved to keep a Sabbath. Those long days were broken in the middle by a repast of bread and wine and cheese, after which François would nap for an hour or two, and one of the twins would take a walk outside. On his return, he would share his impressions of his day and the scenery with his brother. How they wished they could explore their environs together—as they liked to do all things—but they knew that would be far too dangerous. The Geraud Vineyards employed too many workers and one never knew where they might be toiling.

All and all, they were content. They had a safe place to live, plenty of good food to eat, and the honor of learning such a special trade. And they found in François not only a teacher and friend, but someone to help ease the grief of losing their father. In fact, the more time they spent with him and the better they got to know him, the more he reminded them of their own dear father. There was even that same underlying sense of melancholy that had always been part of Nikolaos. They tried not to think too much about that, though, because it made them consider what it would be like to lose François too.

Impossible! Michele thought, consulting the calendar on Remi's desk. *It can't be a whole year since the boys came to us!* But there, on paper, was the proof. Yes, if she stopped to ponder, she could remember the passing of the seasons, the gathering and processing of another year's vintage, the holidays and small celebrations that had marked the passage of time. But so happy and secure had she been all these months, her waking hours seemed to flow past like water. She wondered if it had fled as fast for the boys—they too seemed happy and secure and had certainly learned enough for four men in a decade. *A year!* she thought. *That's certainly worth celebrating.* She smiled. *But that's not all we'll be celebrating this evening....*

At the sound of a voice—"Are you ready?"—Michele glanced up from her reverie and saw Remi in the doorway, holding the tray with the glassworkers' meal hidden beneath a white linen cloth. In the soft lamplight, his face looked more handsome than ever, and Michele felt her heart speeding up, just looking at him and thinking of their evening's mission. Suddenly a little breathless and shy, she glanced away from him and picked up the ice-blue figurine waiting on the desk. It was cool and smooth in her hands, helping her feel more solid and steady too. "Yes," she told Remi with a smile, "I'm ready."

Out in the workshop, François listened to the approaching footsteps and giggling, but he waited until Michele tapped their code softly on the door before he called, "Dinner's here, boys" and swung open the heavy door. Demetri and Theo stepped quickly from behind the partition. François, too, was eager for his supper, but he was suddenly caught by the appearance of the newly arrived couple. He had never seen either of them look so vibrant: Remi's face—grinning, as they say, from ear to ear—was more flushed than the heat of the workshop warranted, and he clutched the edges of the tray so tightly, his knuckles were nearly as white as the cloth.

And Michele! François's heart squeezed almost painfully at the sight of this child grown to womanhood, her radiance undimmed by her downcast eyes and shy smile and the way she cuddled close against Remi's side, even though neither had their arms free to put around each other. It was then that François saw she was gazing down at something she held in her hands. He blinked and squinted to see better through the dimness of old eyes and felt his heart squeeze again as he made out the object and realized its significance. It was the figurine he himself had given Remi a year ago: two loving doves, embraced at the neck.

Theo was reaching to take the tray from Remi, but François said, "Wait. I think our Remi has an announcement to make."

"We were going to wait until after you'd eaten...." Remi protested.

François chuckled and said, "I do not think this announcement can wait that long. Please...."

Remi laughed with some embarrassment. Letting Theo take the tray from him, he put his arm around Michele and said, "Very well." He looked at each of the men in turn. "My friends, you are my only family. Not of my blood, but we share a much stronger bond. Where family can sometimes quarrel and be cruel to one another, that could never be the case with us. To need and rely upon—to **trust**—one another is the greatest gift of friendship. This gift we all share."

Focusing on François, Remi continued, "You, my dearest friend, have always been like an uncle or a second father. Not only were you Father's closest friend, but also my friend as well."

Remi turned his attention to the twins and said. "And you, Demetri ... Theo, my long-lost nephews—my little brothers—my only regret is that we weren't able to spend your early years together. But here we are now—all of us. I'm so glad you are here to share my joy as I announce my intention to marry my dearest Michele."

All the time he was speaking, she had stared at the entwined glass doves in her hands, and now she looked up shyly, hoping to see approval on all the faces. This she found—and more—in their silence, tender smiles, and misted eyes. The boys' reserve was customary, but it wasn't like François to keep so quiet.

Little did she know the emotional tides sweeping that old man. François felt as if his heart would burst. He moved close to Remi and took the younger man's free hand. Holding it tightly in his own shaking hands, François kissed it and looked deeply into Remi's eyes, wishing he could tell the other all he felt and why. Then the old man reached for Michele and drew her close as he began to sob. Somewhat surprised at this response to the happy news, the others treated the moment with reverence, standing with heads slightly bowed, as if in silent prayer. Moments later—still unable to speak—François released Michele and patted her shoulder as if trying to explain, then went to the door and slipped outside.

When the door clicked quietly closed behind him, the twins began to celebrate the news in their own exuberant fashion. Food forgotten for the moment, Theo set the tray on a nearby table, swept the stunned Michele up into his arms, and began dancing around with her while she clutched the figurine to her chest to keep from dropping it. Seeing this, Remi laughed aloud, a sound which ended in a startled yelp as Demetri grabbed him up in the same manner and followed Theo's lead. The brothers whirled about the room, singing—at the tops of their lungs and mostly off-key, what might have been some kind of Greek wedding song—until Remi and Michele were weeping with laughter.

In all the merriment, François was momentarily forgotten. Outside, he leaned against the building and gazed upward toward the skies. The near-full moon shone brightly enough to illuminate this part of the forest, and the stars were visible even to his failing eyes, further blurred by tears.

Only three *times in all my life*, François thought, *have I felt this way*. His soul seemed filled with all the happiness a man could endure. *And each time it is because of Michele!* There was tonight's news, of course, and fourteen years earlier, her move to this estate with the help of his dear friend—Remi's father—Paul Geraud.

And then there was the first time Michele had inspired so much happiness in François: the day of her birth. How well he remembered the way Charlotte glowed as she moved the blanket aside so he could see that sweet infant face framed with black curls, telling him, "We have a daughter." François had thought his heart might fly apart, unable to contain so much love and relief and pride.

At the time he'd never guessed he would be forced to keep his relationship to Michele a secret, that all these years later, he alone would know the truth—a secret he intended to carry to his grave, as Paul had. And now his Michele would marry Paul's son Remi—the finest son-in-law a man could hope for. So at last, with this announcement, François felt all the pain of holding that secret—and denying himself his full share of Michele's love—melt into happiness. Thanking God and making the sign of the cross, he dried his eyes on his sleeve and turned back to join the celebration.

Inside the workshop, he found both Demetri and Theo dancing with Michele while a grinning Remi looked on, clapping time to their imaginary music. Sensing the old man's arrival, Remi turned toward him, his grin growing even wider, and he approached.

Before François could speak—he had yet to offer even the smallest verbal congratulation—Remi stepped close and gripped his shoulders warmly but gently. "Truest friend of my father—my own friend and protector—may I ask a favor? Since you are the closest either Michele or I have to a father, would you do us the great honor of giving away the bride?"

François felt his mouth fall open with the shock of this request, and he had to remind himself it was just coincidence ... his secret was still safe. Still too deeply moved to speak, he grasped Remi's arms and nodded his assent. Then he dragged the young man to the center of the floor, and they both joined the dancers, each taking turns waltzing Michele around the room. When, exhausted, she reminded the men of the supper growing cold, the dancing ended. Beneath the cloth was not only a feast of stuffed partridges and trimmings, but also several bottles of Remi's best champagne for toasting the occasion.

The festivities might have lasted all night had not Remi and Michele reminded the glassworkers that they needed their sleep if they were to work well on the morrow. Remi suggested the three simply take the day off, but François,

Demetri and Theo just stared at him as if they couldn't comprehend the idea of not working.

Since neither Remi nor Michele was walking as steadily as usual, they decided to leave the precious doves figurine at the workshop. "Here," Remi said to Michele, bowing grandly and offering his arm, "take my arm, young lady, and I'll see no harm comes to you on the way home."

Giggling, Michele dropped into a wavering curtsy. "My hero," she teased, glancing upward through her long eyelashes in a mockingly flirtatious manner.

Everyone laughed at this, but Remi saw something more than girlish playfulness in her eyes, and it made him feel warmer than any dancing or laughter or wine had done. "If you'll excuse us," he said to the others, though his eyes never left Michele, "we'll be on our way."

They were quick to depart in a last burst of exuberant well-wishing and held hands as they picked their way along the path by the moon's light. Their haste and tipsiness led to some accidental collisions of arms and hips, which then became a game of bumping hips to see who might make the other step off the path. But they both knew it was more than a game. There was a certain boldness in the touches and the way neither of them was quick to break the contact.

When they reached the steps of the house, Remi could restrain himself no longer. He halted and pulled Michele toward him by the hand he held. She came eagerly into his arms, lifting her face for his kiss. Passion was quick between them, and she melted against his body as if they could become one person. Remi's hands stroked her back, hot beneath the silk dress, and moved lower to new delights, and still she did not resist.

With a little groan of crumbling resolve, he swept her up into his arms and rushed up the steps two at a time. With a sharp thrust of his boot, the door burst inward, and Remi carried Michele into the house and kicked the door shut behind him. She had tucked her face down in the hollow of his neck, hiding her eyes, but her breath was hot and quick on his skin. He hurried up the long flight of stairs and down the hallway, past her room and to his own. There he paused, breathing heavily from exertion and anticipation, but torn about what to do.

"Michele," he said—his voice low and hoarse—and waited until she looked up into his eyes. "If you wish, I will honor your virtue. I have waited this long...."

She pressed so tightly against him he could feel the hardness of her nipples even through their clothing. Her eyes looked deep enough to drown in, and he could see no hint of fear or doubt in them. She pulled his head down to her face, and her lips caressed his ear as she whispered, "Not as long as I, Remi...."

Crushing her even closer in his arms, he carried her quickly into his room and closed the door behind them.

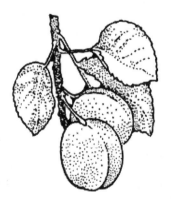

CHAPTER 11
MONTEREY, CALIFORNIA — 1885

It was evening when Dolce brought Antone down to the harbor at Monterey, and almost all the buildings were dark and deserted for the night. Looking ahead, though, he could see lamplight in the windows of Lidakis Glass, and he smiled as he anticipated this unplanned visit to the Greek twins. He dismounted outside and pounded on the door as if he were three times his size and "chewing nails"—as one of his English-speaking friends might say. There was only silence from inside the warehouse, but it was the held-breath silence of the trapped and wary.

Antone could recall several other occasions when he'd done something unexpected around one or both of the brothers and had seen an overly startled reaction. As if they had something to hide or were hiding from something. This was a curious thought, considering how likeable and honest the men had proved themselves to be.

"Theo! Demetri!" he shouted. "This is no way to treat a customer ready to increase your business! Push the girls out the back door if you have to, but let me in!"

The door swung open immediately—as if they'd been standing right there with their ears pressed against it—and Antone was grabbed by two sets of brawny arms and hauled inside, despite his protest of "My horse ...." Full of smiles, exchanging friendly curses, the three bumped together more than embraced, greeting one another in the European fashion of kissing on the cheeks. Relief was plain on the brothers' faces, as well as their usual joy at seeing him. Finished with the greeting but still beaming, Theo said, "I'll go take care of your Dolce" and went out the door.

While he was gone, Antone stood, gazing appreciatively around the glassworking warehouse. It was a huge building with room at the back partitioned off as living quarters. The furnaces that melted the glass were never allowed to go out (when the brothers were away on deliveries, they hired a boy to come in and keep the fires going), so the room was always too hot for any kind of jacket. Antone shed his, glad it was a cool coastal night. He didn't know how his friends could stand it in the summer, but perhaps their years in Greece and southern Italy had given them a different tolerance. The heat intensified the smells too, but luckily, at present, the dominant aroma was of cooking.

"I see my order has been keeping you busy!" The open shelves along one whole wall were full of the wide-shouldered bottles he'd ordered. He walked over to one part of the floor where wooden crates were being assembled, noticing each one was divided with wooden slats, allowing the bottles to sit individually without rubbing together. "These should work just fine."

Demetri had been watching him and nodding, but now he started as if pinched and said, "The soup!" and hurried to the farthest furnace, where a cauldron of something other than glass was bubbling. He used a long wooden spoon to stir it and there looked like enough to feed an army.

"So that's what smells so good!" Antone exclaimed.

"Mydia," Demetri told him, nodding. "Mussels—our father taught us to cook this recipe."

By the time Theo returned from bedding down the horse, Theo was ladling the steaming soup into huge wooden bowls. These they carried back to the living quarters to a table already graced with spoons, wine bottles and glasses, and a long, thin loaf of crusty sourdough bread. They ate in reverent silence. No words were important enough to interrupt focus on the tastes and textures and aromas of the meal. Antone mopped up the last of the hot, spicy soup with a last bit of bread, popped it into his mouth, and sighed as he chewed. "Delicious!" he said.

The brothers, also finished, pushed aside their bowls and gave nods that were both agreement and acknowledgment of the compliment. It was their turn to take Antone off-guard. "Have you kissed your Bella Flora again?"

Antone stammered, feeling his face go hot, especially remembering those latest kisses in the winemaking barn.

Theo and Demetri, sitting on either side of him, both reached out to clap a shoulder as they laughed affectionately. "And have you told her you love her?"

Antone nodded and told them shyly but proudly, "We talked of marriage."

"Ha!" the twins said in unison and thumped the table in their glee. Teasing, Demetri asked, "And have you mentioned this to your families yet?"

"Are you crazy?!" Antone had to laugh at the thought. "We're a long way from that. But the richer I am, the easier it will be. And that's why I'm here on another business trip instead of at home trying to find ways to steal some time with Flora." He told them about how their bottles were to be used as signals for such meetings, delighting them both. They pounded Antone's shoulders so vigorously, he feared he'd have bruises.

"Now this deserves a celebration!" declared Demetri, and he went across to an eight-foot section of the wall that was draped with a heavy curtain. He pulled it back slightly and removed something that had been behind it. Antone was curious. He'd never seen what was behind the curtain, and he'd always wondered .... These Greeks seemed so open, yet there was much about them that remained a mystery to him. As carefully as he looked, he got only an impression of shelves with objects of many colors, some smooth enough to gleam as they reflected the lamplight. Then the curtain fell back, and Demetri returned to the table.

Meanwhile, Theo had gone to fetch another bottle. "Oh, no!" Antone laughed, recognizing it. "Not the oúzo! Don't you remember what happened last time?"

The twins laughed. "We'll take pity on you," Demetri said, and setting three glasses on the table, he added, "Bring the water, Theo." He poured a healthy dollop of the pale Greek liqueur into each glass. Antone was just beginning to take notice of the glasses, which he had never seen before. Emerald-green in color, the goblets were tall and graceful with delicate stems and intricate decoration on each flaring bowl and foot. Intrigued, Antone leaned forward, trying to discern the patterns, and at that moment, Theo added the water, and the oúzo became cloudy.

"Oh!" Antone gasped as the scene came into view—lily pads, lotuses and swans swimming against the milky liquid—and he felt as though he were seeing it from under water. It was a glorious effect.

"A toast!" cried Demetri. "To our glass bottles and anything else that brings Antone close to his Flora!"

"S*alute!*" they all sang out in Italian, and Antone took a great gulp of the sweet, licorice-flavored drink and was struck with the irony of toasting in Italian with a Greek liqueur. As if he could read the thought, Demetri said, "Our father taught us about o*úzo;* he never lost his taste for it all those years in Italy. And Hylas never set sail for Napoli without bringing him a case."

Antone's mind seemed to swim like the oúzo in his glass. It was heady stuff, especially after the wine he'd had with the soup. He wondered who Hylas was, but didn't want to pry.

"Drink up, my friend," commanded Theo, and they all drank until they'd drained the glasses. Antone was feeling decidedly lightheaded, and the brothers took great pleasure in teasing him. "Which makes you drunker—oúzo or beautiful Flora?"

Wishing to steer away from this subject when he was so vulnerable, Antone raised his glass again, admiring the beauty of the now-empty goblet against the glow of the lamplight. As he spoke, he never looked away from the wonders of the emerald-green glass. "My friends," he said, "you have something here. It's not even what I came to discuss, but something even more valuable." He picked up and studied the other two empty glasses, seeing that they were not identical. They were obviously of a set, all of the serene lilypond, but each unique. "You made these, right?" he asked, just to make sure before he got his hopes up.

Mystified, the twins nodded.

"Can you make other things this fine?"

Demetri walked back over to the draped wall and pulled back the curtain. Antone gasped and leapt to his feet. His chair crashed to the floor behind him, but he didn't even notice. "My God!" he breathed, with reverence.

The shelves were packed with pieces of glass art. Many had practical uses: plates and bowls; pitchers, jars, and specialty bottles; decanters, tumblers, and more goblets; vases and lamps and matched candlesticks; sugar bowls, stoppered perfume bottles and paperweights. The array of colors was spectacular, ranging from purples and blues so deep they almost appeared black all the way through every imaginable shade to pieces almost entirely crystal clear. The lamplight glowed on ruby and sapphire, emerald and amber and topaz and aquamarine. As if by a magnet, Antone was drawn to those shelves, and on closer inspection, found many other treasures: freeform expressions of birds and animals, flowers and people, seashells and fruits and whimsical figures impossible to define.

"My God," Antone murmured again. "May I touch them?" Gaining permission, he allowed his fingertips to trace certain graceful lines and knobby textures. He touched the embracing necks of an especially impressive pair of doves. "Exquisite .... All of it." He turned to stare in awe at the twins. "Why have you never showed me these?" he asked. "Do you sell them?"

Theo and Demetri looked at each other and shrugged. They turned their attention back to Antone. "We sell bottles," Demetri said. He pointed. "Those we do ... for pleasure."

A vision—no doubt facilitated by the oúzo—appeared before Antone's eyes. A spacious shop with walls lined by shelves of Lidakis glass creations. Except the shelves, too, were of glass, and behind them, the walls were mostly window panes, so the sunlight pouring through illuminated the colored glass objects as if the whole room were formed of stained glass windows. And there were people crowding in, all richly dressed and eager to possess such treasures.

Antone started laughing. "Oh, my friends. You're about to be very rich. And you're about to help me get that way too!"

SANTA CRUZ MOUNTAINS —1885

Antone reined Dolce to a halt and enjoyed a long last view of the Pacific Ocean, all those miles away. From high up on this ridge, it looked even more calm and blue than it had while he was following the road along its edge around Monterey Bay. When his soul had soaked up enough of that salt-scented air and panoramic beauty, he turned Dolce back onto the road, and they moved into the redwoods. Under the trees, the temperature dropped, and it was already becoming dusk. He urged the honey-colored mare into a trot; they'd better hurry if they wanted to find Sven Heglund before dark.

Antone could hear his destination long before he could see it. Mostly it was the axes and the singing of the saws he heard, but there were other voices too, muffled by the trees and swept away from his ears by playful air currents.

He waited until he heard just the sounds he was expecting; then he swung down out of the saddle and took hold of the bridle's cheek straps. The mare's intelligent eyes regarded him with interest; this was something new. Antone spoke to her soothingly and warned her, "Wait now. Don't be afraid. Just a big noise." The terrible sound of splintering wood came first, and then a long roll of deafening thunder. The mare did fling her head up with a startled snort, but Antone held on and kept reassuring her. Before the thunder ended with a crash that shook the earth beneath their feet, the mare was standing still but definitely wary, her head turned toward the sounds, nostrils flared to taste the air for danger. Then there came faintly the sound of men whooping and shouting, and as the last echoes died away, Antone swung back up on Dolce and turned her in the direction of the noises. She went willingly but with a nervous bouncing to her gait.

They followed the road till it bent around and opened out in a large cleared area. There lay the enormous redwood tree that had just been felled. There were a number of woodsmen about, listening to orders being delivered from the top of the big tree's stump, which rose six feet off the ground and was as big around as a small house. Up on that stump stood a giant of a man with shoulders like an oxbow straining the fabric of his red woolen jacket. The long blond hair straggling past those shoulders was two shades lighter than the full beard and mustache on the sun-browned face. Sven Heglund was unquestionably the biggest man Antone had ever seen, but as he came riding up, Antone called out in English, "Hey, Tiny! What's for supper?"

The man froze in the middle of bellowing orders and pivoted, like a bull trying to catch an annoying fly buzzing at its flank. But when he saw who was approaching, Sven's bearded face broke open in a gap-toothed grin, and he exclaimed with obvious delight, "Antone!" His arms spread out to indicate the stump. "Ever been up on one of these?" Grinning back at him, Antone shook his head. Sven motioned for him to come on up.

Scaling that mammoth stump was no easy chore for Antone. It was hard to get a boothold, and at one point, the shaggy, rust-red bark he was gripping pulled loose, and he slid halfway back down, banging his chin on something sharp. Blood sprang from the gash, flowing down his chin and neck as he began pulling himself up again. Observing all this, Sven let out a robust laugh, then leaned down and grasped Antone's upper arm (like a fist around a sausage) and hauled him the rest of the way up with one mighty jerk. Antone gasped at the wrench in his shoulder socket.

Still laughing, Sven pulled a none-too-clean kerchief from his pocket and slapped it against Antone's chin, sending a bolt of pain through Antone's head. Then he grabbed Antone in a giant bearhug, pounding him on the back, and the coarse wool of his jacket rubbed against Antone's chin until he thought he would faint. Sven held him at arm's length. "Good to see you again so soon! You hold that to your cut while I finish here. Then we'll all get some supper."

Antone did as he was told—one hand holding the cloth to his chin, the other massaging the strained shoulder—and while Sven completed his instructions for beginning the next day's work, Antone stood breathing in the sharp scent of freshly cut timber and gazing at the world from his new perspective. The stump itself was impressive enough: the rich pink wood radiated out from its center in a series of growth rings—perhaps 2000 of them—and each represented a year that tree had withstood the elements. And then there was the view. Like working on the roof of the new barn, it was strange to be looking down on Dolce, who stared up at him with ear-pricked interest. As he dabbed at his wound, the bleeding slowed and stopped, and the pains in his head and arm began to ease.

When Sven was finished and his crew had dispersed to store their tools for the night, he clapped Antone on the shoulder and said, "Let's go!" The descent from the stump was easier, and Antone made it to the ground without mishap. Sven had a horse tied nearby, and they rode, talking, the mile to the base camp. Here there were barns and bunkhouses and a blacksmith shop for shoeing the horses and teams of oxen. When the horses were put away, Sven and Antone headed straight for the cookhouse. By the time they'd washed up outside, the wagon with the rest of the crew had arrived. Inside, Antone sat among the woodsmen, putting away sizable portions of beefsteak and potatoes and beans and wild greens and hot, black coffee. By the time Joon Shing, the Chinese cook, brought in several dried-apple pies—still warm from the ovens—Antone didn't think he could eat another bite, but he managed to polish off a huge slab anyway.

Afterward, as the woodsmen retired for the evening, Antone followed Sven to his office to talk business. The big Norwegian poured them both some brandy, and they sat sipping it as they negotiated and came to agreement.

Seeing him out among the trees, working alongside his men, many people would be surprised to learn Sven Heglund was a very rich man—the sole owner of the Heglund Mill over on the coast and all its timber holdings along the San Lorenzo River. Rather than hiring foremen to run his crews in the woods while he sat shuffling papers in a city office, he'd chosen to hire office people while he remained free to enjoy the work and atmosphere he preferred.

"Ninety thousand board feet of timber," Sven said slowly. "It's a big order, and I'm much pleased to fill it. I'll make sure it's ready for shipping by the date you mentioned."

"And if all goes well, there will be more orders coming." Antone removed the money belt he wore beneath his shirt; it contained the cash he'd been paid in Monterey by the Fortunallo Company to acquire redwood lumber for export to Europe, where it would be made into wine vats.

Sven's eyes widened as he watched Antone count out the money. The belt was still plenty fat when Antone strapped it back on. Sven saluted Antone with his glass. "Looks like you made a good profit on the transaction."

Antone nodded; he had no reason to hide any of the details from Sven. Then he grinned. "A very good profit."

Sven laughed heartily. "Me too!" They laughed together and lifted their glasses in a toast. "To good business," Sven boomed. "And to good friends!" They drained the glasses and smacked them down on the table and then clasped hands—the only contract they would ever need.

Dolce moved quickly through the hushed cathedral of redwood forest. Her hooves made little sound on the carpet of shed needles, so it was easy to hear the voices of the birds singing to the morning. Mist rose up like fairy fog from the forest floor and accentuated the shafts of sunlight that managed to stab through the thick canopy of branches.

Shifting his position, trying to ease the soreness in his arms and shoulders—a result of his visits with two Greeks and a Norwegian—Antone yawned. He was not well-rested (thanks to a night in the Heglund bunkhouse with all those champion snorers), but he was well-pleased. Everything seemed to be falling into place. It never ceased to amaze him how one transaction could blossom into more and more opportunities.

The Fortunallos, family friends in Monterey, had made most of it possible. Months ago, during a visit, Antone had mentioned how his own family was considering a change of focus from table grapes to winemaking. Dante Fortunallo proved quite encouraging (at the time he was sampling a keg of wine Antone had brought as a gift), and he should know what he was talking about: his very prosperous business was the import and export of wines and information on viticulture. He praised the sample of the Mellini product and added, "I can tell you boys have let this age properly—unlike the majority of impatient vineyardists around this state. No wonder our California wines have such a spotty reputation. But one day that will change ... perhaps your vineyard will be part of that." An intoxicating thought!

When Antone told Dante he'd been making his vats out of redwood and explained the special properties of the wood, the man was very intrigued and said some of his colleagues in Europe might be interested in obtaining such timber. The next thing Antone knew, he was brokering redwood from his resource Sven Heglund, and the success of that trial venture had resulted in this current trip to acquire ninety thousand board feet.

Meanwhile, Dante had also introduced Antone to the Lidakis brothers as a source of bottles. That—like most commercial dealings of the congenial and charming Antone—had led not only to good business but also to close friendships. It had been part of the plan to stop at the Greeks' to order another wagonload of bottles (the first shipment was nearly filled with wine that had been kegged for several years on the Mellini farm).

But another surprise awaited him. When he had beheld that decorated emerald-green goblet and then that wall of exquisite glass creations, he saw an even brighter future unfolding before him. He could picture Bella Flora wine

117

being poured into Lidakis glasses in thousands of homes full of the Greeks' inspired glass objects. And when he'd discussed his idea with the twins two nights ago, they were so thrilled that he even liked their work that they just kept looking at each other and laughing joyfully. They made it clear they wanted no part in selling the glass. "We make them," Demetri said. "You sell them." Which was just what Antone had been about to suggest. He could envision a glass shop in Monterey and one in San Francisco, where so much California wealth and art-appreciation flourished.

And he, as the broker of wines and glass and redwood timber, would become rich beyond even his previous fantasies. He would be able to afford a large, elegantly furnished home, and he could visualize Flora there, her innate beauty enhanced by fine clothing and jewels. The home didn't have to be in Santa Clara; if their relatives didn't approve their marriage, then they could live in Monterey or San Francisco—or wherever they wanted!

Smiling to himself, Antone lifted his reins and touched the mare with his heels. She sprang forward at a canter, as eager as he to be home.

CHAPTER 12
SANTA CLARA VALLEY — 1885

Flora's body knew the rhythms so well, she could let her mind wander to more important matters. While her bared arms pumped like pistons and her hands dunked Papa's shirt in the soapy water and massaged it vigorously against the metal ribs of the scrub board, her thoughts were across Page Street in the Mellinis' winemaking barn where she hoped to be that night. For—at last!—the green bottle had appeared this afternoon in Antone's window. He'd arrived back by noon on Saturday, but a big rainstorm that night—and through the next—had kept them from meeting.

I sh*ouldn't hate the rain,* Flora thought guiltily. *This spring has been so dry, and the apricots need the water.* But it was difficult to have waited so long for his return, to know he was over there in that room with the window facing hers, and not be able to meet. And even when the rains were past, still the signal did not appear. Flora had no way of knowing why he couldn't—or wouldn't?—meet her Monday night, and when she arose this morning, still there was no bottle in the window. She'd just begun to tell herself he probably didn't **intend** to meet with her again. Perhaps his family had found out and made him promise not to see that Croat girl again. Or worse yet, maybe it had all been a cruel joke on his part ....

But then, an hour ago when she'd gone into her room to gather items that needed washing, she couldn't help casting one last forlorn look across the street ... and there it was! How her heart leapt at the sight, and she quickly put her own amber bottle—its purpose disguised with a handful of bright poppies—in her window. Then she almost ran back to the yard to the waiting washtub and scrub board.

For now she had only to get finished with the laundry in time to take a bath before Papa got home. She **could** haul the bathing tub to her own room instead of the kitchen, but it wouldn't be as warm in there, and the idea didn't appeal much. So as she scrubbed the life out of Papa's favorite shirt, her thoughts were on the delights of bathing—and of taking some pleasure with Antone—when the voice interrupted them.

"I hope I'm not being too forward ...?"

Startled, she snapped upright and half-turned to see who was there.

"Please forgive me," Karsten Tipanov said hastily. "I didn't mean to startle you."

Flora laughed at herself. "I was a million miles away."

"Would that I could be ...." Karsten said wistfully, then seeing her puzzled look, he waved a dismissive hand. "Never mind. I see you are busy, and I have no wish to impose, but could we speak for a few moments?"

Flora reflected it was fortunate the two of them had no interest in each other romantically. Otherwise, she'd feel embarrassed to be caught so sweaty and disheveled. But she was glad to see him. It'd been very nearly seven weeks since they'd had dinner together, and since then, she'd seen him only briefly at church, and they'd hardly had time to speak together. She was looking forward to getting to know him better, so they could be friends as they'd hoped.

Using the back of her hand to brush some drops of perspiration from her forehead, she told him, "I really must finish this laundry as soon as I can, but if you don't mind talking as I work ...?"

"No, no," he assured her. "And please tell me if I can assist you."

"I'll do that," she promised, and began to run Papa's shirt through the wringer into the tub of rinse water. "What shall we talk about?"

Karsten hesitated, as if he didn't know where to begin. Flora picked up another of Papa's shirts and pushed it down into the soapy water. "I just don't know what to do," Karsten said at last. "I can't make up my mind without talking to someone, and you were the only person I could think of who might understand. You were so sympathetic and kind when we spoke before ...."

Flora smiled to acknowledge the compliment, but she remained silent as she rubbed the shirt relentlessly against the board. She waited for him to choose his own way.

"It's about Ruzena ... the girl I love."

"Ah," Flora said, as she had that first night.

"I can't stand being here without her." He had started out slowly, but now the words came out like a stream undammed. "I think of her all the time—of being near her, of how her hair smells and how her laugh sounds and what it's like to touch her skin and kiss her and never want it to end." He stopped abruptly, embarrassed. "Please forgive me if I've said anything improper."

Flora cranked that last shirt through the wringer. "I'm not offended," she told Karsten and signaled for him to help her dump the washtub's water into a ditch that channeled it away from the yard. "I understand your feelings ... exactly." Still unsure what he expected of her, Flora didn't press. He helped her carry buckets of clean water to fill the emptied tub, and she couldn't help being a little amused with his actions. One could tell he was the product of a rich household, for all these tasks were obviously new to him and his clothes too fine to risk around soapy water and the splatter of mud.

As Flora began to scrub the clothes in the first rinse water and send them back through the wringer to the second, he finally started getting somewhere. "I don't know what to do," he said, as he had at the very beginning.

"What **might** you do?" she asked.

"I could give up and try to forget her." He considered this a long moment. "I've actually tried," he admitted guiltily. "The task of convincing my parents just seemed too large. But my feelings for Ruzena are stronger and more certain now than before I left. And her letters prove it is the same for her."

Flora nodded. "Or?"

"Or I could send her the tickets to come here." He paused, looking a little embarrassed. "Ruzena is not very educated yet, and she has no English at all. It would be frightening for her to make the journey alone—by ship to New York and by railroad to San Jose—and I would be terrified waiting for her."

Curious, Flora asked, "If she's not educated, how does she write letters?"

"Her priest reads my letters to her and writes what she dictates to send to me." He laughed ruefully. "That limits very much what we can say to each other."

Flora smiled sympathetically and thought how fortunate it was that both she and Antone had attended American school and learned English. "Is there any other thing you can do?"

"I could go there and get her and bring her here."

"You have the resources?" It was strange to think of anyone she knew having the money for passage to Europe and two passages back.

Karsten made a dismissive gesture with his hand. "Money is no problem."

"What is the problem then?"

"My parents. They think Ruzena is beneath us. They have forbidden us to marry."

Flora pondered this as she finished the first rinse and got Karsten to help her dump that water. As she started working on the second rinse, she said, "The commandments tell us to honor our parents, but sometimes I wonder what that means. Are we not free to choose our lives?"

"My parents say they are older and wiser. They have had experiences I have not and so their judgment is better."

"Perhaps. But don't you think times change and young people need to try new ways to improve upon the old—even if they make some mistakes?"

Karsten pondered this, as if it had never occurred to him. "But they say it will ruin our life—our family—for me to marry someone below our station. I don't believe that, but they do, and I want them to have a happy life."

"And what of **your** life?" Flora stood upright from the tubs and wiped her hands on her apron. She stood looking past Karsten into the distance; from this location, she could only see part of the Mellini house, but she could see the window with the green glass bottle in it. When she spoke again, it was very softly, almost as if to herself: "To whom do we owe our lives? To our parents ... or to ourselves?" She brought her eyes back to Karsten's, then asked, "And if we live a life our parents choose instead of what is in our hearts, how will we feel when our parents are gone and we are still trapped in that life we did not want?"

Karsten stared at her as if Minerva herself were speaking. "You are so wise!" he said. Flora laughed aloud at this, but he shook his head and told her, "It's all so clear now. I'm going back to Hvar and get Ruzena." It was obvious his mind was racing ahead, making plans. "I can't tell my parents before I leave or they will try to prevent it—even though I'm twenty years old and I have my own money." He paused for a long moment, his thoughts in the future. "I will tell my parents I'm going to spend some days in Sacramento. But I'll get the train in San Jose, and I'll post a letter to them explaining where I'm really going and why. By that time, it will be too late for them to stop me."

As he spoke, Flora saw a subtle shift in his being. He stood up straighter than before, and there was a new certainty and determination in his eyes. He focused on her and gave her a wide and hopeful smile which lit his rather plain face like a lamp. "Thank you, Flora," he said earnestly. "No one has ever done me a greater service than this, and I will remain in your debt as long as I live." He bowed, and taking one of her hands—still damp and red from the cold wash water—kissed it.

She laughed self-consciously and gave a little curtsy, saying playfully, "It was my pleasure. I look forward to meeting your wife Ruzena."

Straightening again, releasing her hand, he laughed aloud and repeated with wonder in his voice, "My ... **wife!**" Suddenly he was in a hurry. He thanked Flora several more times as he backed away, excusing himself with a last "I have a train to catch!"

When he'd turned and hastened off up Page Street, Flora finished wringing the clothes from the second rinse and tossed them into a wicker basket. With some trepidation, she considered what she had done: convinced a lovesick young man to defy his parents, take a journey half-a-world away, and make a marriage they opposed. She took the basket to the clothesline and began to pin the shirts up beside the other items already hanging there. Remembering with what confidence she'd spoken of making a stand for one's own life and love, she thought of Antone and mused, If only *I can be so brave in my own life!*

"Who was that?" a voice asked, and Mattiza Stanich took a shirt from the basket and stood beside her, pinning it up on the line.

"Matty! You startled me. You know him—Karsten Tipanov. His papa owns the new distillery in town." She gave him a teasing smile. "If you were in church more often, you'd recognize the new people ...."

Matty regarded her with his solemn grey eyes and asked, "He's not courting you, is he?"

Flora laughed at the irony of it. "Oh, no," she assured him. "In fact, he'll soon be on his way back to Dalmatia to marry the girl he's in love with. His parents don't approve."

"Good," Matty said, but Flora wasn't sure what he was referring to.

Flora wondered suddenly about Matty's parents ... the violence his mother had endured. Had their marriage been one arranged by the families, or had Eliska once been in love with Vlach? And what would it be like to have such a father as Vlach Stanich? The thought made Flora shiver, but at least Matty was safe from him now. Only two weeks ago in a drunken rage at a local saloon, Stanich had beaten another patron so savagely he'd been convicted on assault charges and sent to prison. Since his health was so poor it was unlikely he'd live out his sentence. Matty was now on his own and managing the pig farm much more successfully, since Vlach wasn't drinking most of the profits.

"What do you think, Matty?" Flora asked. "Should we marry the person we love, even if our parents disapprove—even if it causes pain and discord?"

Matty pinned up the last shirt and turned to her. He was as serious as she'd ever seen him. "I think love is the most important thing. And real love— true love shared—will overcome everything else ... eventually."

Flora smiled at her childhood friend, wishing she could tell him about Antone, but she couldn't ... yet. "I hope you're right, Matty," she said softly. "Oh, I hope you're right."

The moon was very nearly full, so Flora could see Antone as soon as he stepped onto Page Street, and she left the deeper shadows beside the house, moving to meet him. He took her hand and brushed his lips on hers before they hurried across the well-lit yard and into the winemaking barn. It was as dark as outside in this part of the barn, but a lamp was burning back in the alcove.

As soon as the door closed behind them, they were in each other's arms, and their mouths let the hungry kiss express their greetings. They pulled apart somewhat, both panting and laughing a little at their own eagerness. "I missed you!" Flora said.

"I can tell," Antone teased, and then, still holding her in the circle of his arms, his face growing more serious, he told her, "I missed you too. I cannot count the times I thought of you ... of kissing you ...."

The second kiss went on a long time, and Antone's hands roamed across her back but stayed above her waist and Flora knew he was attempting to maintain control—as she had vowed herself—so that nothing went too far or too fast.

In recent days, Flora had given a good deal of consideration to these matters, wondering what God thought of the things that she and Antone were doing. She had no feeling she was doing wrong, for she was convinced it was God's plan that she fall in love with her Italian neighbor and that they express that love in joyous ways. If God didn't want them to kiss and touch, would He have drawn them together and given them such intense feelings for each other? And surely He wouldn't have made it all feel so heavenly, would He?

Shortly after that, Flora made a bargain with God. One day as she helped Papa in the apricot orchard—cutting away the new sprouting branches at the base of the trees before they could steal vital energy and nutrients—Flora found herself missing Antone's touch, and she began to pray to be guided in her actions as she explored their blossoming love. *Dear Lord, I promise I will obey*

Your wishes if You only make them clear to me. I will not do anything You tell me not to. She felt confident in this arrangement since, all her life, when she began to do something wrong—whether she knew beforehand or not—a little voice would say, "Don't." Perhaps it wasn't God Himself, but at the very least it must be some saint or guardian angel doing His will and watching over her. And because this bargain worked so well, she'd spent little time in the confessional. Why should it not work now, when she was with Antone, whom God had sent to her?

When the kiss ended, Antone's voice sounded very deep and breathless as he said, "Shall we sit and talk awhile?"

She gave him a sultry look and said, "I don't want to, but I think we should." They walked to the back of the barn where they'd sat before, and Flora saw he'd spread a blanket over the bales of hay to make the seating a bit less rustic. He offered her wine, but they both decided it would be wise to avoid any other intoxicants. He turned up the lamp to further chase temptations, and she saw for the first time the mark along his jawline. The gash was healing well—despite the application of Sven Heglund's much-used handkerchief—but was still noticeable. "What happened?" she asked.

"It's the mark of one of my many adventures this trip," he replied. "Shall I tell you about them?"

"Oh, yes! And don't leave anything out. So far, I only dream of travel, so take me where you went."

Antone proved to be an accomplished storyteller, despite having to translate his narrative into English. He told her of his latest visit to the Fortunallos and the money he was given to order more redwood lumber. He described his visit with the Greek twins so well, she could taste their mussel soup and oúzo and hear their joyous laughter and clearly see the glass which had so enraptured him. She thrilled to the thought of Antone having wealth that would set them free to share the life they wanted together. She tried to picture the redwood tree large enough to create thunder as it fell. She could see the brawny woodsmen with their axes and the Norwegian giant Sven standing on a treetrunk as big as a house.

And at the end of the stories, she was so moved by his adventures and his efforts to secure their life together, she reached out and softly touched the healing wound on his face, then leaned to kiss the mark. These touches were all that was necessary to remind them what they'd most like to be doing, and when her lips left his chin, they were easily captured by his own.

The kiss deepened more quickly than they had anticipated, and very soon their hands had begun to move against fabric, exploring what was beneath. Flora began to unbutton his shirt, wanting to touch again that soft dark fur across his chest. And when he undid the buttons down the front of her dress, she could sense his surprise and excitement when he found she hadn't bothered with a camisole at all.

And then there was the exquisite moment when their bodies pressed together and she felt for the first time the fur and bare skin of his chest against her breasts. Her mouth was crushed by his and they lay back against the other blanketed bales so that their bodies could make more contact than in a sitting position.

The fire was bright in them both, and Antone wondered if maybe they'd better not stop now. He didn't want to. He'd been this far—farther—with Concetta, but it had never been this good. His mouth wandered from Flora's, kissing her chin and creamy throat and shoulder and collar bone and the beginning swell of her breast, and he heard the wondrous sound she made as his mouth found her nipple.

But there was another sound—the door banging open and a rough voice: "Antone!? Are you in here?"

The passion left them in an instant, and they pulled apart, tugging at their clothes to fasten them. Antone wildly signaled for her to roll over behind the last bale of hay. He managed a sleepy, disoriented voice. "What? Uncle? I'm in the office." He tossed the blanket back so it not only was less noticeable, but concealed Flora. "I fell asleep ...." By the time Gregorio reached him, Antone was seated at the table and had most of his shirt buttons fastened. Thanking God above that the light was lit and a ledger left open on the desk, he rubbed his face as if just awaking.

"You look like you've been spending time with Concetta," Gregorio observed, rather perceptively.

"To tell the truth," Antone said with his best attempt at a leering grin, "I was just dreaming of her. You woke me up at a most ... inconvenient ... moment."

Gregorio laughed, a short, rough bark with little humor in it. He actually apologized. "Sorry, then. A fellow needs those dreams ... especially if he isn't man enough to lie with a woman yet." He was very unsteady on his feet (Antone had thought he'd plied his uncle with enough strong drink to keep him unconscious all night), and he was looking none too well himself. "Let's go. It's late."

"You go on, Uncle. The least you can do is let me ... finish ...."

Gregorio tried to laugh again, but his coloring was looking very bad and beads of sweat popped out on his swarthy skin. "All right. I'll go ahead. I have to puke anyway. Don't be long." He began weaving toward the door, but his voice trailed back. "It's time everyone in this household was in bed."

All this time, Flora lay trembling beneath the blanket, trying desperately to understand what the men were saying in Italian. She wondered what would happen if Gregorio found her here. And frightened as that made her, she was almost equally angry. The indignity of cowering under a blanket in some barn

... of having to hide the love she felt for Antone! It was all unfair. She wasn't sure what they could do, but she was determined that this humiliation would never happen again. Suddenly realizing she hadn't heard either voice for almost a minute, Flora held her breath, wondering what would happen next.

A hand pulled the blanket away from her face, and she saw Antone bending above her with one finger pressed against his lips in a shushing gesture. He helped her to her feet and pulled her into his arms in a protective and somehow apologetic embrace. She leaned into him, weak with relief. He put his mouth to her ear and whispered, "I must go very soon or he will be back to look for me. Can you get home on your own? I will get him in the house and distracted if you can find your way."

She nodded. It wasn't far and there was plenty of moonlight. He led her to the very back wall and moved some kegs to reveal another, smaller door.

"Follow the barn wall around to the front and stay there at the corner until you see we are inside the house. Count to ten slowly, and then go as quickly as you can."

She nodded. It seemed a reasonable and safe plan. They brushed lips and then she ducked out the door, but he caught her hand and pulled her back so her ear was close to his mouth again. "Can you meet me tomorrow night, Flora?"

She didn't hesitate. "Yes."

"We'll figure something out," he said. "I promise ...."

She nodded and he let her go into the moonlight.

Flora had no trouble making her way to the front corner of the barn where she squatted down to be less noticeable if anyone happened to be looking. She watched Antone trying to get his uncle up the steps of the house. Gregorio sounded sick and querulous and Antone kept trying to shush him. They disappeared inside.

"*jedan ... dva ... tri ...* " she counted, "*četri ... pet ... šest ....* " All seemed quiet and safe, but still she counted slowly, "*sedam ... osam ... devet ... deset !*" She darted quickly out to Page Street and across into her own territory, and the main thought in her mind was: *I'll see him again tomorrow night, and we **must** find a safe place to be together!*

CHAPTER 13
CÔTE D'AZUR, PROVENCE — 1878-1879

It was a magical night. Peter Depêche felt it as soon as his bare feet touched the beach sands. He'd never seen a full moon look so large or so bright, and beneath it, the seacoast lay unusually still and hushed. Nor had he ever in all his sixteen years seen this much beach. Generally, there was not that much difference between high tide and low tide along the edge of the Mediterranean, but tonight the sea was retreating a long way from the shore, leaving a wide expanse of shining-wet sand and great tumbles of black rock.

Peter grinned happily, glad he'd brought a sack as well as his net. Old Man LaPorte—who owned a cafe struggling to be a restaurant—was always eager to serve fish freshly caught during the night, and he paid especially well for the delicacies that were harder to find. Peter hurried toward the rocks, but as soon as his feet stepped onto the wet part of the sand, he felt compelled to look off to his right, and he noticed the way was clear to Hidden Cove. Most times it was cut off completely by the sea, and the way down from the cliffs was treacherous to risk for so little reward (the only thing it seemed to offer that wasn't available elsewhere was privacy). But perhaps its rocks would reveal caches of shellfish. At any rate, Peter found himself inexplicably drawn there.

Once past the point and on the more sheltered beach of Hidden Cove, the atmosphere seemed even more hushed and still. Peter felt as if he had entered another world. He had always been attuned to the more mystical aspects of life, a person who trusted his intuition and believed in his dreams—especially those that recurred. When he was only five he had dreamed four times that he would find a coin inside a fish, and he did. And at twelve he had dreamed ahead of time that his father would be promoted at the foundry, and he'd wished later on that he'd told someone, because after it happened, who would believe he hadn't made it up? There were two dreams he'd had many times, but he never told anyone because he feared then they might not come true. One dream was of a girl; she was lovely, but her features always eluded his memory upon waking, except for an endearing small gap between her front teeth. The other dream was of a boat—**his** boat—from which he could fish more easily and profitably. No one in his family wanted him to follow his father into the foundry, so they insisted he keep on with his schooling during the day instead of working at something that could substantially add to the family income. His night fishing trips helped some, even beyond what he brought to their own table.

Moonlight splashed on the tops of the waves, and Peter fancied it looked like a silver road leading to a destination. It beckoned him, and he responded. He waded out to the nearest rocks and scrambled up onto them, stuffing his sack with the shellfish he found. But still he felt the draw, and he moved farther and farther from shore, gathering creatures as he saw them, but not lingering in any one place. On the edge of the most distant rock, he gazed out at the silver road which still lay before him, and then something happened he could not explain. It was almost as if a great hand touched his shoulder and then pointed, showing him exactly where to look. Below him, in the dark water, something reflected the penetrating moonlight and glimmered up at him.

On this warm summer night, Peter wore only an old pair of trousers cut off above the knees, and without hesitation, he secured his sack on the rock and dove into the water. Down he went to the white gleaming, and saw ... a boat! Excitedly, he made for the surface, filled his lungs for a longer dive, and pushed himself back down for a better look.

The boat of his dreams lay calmly on the sandy surface; it had run aground somewhere, and a hole was torn in its bottom, but other than that, it looked to be in good condition.

Peter came up out of the water like a swordfish leaping onto the rocks. He grabbed the sack and moved as quickly as his bare feet would take him over the sharp surface. Once on the beach, he dropped the sack and ran toward his home. He knew the tide would not be favorable for long.

He slipped into his parents' bedroom and shook his father's shoulder to wake him, whispering, "Papa, I need your help. Please!"

He'd never been one to raise false alarms or ask frivolous favors, so his father rose and followed him into the other room. In a low but excited voice, Peter told him about his discovery, ending with the breathless question, "Can you help me tow it out?"

Jacques Depêche struggled with the temptation of more sleep before going to work. The boat probably belonged to someone else and must be returned, but how could he refuse this son who was such a source of joy and pride to him? He nodded. "I'll get dressed. We'll need rope—and the mule."

Peter's face broke into a glorious smile, and he raced out to gather what was needed. Têtu was his uncle's mule, stabled at his house next door, but they were free to use it anytime. Jacques wasted no time and soon appeared, and they both swung up on the mule's bare back and thumped their heels against his ribs. Têtu was none too pleased to be awakened for a seemingly pointless jaunt into the night carrying a double load, and he showed his displeasure by pinning his long ears back and refusing to move faster than a bone-rattling trot. Father and son shouted and cursed at him and slapped him with the ropes, but he took them to Hidden Cove at his own pace.

Peter was terrified the mule would be equally intractable when it came to pulling the boat, but once he was hitched up—after several ropes were lashed together and Peter had dived down to secure one end of the rope to the boat's prow—Têtu performed exactly as directed, perhaps even heroically, considering how he went to his knees in the sand several times at the beginning, trying to get the craft dislodged. It was not an easy process, but the night's magic lingered, and with Jacques working the mule on the shore and Peter maneuvering the craft around the rocks, they accomplished the near-impossible in a very short time.

But as soon as they'd dragged the boat above the highest tide mark, Jacques said, "I must hurry, son, if I am to get to work on time." He hardly gave the boat a glance; he didn't want to start dreaming it could actually be theirs.

"Isn't it **wonderful**, Papa!? Can we keep it? It shouldn't be hard to repair."

"Yes, it is wonderful, and if no one claims it, then you can keep it. But first we must post a notice on the wall in town. If no one claims it, then it is yours, and you can fix it up. But I wouldn't work on it until you know it will be yours. It will be safe here in Hidden Cove until we know for sure. Now, let's go. Already the tide is at the point. I hope this damn' mule is willing to wade through it."

The last thing Peter wanted to do was leave that boat, but his father was right about the tide, so he gave in to that wisdom, and they both left Hidden Cove on the back of a very disgruntled mule (who tried to pitch them off when he was knee-deep in water rounding the point).

Undoubtedly, it would have been wiser, too, for Peter to follow his father's advice about repairing the boat, but the boy knew in the core of his soul that the boat was **his** and that no one else would claim it. The magic night had given his dream to him at last, and with it, he was to make a better life for his family. So he pretended to follow his father's advice—he **did** post a notice, spreading the word throughout town, and he would've surrendered the boat in a moment if the true owner had ever appeared—but secretly, he spent all his time out of classes working on the boat. He worked alone, and was glad that the tides returned to normal and kept the cove less accessible. He fashioned a rope ladder that he could use to get himself and his tools and materials down by way of the cliffs.

The boat already had a name—Ste*lla* was written along her bow—but as soon as the broken boards were patched and Peter painted them white, he also painted over the old name and added her new one: *Magique.*

By the time everyone in the town agreed Peter could claim the boat, it was completely repaired and ready for the water. His father Jacques and one of his uncles came down the rope ladder to help push the craft into the waters of the cove. Peter knew his father was annoyed to find he hadn't waited on the repairs, but Jacques didn't comment on that, since all seemed to have worked out for the best.

Once Peter began using the boat, its reputation grew. Everyone knew about Peter Depêche's "magic boat" that never came in empty and always attracted the very tastiest treasures of the sea. Legends began—stories about how fish would leap into the Magi*que,* begging Peter to put them on the tables of Henri LaPorte. (Peter was fairly certain LaPorte himself had started **that** legend.)

They all prospered. LaPorte served full dinners every night, and his patrons raved and spread the word. As soon as Peter finished his schooling and devoted himself to the M*agique* full time, he began bringing in more money than his father, and they always had more seafood than they could eat. Nightly they feasted on various types of shellfish, octopus, squid, eels, or any of a hundred kinds of fish—whatever was in season. Peter's mother Natasha could cook as well as LaPorte himself, and her talents flourished with the sudden bounty provided by her son.

Well-aware his father had always hated working at the foundry, Peter begged him to quit and help with the fishing, but Jacques knew the M*agique* was an operation big enough for only one person, so he made excuses and continued in the hellish atmosphere that had over the years robbed him of his youth and much of his pride.

Peter agonized, searching for a way to free his father. It was LaPorte who suggested it, asking one day, "Do you think the magic would extend beyond that one boat? If you think you can double your daily catch, I will provide you with a second boat. Do you know someone who could be your partner?"

Never had Peter seen his father look as happy as the day he quit the foundry—and told his boss exactly what he could do with the job. And the two Depêches found there was more than enough magic for two boats. Soon LaPorte's seafood was so sought-after, he began to cater large banquets and parties, even traveling to other towns and villages and private homes.

Peter and Jacques, though they loved the boats and working at sea, found great interest in the restaurant and catering businesses. The younger man was drawn to the latter—which involved travel and viewing some very impressive homes—while his father had begun to fantasize about owning his own restaurant.

At present Jacques was content to fish. There was a holiness in his life now, and the sea was his cathedral. The bounties of the ocean renewed in him the love of life he thought he'd long lost slaving in the foundry. He felt young and strong as a bull again, and his wife Natasha teased him that he hadn't wanted her so much since they were seventeen. And when she warned, "I'm not too old to give Peter a baby sister," he had laughed and asked, "Why don't we try?"

Yes, the sea was good for him, but he looked forward to a time when he would open his own restaurant. He could picture himself greeting his customers and making sure their food was served exactly to their taste. His establishment would be even more famous than LaPorte's, and he would call it after his beautiful wife with the exotic Russian name: Natasha's. And Peter could continue his work with large parties.

The boy had grown into a fine, self-possessed young man, much sought-after by the girls of the town and countryside. When Jacques saw the polite-but-steadfast Peter continually turn away these advances, he began to worry. But when he hinted at the subject to his son, Peter only laughed affectionately and reassured Jacques, "Don't worry, Papa; I know exactly who I'm looking for. All I have to do is keep looking till I find her."

Peter was taller than his father now, with the same sea-colored eyes and black, curly hair but without the silver that now streaked Jacques's. His face was more rugged than his father's but just as tanned and attractive. Jacques was certainly proud of his son, though he did despair of Peter's youthful disregard for formality: he went about most summer days clad only in trousers cut off above his knees. Except for his confident manner, he appeared to be a vagabond, which hurt Jacques's pride some. But it didn't seem to bother most people, especially the young. He had the respect of his male peers, and what girl **wouldn't** be eager to get a closer look at his rippling muscles and well-shaped legs?

But Jacques liked to see him as he was on this day—more than a year after finding the boat in Hidden Cove—perfectly groomed and dressed in a fine suit, as was Jacques himself. There would be no fishing today. They were off for a five-day adventure in the countryside. Peter was assisting LaPorte with a wedding, and he'd convinced his Papa to accompany them so he could see how much fun such events were—including lodging at a private estate—and how many business connections one could make.

And Peter, sitting at the breakfast table with his parents, couldn't help reflecting how rich his life had become since the night when the moon showed him where to find a magic boat.

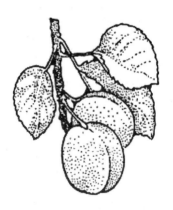

CHAPTER 14
Santa Clara Valley — 1885

As soon as Antone reached Flora, there in the shadows of her house, he enfolded her in his arms and held her close but tenderly. "I am so sorry about what happened last night," he whispered. "That must never happen again."

Flora clung to him; she was in full agreement. "What can we do?"

"We need a safe place to meet. I thought if I could keep my uncle drunk enough, he wouldn't wake and miss me. We've found out we can't depend on that. Besides," he said in a lighter tone, "I can't very well get him drunk every night—that's how often I want to be with you—and even if I could, he's worse than ever to be around the next day. He's like a wolf with a sore tail. So it won't be safe for us in the wine barn **or** our animal barn—or anywhere on my farm. What about **your** barn?"

Flora considered. They could see the barn from where they stood. It was out of sight from her parents' bedroom, but within view of the Stanich house, despite the line of trees—apple, persimmon and fig—that marked the edge of the Bogdonovich property. It should be safe enough, though more dangerous on moonlit nights like this. She smiled up at him. "Let's try it and see."

He grinned and squeezed her hand, and they moved quickly and quietly toward the barn. She had a few brief moments of anticipation, thinking what it would be like to be kissing Antone—feeling his bare skin against hers—secure in her own barn, surrounded by the familiar sounds of Ilka and the horses munching their hay. But in an instant, that image was shattered.

The peaceful night broke open with the sound of vicious barking. Vučak! How could she have forgotten the neighbors' watchdog—who considered the Bogdonovich barn part of his protectorate? She tried to quiet him in a low, desperate whisper, "Hush, Vučak!" But he paid no more mind this time than he ever had. Flora pulled Antone away from the barn doors, which were bathed in moonlight, and into the more shadowy area on the south side of the building. Still the barking continued, and if anything, it sounded louder and more insistent. "Speaking of wolves ...." Flora muttered. "That's Vučak. His name means 'wolf.' He'll never let us in the barn, and even if we got in there, he wouldn't quit. He won't quit now until we leave."

"We'd better go then," Antone said nervously. "Who could sleep through this?" Hand-in-hand they dashed across the moonlit yard till they were hidden from view by Papa's toolshed. The barking ceased, the dog gave a self-satisfied snort, and silence ruled the night again. Antone pulled Flora into his arms and held her; his voice came out in an anguished whisper, "There must be somewhere we can go. Is there no place in this world for us to be together?"

Flora pondered. If only Papa hadn't nailed his cellar shut! The doors were nearly beneath her parents' bedroom window, but she was convinced they could have been quiet enough to slip inside and out again without detection. And even if she could have thought of a way to unnail the doors without being seen or heard, Papa would soon find out. (On more than one occasion since he'd stopped drinking, Flora had seen him test those doors, testing his own resolve.) No, the cellar would never do, nor any of the outbuildings.

Where?! Flora cried within herself. Could life—could God—be so cruel to give this love to her and Antone but not provide a safe place where they could be alone to explore it together? *Where?!*

A memory from childhood touched her mind. "I know!" she whispered, tugged on Antone's hand, and began to lead him toward the orchard. He followed her without question. They moved silently between the rows of apricot trees, now well-leafed and bearing numerous clusters of small, green fruit. On the far side of the orchard was an uncultivated strip of grasses and wildflowers, and at the far edge of this, one could see the white grave markers for the two Bogdonovich babies that hadn't survived. Flora led Antone past these and to the edge of a steep bank. Some eight feet below them flowed a lazy little creek that at times in its past had flowed fast and furiously to cut such a steep niche for itself.

And at one of those times, it had undercut the root system of a huge old oak, causing it to topple sideways, ripping partially free of the earth and lifting most of those roots into the air. But the oak—though lying helpless on the ground—had clung tenaciously to its life through the few roots still penetrating the bank, and eventually it began to flourish once again. Before the elements could steal away the soil clinging to the fan of exposed roots, the seeds of new life took hold there and laced the skeleton with leafy green. As small children, Flora and Mattiza had played there, pretending it was their house and making improvements as they grew and needed more space. They had cut away many of the inner root branches and even carved back into the base of the tree a bit (which hadn't helped the tree's health, but this, too, it had survived), and Flora had pulled trailing vines of a nearby brambleberry bush and guided them among the roots as if it were a trellis.

There now was a riot of bramble canes entwined in the old roots and trailing down in front like a leafy waterfall. In the moonlight, Flora could see the buds that would soon burst into sprays of white blossoms, and these, in turn, would become succulent blackberries in the height of summer. Though neither of her parents ate these berries ("Too many seeds!"), she came several times a season to pick and eat her fill.

But she had quite forgotten her childhood hideaway. She picked her way slowly down the old path to the streambed and stepped up to the veil of brambles, carefully pulling it aside and peering into the nook behind it.

Antone had followed her down, and he made a low sound of surprise as he reached to help her, then grunted when the thorns nipped his hand. But he held the curtain back so Flora could crawl under it and explore her childhood playhouse.

It was damp and cool inside, not at all the warm retreat of her summer days, but there was room for two adults—if they sat very close together. She called back over her shoulder, telling Antone what she'd found, and he shed his jacket and handed it in to her. She spread it out as much as she could and sat on one side. Antone slipped in beside her and sat with his arm around her. "If we had some blankets ... " Flora mused. "But Mama is so ... thrifty ... keeps track of every household article; nothing is ever thrown out. Old blankets become padding or pot holders or some other useful item."

Antone nodded. "I can probably find a couple that won't be missed," he told her. "I am getting many new ideas about how to make this work for us, and how to overcome the difficulties. My Uncle Gregorio is already suspicious, and he will start watching to see if I am often missing, especially if he doesn't find me anywhere on our property."

"What can you do about that?"

"One thing Uncle Gregorio always rides me about is getting a girlfriend." Antone tightened his arm affectionately about Flora. "Of course, he thinks that should be an Italian girl. Anyway, he won't be able to say much against my leaving the house on such a mission."

"But how could you maintain such a deception?"

Antone shifted uncomfortably. "There's an Italian family I know south of here, on my way to the coast. One trip, my horse—before I got Dolce—started limping and I stopped at a farm, and the family took me in for the night. They have a girl my age named Bianca."

"Is she pretty?" Flora asked, sounding very casual.

But Antone recognized the undertone of Flora's voice and couldn't help teasing her. "Oh, yes! **Very** pretty!" He felt her stiffen beside him and gave her another squeeze and nuzzled her ear as, relenting, he assured her, "But not nearly as pretty as you."

Flora's demeanor softened, and she leaned against him again. "So what about this Bianca?"

"I will tell my family I am going to visit **her**. She lives some distance away, so that will give me an excuse to leave earlier. I'll come here—I'll have to bring Dolce—and meet you."

Flora was nodding. "And I will come as soon as my parents are asleep enough. Dolce can graze up on the bank ... she can't be seen from the road there." She pondered more details of the scheme. "Won't your family find out from Bianca's?"

"No. They live far enough away that they are part of another community and attend another church. Our families are unlikely to meet."

They stared at each other and smiled, both feeling the strengths of the plan. It was very dim in their hideaway, but their eyes had now adjusted to it. The bramble curtain blocked out most of the moonlight but bits filtered through the leaves and illuminated tiny sections of their faces. Antone touched one of these that looked like a teardrop on Flora's cheek. "We should go back soon," he said regretfully. "There's not much night left, and we must get enough sleep so that we don't attract attention to ourselves."

"Not just yet," Flora pleaded, her own fingers touching the pattern of moonlight on his lower lip. That soft touch and the longing in her voice made it impossible for Antone not to kiss her.

But it remained a long, sweet kiss, more pure than passionate, and when it ended, Antone looked deep into her eyes and whispered, "I love you, Flora."

"Oh, Antone!" she murmured, and he could see the moonlight sparkle on the sudden tears in her eyes. "I love you too ...."

They kissed again, and sitting as they were, side by side, it was easier to keep this kiss, too, on a more spiritual than physical plane. As they moved, trying to make more contact, they were suddenly poked by bits of root, elbows encountered damp patches of earth, and Flora's ankle brushed against the curtain of thorns. Their mouths came apart in laughter, and they sat up again, rubbing the offended areas.

"Next time we'll be more comfortable," Antone promised. "Leave it to me."

"Tomorrow night?" Flora asked hopefully.

Antone shook his head, and his voice was full of his own disappointment. "No. I think we'd better wait till the next night. I need some sleep and time to—what do they say in English?—lay the groundwork ... with my family."

Flora nodded, seeing the wisdom in this, feeling her own need for sleep. "Friday night, then."

They struggled out of the little tree cave, Antone cursing softly as the blackberry prickles caught and held his shirt sleeve and shoulder when he tried to hold the curtain open for her. Flora made him stand patiently as she worked the brambles free, asking, "How would you explain so many tears in your shirt? Would you tell Gregorio that Bianca has claws like a cat?"

Antone laughed uneasily, sensing that, despite all logical reasoning, Flora was jealous of Bianca, and he felt a little chill when Flora spoke Gregorio's name aloud, a sense of foreboding, as if somehow his unpleasant uncle could reach out and touch their love with disaster. Antone shivered. "Please, Flora, don't say my uncle's name out loud anymore."

"Why not?" she asked, but she had felt the same dark foreboding and hoped that Antone would somehow dispel this.

He shook his head ruefully. "I can't explain. It would only sound silly. But please don't speak the name again." When Flora nodded her agreement, Antone said, "I told him I was going for a walk tonight. Perhaps I should follow the creekbed to the road and walk back that way. Do you mind? Can you get back safely by yourself?"

Once again, she was disappointed, but let the wisdom be more important. "I know these orchards and fields and this creekbed like the rooms in my own house."

"Then we'd better go ...."

They kissed briefly and whispered, "I love you" to each other and parted. Flora scrambled up the creekbank and watched Antone make his way along the stream, using rocks as stepping stones to cross from side to side when he needed. Flora strained her eyes to follow him, admiring his athletic grace and savoring the joy of loving someone so beautiful. When the creekbed made a turn and Antone stepped from her view, Flora sighed and began the walk back alone to her empty bed.

Two nights later, Flora lay in her bed with the covers pulled up to her chin, even though there were beads of perspiration on her forehead. Underneath, she was fully clothed and ready to run to the creek as soon as her parents were asleep. But that could take some time. They'd been making love for hours, now. At least it seemed that way, and the sounds coming to Flora's ears through the bedroom wall didn't help to make her feel any cooler or more relaxed. They were exciting and intriguing sounds, all the more because Flora knew they were attempting to be discreet. What pleasure they must be sharing to so overstep the bounds of decorum. Of course, they thought **she** was asleep, having come to check on her some time ago. Since Papa quit drinking, her parents' lovemaking was a near-nightly celebration of their new life together.

Flora lay listening to the noises, trying to imagine from her limited experience what they were doing and whether she would enjoy such things as much as they. And after those sounds peaked and ceased, there was a short silence followed by low laughter and then murmuring voices. *Why don't they just go to sleep!?* Flora thought impatiently. She could hear the big clock ticking in the parlor, counting away the seconds of her life.

Sometime shortly after the clock chimed eleven, the voices fell silent and soon she heard Papa snoring. She slid out of bed and arranged the bedclothes so that a cursory inspection would conclude she was still sleeping there. She straightened her skirt and blouse—the darkest outfit she owned, hoping to be less visible in the moonlight—and swept her hair up into its bun, then grabbed her shawl and moved silently into the parlor. Her parents had closed their door so she didn't worry about being seen; she just hoped her mother would sleep as heavily as Papa and have no reason to check in on her through the night.

Once safely out of the house, she ran for the orchard and made her way between the rows to the grassy strip on the other side. She stopped short, breathless, when she saw a huge shape looming there, but then it shifted position and she could see it was Antone's mare Dolce. Flora spoke quietly to the horse to avoid startling her, and she lifted her head from grazing and blew softly through her nostrils, as if in greeting. Flora could see Antone had removed the bridle and hung it on the saddlehorn, and soft rope hobbles on her front feet would keep her from roaming far.

Flora hurried to the edge of the bank and started down the path, whispering, "Antone ...?"

He was there in a moment, enfolding her in his arms and his kiss. Then he just held her and murmured, "I thought you'd never come!" She gave a low laugh and told him what had kept her so long as he led her the rest of the way down the path.

When they got to the bower, she could see he'd been busy. A length of rope held the curtain of brambles to one side and beyond it, she could see he'd been smoothing out the back wall, cutting away those bits of root that had poked them. But best of all, there were several thick blankets spread on the ground for them to sit on, and Antone proudly showed her that underneath, he'd thought to put a large piece of oilcloth to keep the earth's dampness from the blankets and their bodies. "It's wonderful!" Flora told him and went to sit inside. She bounced herself gently on the blanketed surface and proclaimed, "It's nearly as soft as my mattress at home."

Antone laughed and sat down beside her. He made no move to let down the curtain but instead, stared at her in the moonlight. "You are **so** beautiful," he murmured, and reached out to her hair, touching it where some stray wisps curled along her cheek. Then he leaned closer and began to pull the hairpins out and put them in his shirt pocket. Her hair tumbled down, and he pushed his hands into it on either side of her face and combed through it, feeling the silk of it run between his fingers. Then he brought his hands back to where they began, pushed into her hair on either side of her face. He bent and kissed her, and her arms came up around his neck.

It was a long kiss, and both seemed determined to make sure matters did not progress too quickly. They had made a pact to find pleasure together without the marital act of intercourse, and they were wise enough to know they must go very slowly and very carefully. At the end of the kiss, she cuddled close against him with her head beneath his chin, and they leaned back against the wall of smoothed roots, appreciating the feeling of simply lying in each other's arms.

They talked awhile; when she asked, Antone described telling his family about the imaginary relationship with Bianca. Like any good storyteller, he embellished the account somewhat, making it more humorous than it actually was, and was rewarded by Flora's sweet laughter. And he down-played the encounter afterward with Gregorio, who had taken him aside after the announcement he was courting someone.

"So!" Gregorio said. "At last you find your manhood! Well, since your own papa probably won't tell you these things, I guess it's my job to give you some pointers." Antone was sickened by what followed, but he made himself stay and listen because this was the friendliest his uncle had ever been, and it was very important not to arouse his suspicions if the plan was to work at all. He could only hope his face didn't show his true feelings as he listened to his uncle's advice about how to treat his paramour and what he should do to her as part of the lovemaking. Antone understood now why no decent girl would have anything to do with him. And Antone had to wonder what things had happened to Gregorio that he would have this twisted view of sexuality—the word "love" was never mentioned—and of life itself.

At the end of his story, Antone kissed Flora to taste again the purity of her spirit, chasing the last shadows of Gregorio from his thoughts. After this, Antone played again with Flora's hair, telling her, "You look so different with your hair down ... you're even lovelier and more desirable. It's strange to think we only see a little bit of what people look like because of clothing and hairstyles. Our faces and our hands, that's what the world sees. Sometimes our arms if we roll up our sleeves, and delightful barefoot girls like you teach us what pretty ankles look like."

"I have my curiosity too," Flora admitted shyly.

"What do you mean?"

She looked away from his eyes. "For a long time, I have wondered if your back is smooth like my papa's—or do you have that wonderful soft fur there too?"

He studied her a moment, then grinned and sat upright, unbuttoned his shirt and pulled it off. He faced away from her. "See for yourself." He waited, and after a moment, he felt her first tentative touch. Then her hand stroked across his back in such a delightful way it covered his skin with *pelle d'oca*—goose flesh. She tugged on his shoulder, turning him to face her, and moved a little out of the way so more moonlight fell across his bare torso. She let her hands and eyes explore his shoulders and the muscles of his chest, skipping lightly across his nipples, and down across the lean tightness of his abdomen, stopping just above his belt. Still staring at his body, she said, "**You** are beautiful."

It was too much for Antone. He began to unbutton the front of her blouse. He watched her eyes to see if she might change her mind, but she looked back at him calmly, and it was she who pulled the tails from her waistband so he could remove the blouse completely. She wore nothing underneath and her nipples tightened with the sudden cool air ... and her excitement. She made no move to cover herself, and let him turn her more into the moonlight so he could view her better. At first he used only his eyes, feasting on the splendor of her body. He shook his head in wonder and said, "Breasts! How could God have known to create something so beautiful to look at?" That made her smile, but when his hands touched her and began their exploration, she lost the smile, her eyes closed, and she let her head fall back with a small soft sound of pleasure.

When Antone saw the arch of her throat, so pale and lovely in the moonlight, his mouth went there first, and then he pulled her close against him. His lips found hers and they clung to each other in a long and passionate kiss while their hands moved across the bare skins of each other's backs and arms. Then Antone whispered in her ear, "*Io ti voglio bene.* That means 'I love you' in Italian, Flora."

She kissed his ear and told him, "In my language, I would say *Ja te ljubin.* I love **you**, Antone." They kissed again, and Antone struggled with himself, wanting more, knowing Flora wanted more, but knowing if he went further now, he might lose the self-control he'd pledged. Groaning a little, he told her, "We should stop now."

She nodded, clearly as reluctant—but as committed to their agreement—as he. They lay together, still unclothed from the waist up, and tried to talk about their everyday lives until Antone said, "If we're to get any sleep, we best get home."

They shared one last skin-to-skin kiss and whispered their love in their native languages and in the one that bridged the two. Then they pulled on their clothing, and Flora did the best she could—without a brush—to sweep her hair up into the bun and place the pins as Antone doled them out from his shirt pocket.

Flora's thoughts were already on the future. "Tomorrow night?"

"Perhaps. Watch for the bottle in my window, and keep your own there if you can meet me. We must always check each other's window just before we come here, in case something unexpected might keep us from leaving." He cupped her face in his hands and gave her one last quick kiss on the lips. "I'll straighten up here," he said, "and hide these things in case anyone happens upon the place. You go on and get some sleep. *Buona notte* ... good night ... Flora."

She turned in the opening of the bower and smiled impishly at him. "*Laku noć, Gospodin Mellini*... good night, Mr. Mellini." Then she ran quickly up the path and disappeared over the edge of the bank.

Over the next few weeks, all the month of May and into June, Antone and Flora met as often as they could, and the only business trip he had to make during that period fell at a convenient time on Flora's calendar. Almost always, Antone was there before Flora and had their place comfortably prepared. (One day during the time that he was gone and she missed him so badly, she had risked a daytime visit to the bower and found he'd rolled up the blankets in the oilcloth and pushed it into the very farthest, darkest corner. So even if someone happened to push aside the brambles and look behind them, they'd be unlikely to see anything unusual.)

He brought her gifts: a tortoiseshell hairbrush that could be left there in the bower, more hairpins to replace those that disappeared, flowers, sweets, and other things his family might expect he would buy for his sweetheart Bianca—none of which Flora could take home with her. Nor could she easily reciprocate. She never went alone to the shops in town, so there was no opportunity to buy things without raising her parents' suspicions. And though Antone insisted, "Your company—your love—are gifts enough," still she wanted to give him more. When she could, she brought a little snack for him, something left from dinner, to introduce him to the foods she would be cooking as his wife: smoked meats and pepper cakes, cheese-and-spinach-filled pastry called *burek,* and his favorite, *ajvar* ... a spicy combination of eggplant, sweet peppers and garlic. Laughing, Antone had teased her more than once: "Are you sure you're not Italian, lady? Trying to feed me all the time?" It was harder for him to bring food, but more than once he supplied ripe cherries from Mellini trees.

And there were other hungers to reckon with. They made a valiant effort to keep their passions under control, to make sure their time together focused on sharing all aspects of their lives, not just their physical desires. They talked about those lives—what had been, what was, what they hoped would be—and it only served to deepen the love and respect they felt for each other. They dreamed together of their wedding—in their fantasies, they both managed to believe it possible to have a ceremony happily attended by both their families—and how they would raise their children. They taught each other words and phrases from their parents' native languages, and they worked at improving their English as well. He called her his *amorosa* ... sweetheart, and she called him *dušho moja* ... my soul, my life.

But always, there was the craving of the flesh to tempt them, for more than almost anything, they yearned to lie together as man and wife, to consummate their love with that ultimate act. They did not rush; they constantly drew limits and stuck by those at the time, but it seemed every meeting started closer to the last limit and went beyond it so that a new limit had to be drawn, and each brought them closer to the inevitable.

Though God had not yet sent a message that Flora was doing wrong, both she and Antone worried that they might be overstepping some limit without knowing it. Both of them wanted to share these pleasures without guilt. After an especially moving mass which focused on the subject of love as described in the thirteenth chapter of First Corinthians, Flora offered a way that they might demonstrate their commitment to each other and to the sacrament of marriage. Antone readily agreed, and the next time they met, they performed a ceremony in the bower to marry themselves in the eyes of God—a temporary measure until they could do so in the eyes of the Church and the law.

First, Antone recited his vow: "Flora, I will love and honor you all the

days of my life. In the name of the Father, the Son, and the Holy Ghost, Amen."
She repeated this, saying his name.

Remembering the passages she'd heard in the mass, Flora translated
them from her Bible into a more modern English phrasing so she and Antone
could read in unison the part beginning with the fourth verse and ending with:
"Love bears all things, believes all things, hopes all things, endures all things.
Love never fails." They finished with another prayer and a kiss to seal this, their
marriage in the eyes of God. And Flora was confident He would guide her
actions from there.

For several meetings they managed to keep their intimacies to bare
torsos, but soon their hands were exploring on the outside of their clothing
below the waist, and then they began to lie together with only their lower
undergarments. They found they could no longer resist the temptation of seeing
each other completely nude. And yet through all of this, they maintained their
commitment to save intercourse for marriage.

They were as satisfied as they could be under the present circumstances.
They thought they had everything under control, and that events were unfolding as they should to take them to their goal of marriage and a happy life
together. They were, after all, young and innocent and hopelessly in love.
Neither had yet learned how unexpectedly—and irreparably—lives can change.

T. Robertson

CHAPTER 15
PROVENCE, FRANCE — 1879

Remi Geraud, resplendent in his wedding finery, took a last, satisfied look at the area where the ceremony would take place. Near the pond, his workers had erected a small, octagonal gazebo. Painted white and decorated with garlands of multi-colored flowers, it was just large enough to accommodate the wedding couple, their witnesses, and the minister. Facing the gazebo and the pond were neat rows of benches for the guests. (Remi had invited nearly a hundred people besides the numerous employees of Geraud Vineyards, and all of them were expected to attend.) Down the center, an aisle leading to the gazebo steps was strewn with petals from the same blossoms decorating the gazebo, a pathway of pink and white, blue and lavender and gold.

The guests were beginning to arrive, and some of the staff he'd hired for the day served as ushers. Remi and Michele had agreed: on this day, their employees were to be treated as guests; all the work would be done by the service catering the reception.

Remi turned and found François standing nearby, regarding him affectionately. Remi took out his pocket watch. "Not long now," he said, a little nervously. François smiled and nodded, and Remi continued, "In a half hour you'll go get Michele?"

The old man took out his own watch and peered at it, then nodded again, assuring Remi, "Don't worry. I'll have your bride here on time."

Remi embraced him, grateful for this steadying influence in the absence of his own father. "I must go check on things ...." he murmured and hurried away. François watched him go. Rarely had he felt as happy as he did today, waiting to see his Michele married to his best friend's son. He went to sit on one of the benches where he could stare out across the pond and the green lawn surrounding it. Through his dimmed eyes, the images blurred together, reminding him of a bright day of emerald water some seventeen years ago.

CASSIS, PROVENCE —1862 – 1863

The Mediterranean expressed itself in many colors, and on this day, it appeared an unusual emerald green. François Avelin stood on the beach, gazing at the sea as he tried to blend the perfect color on his palette. This painting was going well, and he felt pleased with the beach he'd chosen. Here at Cassis—a small fishing port sheltered at the base of Europe's highest cliff—there were three lovely beaches, and the scenery was the stuff of artists' dreams. But perhaps more than the stunning view, he appreciated the fact that the area was practically deserted, and the few others strolling in this little paradise seemed to cherish their privacy as much as he did.

François had been traveling from one coastal village to the next, painting seascapes as he went, trying to master the techniques and subtleties he needed to reach his goal as a recognized and successful artist. It was not a secure life by any means, but he needed little beyond enough food to sustain him and the cost of his materials. France, thankfully, was a country that revered its artists, and perfect strangers often invited him home for meals or gave him temporary lodging and cast-off clothing; when he actually needed money, there were always people who would pay a few francs for a quick portrait. Occasionally someone even bought one of the seascapes. From time to time, he went hungry for a day or sheltered himself beneath a bridge to keep out of the rain, but this life was worlds better than the life he'd fled in his family's glass empire.

For many years, he'd endured the manipulations and tyranny of his parents, learned the trade to which he was bred, and planned to marry the fair Josette Leclerque, the love of his life. When Josette's parents forced her to marry the heir to an even richer glassmaking family and François's own parents castigated him for his heart-broken depression, he vowed to be done with them all—he would live the life he wanted as a painter, and he would never make himself vulnerable to love again.

And so it was, he found himself alone but doing what he loved the most on the beach at Cassis. On his canvas, he had captured the massive cliff meeting the vast expanse of sea, both reminding a man how insignificant he really was. And he was pleased to see he'd duplicated the unusual green of the water this day and the way the light filtered through the clouds as the end of the day neared.

Totally absorbed in applying the last little touches, he suddenly felt certain he was being watched. This was not unusual for any artist working publicly—and at least whoever it was hadn't tried to interrupt him—but never before had he felt a gaze with such intensity. He turned, ready to politely acknowledge the attention but make it plain he wished to maintain the solitude that was his inspiration. He couldn't know that all this was about to end.

"Oh! Pardon me, Monsieur," the intruder said. "I never intended to interrupt you." She was petite enough to be mistaken for a young girl, but there was no mistaking the womanly shape of her body in the dress of rich rose-pink batiste. She carried a matching parasol, and she clearly needed it, for her skin was white as porcelain, in striking contrast to night-black hair, swept up and held in place by several pearl combs. François found himself speechless, but that didn't seem to matter, because his visitor had plenty to say.

"I see now what you've been working on for all these hours," she continued, moving closer to the easel. "It is really quite remarkable the way you caught the flickering of the light in the clouds. Why, I feel I can almost see the movement in it." Her eyes had been on the canvas, but now they came to meet his. "You are truly gifted."

With a shock, François realized those eyes were the exact shade of emerald green he'd been struggling to find for his brush, and he had the sudden fanciful thought that some higher power had given the ocean that hue today as a signal to him. Caught off-guard by her beauty and her compliments, he began to stammer a humble protest, but she waved one white-gloved hand and went on speaking.

"No, no, Monsieur, I am sincere. I live just up there—in that stand of trees—and I've seen many painters on this beach. Sometimes I come down for a closer look. I see many painters," she repeated and—with an enchanting smile—added, "but not nearly so many artists. You, sir, are definitely an artist."

François gave her a little bow and managed to say, "Thank you very much, Mademoiselle—"

"Madame," she corrected, then held out her hand. "Mme. Charlotte Devereaux."

He took her tiny hand, kissing the white glove that protected it from the sun, and—even though he'd vowed to never love again—he felt his heart sink inside him. She was married! "François Avelin," he said. "Your servant."

With a soft laugh, she told him, "I thought I might be of service to **you**. Struggling artists are usually in need of food and lodging, and I'd like to offer such to you—if you haven't already found a local patron ...?"

François laughed aloud at this and joked, "Oh, yes, I've had numerous offers." Dare he be so bold? "But I turned them down, waiting for someone as charming as you."

She laughed again, and François could not take his eyes from her—the raven hair and perfect heart-shaped face with rose-pink lips and green eyes sparkling. He wanted desperately to paint her, to try to capture those colors and contrasts—that spirit—on canvas. And he knew, too, in that moment that he was already irretrievably in love with her. Inwardly, he groaned. Had God not punished him enough? Giving him such parents, separating him from his Josette, forcing him to waste time working at something he resented instead of learning to paint well at an earlier age. Now that he was finally free of the glassworks and his family—resigned to never finding love again—why had God sent him this heavenly Charlotte Devereaux ... a married woman?

"You may be sorry you didn't accept one of those other offers. I'm afraid there won't be a hot meal tonight. I've idled away my afternoon watching some fellow paint on the beach. But there's plenty of cold ham and cheeses and bread, if you can make do with that."

He packed his equipment and followed her up the sandy hill to her home amid the trees. They came first to a little cottage. "This used to be the servants' quarters—when my family had servants." She opened it up to air, saying, "Put your things here. I'll give you some clean linens up at the house." Then they went on to the main house. It was a large structure, but only a third the size of his own family home. There didn't seem to be signs of anyone else around, which made him a little uneasy, but he assumed her husband would be joining them for dinner. Otherwise she certainly wouldn't have invited a total stranger into her home.

Charlotte pointed out the dining room and showed him where to wash up, then excused herself to the kitchen. When François returned to the dining room several minutes later—with his face and hands scrubbed clean and his thick brown hair slicked back and still damp—Charlotte was already seated at the table. On it were flowers and candelabras with brightly burning tapers, huge platters of food and plenty of wine, but François noticed immediately there were only two places set. He stood by what must be his chair and asked, "Will M. Devereaux be joining us?"

Charlotte looked at him, unsmiling, and said, "No, he will not. Sit down, M. Avelin, and help yourself." François did as she directed. He felt awkward at first, but as they ate and drank a good Bordeaux and Charlotte drew him out, he began to relax and told her considerably more than he'd intended about his life as a painter and the events that had led up to it.

At the end of the meal, they moved into another room to have a brandy. Gazing around, François noted the rather masculine decor and all the nautical items: paintings of ships on stormy seas, an ornately crafted ship's compass, a brass sextant, an antique astrolabe. He realized—though he'd told her practically his whole life story—he knew next to nothing about his hostess.

"And what of you, Mme. Devereaux?" he said at last. "What of **your** life and dreams?" She didn't answer right away, only regarded him with a melancholy look, as if she hardly knew where to begin, so he asked another question. "Your husband is a sailor?"

"A naval officer," she replied, and though he waited for more details, she did not offer any. In the silence that stretched between them, a clock chimed eleven. "It's late, Monsieur. You must be tired. I'll get those linens and a lamp to light the way to your quarters."

He nodded and did not ask more. He was the guest, and it was not his place to pry, no matter how curious he was. She left the room and returned a few minutes later with sheets, towels, and a lantern. As she handed him the linens, their arms brushed accidentally, and they both were surprised at the ripple of excitement they felt; their eyes locked questioningly, and then they both looked quickly away. Charlotte gave him the lantern, careful that they did not touch again, and murmured, "In the morning, please come back for coffee and croissants. If it's sunny, we can eat on the terrace."

François thanked her again and made his way to the comfortable little cottage down the path, but he did not sleep well that night. He lay a long, restless time, telling himself he should just get up and leave, forget about this beautiful married woman and whatever game she was playing. Did she often invite artists to dine alone with her when her husband was away at sea? And did her patronage of the arts go beyond food and shelter—or was she one of those sirens who merely tempted men for her own love of power? None of these images fit his sense of who Charlotte Devereaux really was, but how could he know until she told him more about herself? When, at last, he did fall asleep, he dreamed of ships lost in storms and drowning men rescued by black-haired mermaids with emerald eyes.

The next morning, no one answered his knock on the front door, so he found a path around the house toward the seaward side where he should find the terrace. He heard Charlotte Devereaux before he saw her; the sound of soft, heartbroken sobs came to his ears on the gentle sea breeze. He found her on the terrace, collapsed on a *chaise longue*, her face covered by her hands and a sodden white handkerchief.

François went quickly to her side, crying, "Oh, Madame, what is it?"

At first, she tried to hide her grief and choke back the sobs, but the dam was broken, and she gave herself up to it. François stood helplessly for a few moments, then begged, "Please, Madame! Won't you tell me what's wrong?" She tried to speak, but the words were muffled by the handkerchief she still held to her face. There was room on the edge of the *chaise* for him to sit beside her, and he took this liberty, then gently pulled her hands away from her face, saying, "I can't hear what you're trying to tell me."

"It's so unfair!" she cried and there was such a tone of desolation in her voice, François felt as if some giant hand were trying to pluck his heart from his chest. "For you to finally come, and now it's too late."

He stared at her, uncomprehending, but finding—even ravaged as it was by tears—hers was still the most beautiful face he'd ever seen. "I don't understand ...."

"I know you are the man I was meant to marry," Charlotte told him. "I knew it the moment you turned and I saw your face. It's the face I've been looking for all my life." He could only stare at her, dumbfounded. She pointed to a book lying on the terrace tiles beneath the *chaise*, and François bent to pick it up. It was an old book of tales and fairy stories, well cared for but obviously worn from much use. The book fell open to an illustration of a knight on a white stallion, and François had a little start to see his own face looking back from that page. As he stared in disbelief, Charlotte's voice explained.

"My parents gave me this book when I was very young, and from the very first, I was convinced that was a picture of the knight who would come to marry me ... my future husband."

François had to ask. "And what of your husband ... M. Devereaux?"

"My husband is dead," she said flatly. "I know it in my bones, but no one else will believe it." She sighed. "Wait. Let me start at the beginning."

It was not a happy story. She had come to her parents late in their lives, and by the time she was twenty, they were ill and knew they would not be with her much longer. They wanted to see her well provided for and dreamed there might even be time to see a grandchild, so their patience wore thin about her own dream of finding her perfect mate. When they all met the dashing naval officer Audric Devereaux on a trip to Marseille, her parents were convinced this was the answer to their prayers. His family, too, approved the match, seeing Charlotte as a vivid jewel to decorate their son's life. With both families pressuring her, it was difficult for her to resist, especially as her parents' health declined. She wanted to see them happy, and she did not want to live her life alone. At twenty, she was practically a spinster. What if her parents were right— that it was only a picture in a children's book? What if she passed up Audric Devereaux and no one else ever came along?

Besides, he was certainly a good catch: a golden Adonis already decorated three times for bravery, he had impeccable manners and all the financial resources a bride could ever hope for. He showered her with expensive gifts and flattery, and she was swayed by this attention and her wish to please her parents.

She married Audric in May, and by the first of June, she knew she'd made a terrible mistake. His temper, his libido, and his jealousy ruled their life. They lived in one wing of his family home in Marseille, so that she was constantly under the critical eyes of his parents. He placed impossible restrictions upon her, and the most inoffensive attempts to stand up for herself led to physical violence ... and what happened in the bedroom was far worse. He even admitted he wanted her to hate sexual relations so she wouldn't be likely to stray to someone else's bed. At first, she hid her unhappiness and fear from her parents, allowing them to think she'd made a perfect match. By the time Charlotte knew she needed outside help, her parents had succumbed to a summer heat wave, and she was truly alone. When she tried to drop hints to her mother-in-law, she was met with stony silence and total lack of support.

The only good thing about her marriage was that Audric was often gone to sea. She lived for those times and prayed she would not get pregnant when he was home. Then, a year ago, he sailed away and never returned. No trace of his ship or crew had ever been found. Charlotte was absolutely certain he was dead, but his parents remained convinced he was marooned somewhere and would eventually return. They refused to have him declared dead, so she was trapped in a spurious marriage, and of course, Audric's parents were unwilling to let her obtain a divorce. When she could no longer endure life in the Devereaux house, she ran away to her old family home in Cassis—some 25 kilometers to the east— which they had kept as a holiday retreat.

"I've been here ever since," she told François. "I have enough money of my own to keep this house and live very frugally. His family would know where to look if they really want to find me. But they don't care about me—as long as I don't burst their fantasy that he's still alive ... or disgrace his name by trying to divorce him. And no, nothing legal can be done because members of the Devereaux family can buy whatever they need when it comes to legal favors."

By the time she finished her sad tale, Charlotte had stopped crying and dried her eyes. "So you see," she finished miserably. "It is too late."

"Why too late?" he asked her.

"I have no reason to assume you might be interested in me, but even if you were, I'm ... damaged goods ... I may never be able to overcome my experiences in that man's bed. And I will probably never be free to offer my love to anyone."

François gathered her up into his arms and held her tenderly. "Oh, my dearest one," he murmured. "**Interested** in you? I've been in love with you since that very first moment. If you are damaged, it is no fault of yours, and I am here now to cherish you as you deserve. We will only do what is right for you ... only what you want. And as for being free ... who can keep us from loving each other?"

"We cannot marry," she whispered. "I care not, but I can't ask you to offend God's laws by loving me without His sacrament and blessing."

François looked deep into her eyes and asked, "Do you not believe it was God who brought us together? And which union do you think He would most approve: that unhappy marriage to a tyrant or what He has given us? As far as I am concerned, we are married from this moment forward. If you will have me ...?"

"Oh, François!" she cried with new tears shining in her eyes. "Of course. There is nothing I want more than to be your wife."

"Then you **are** my wife, Charlotte ... as long as we both live."

"And you are my husband, François Avelin," she whispered, "as long as we both live."

François held her close in the shelter of his arms and kissed her black hair where it met the whiteness of her forehead. He wanted so much more, but he would wait for the time that Charlotte was ready. And if that time never came, he would love her and take care of her just the same.

They spent the day talking and walking the beach together, and in the evening, he moved his belongings from the cottage into what had been a guest room in the main house. It was not until they parted for the night that François at last kissed Charlotte. He made sure it was tender and sweet but held the promise of what they could share together.

Over the next week they spent nearly every waking moment together, learning all they could about each other and letting the physical side of their union unfold like a rare and delicate flower. Charlotte craved loving touch, and François spent hours simply holding her or walking hand-in-hand or with his arm around her. The first tentative whispers of kisses began to linger and be touched with the beginnings of passion. He had her lead the way, letting him know when she was ready for more.

By the time she finally told him she was ready to make love, such an unshakable bond of trust had been forged, she was able to lay aside her old fears and emotional scars and come to the physical union as one brand-new and ready to believe in the beauty and joy that could be found there. As for François, he surprised himself. He'd been told so many times by his parents what a selfish person he was that he believed it. He'd never realized the ability he had to be so aware of someone else's needs and put those before his own. And as wonderful as the act had been for him at other times in his life, he felt he was truly making love for the very first time.

They spent the next few months doing little more than eating, sleeping, and making love together. It was as if they were trying to make up for lost time ... or as if they feared their love would be snatched away from them again at any moment. And as they explored, caressed, and cherished each other's bodies and learned how to give each other pleasure, Charlotte blossomed. The student became the teacher, and they charted new territories together.

In some ways it was as if time stood still for them, but in other ways, time certainly moved on. One evening, Charlotte shyly told François she was pregnant, an announcement that led to a night more passionate and tender than any they'd yet experienced. The very next day, François began to paint once again. This time his seascapes were Charlotte. Her entire countenance took on a radiance which astounded him and challenged him to capture it in mere paint on cloth. And as her body responded to the miracle within her—a new glow about her skin, the way her tiny breasts and flat belly began to swell like ripe fruit—François found her more beautiful and desirable—and inspiring—than ever before.

The last traces of Audric Devereaux—the nautical items in the parlor—disappeared from the house, sold for the price of new paints and canvases, and were replaced by François's paintings. Many of these were of Charlotte, but the inspiration carried over and infused many other subjects with his special gift: the sea, the tilled fields, a grove of trees, a vase of flowers—all looked new and unique flowing from his brush.

They continued their lovemaking as long as they felt it was safe, and even after that point, the touching and caresses never ceased. They spent countless hours thinking of names, and decided on Michele for a girl—after Charlotte's mother—or Paul for a boy—after François's best friend who lived in another part of Provence and came to visit once shortly after Charlotte learned she was pregnant.

When Michele was born, François found himself once again astounded by the depth of his feelings. How could such a tiny being—no matter what a lovely replica of her mother—stir his soul to such profound spiritual insights? And when he saw the two of them together—mother holding child—a brush would seem to appear in his hand, and he would paint as never before. The rooms of the house began to look like a gallery with his seascapes and still lifes and his incredible portraits of women and children in the everyday rituals of child-rearing. There were so many of these paintings, he began to paint the figures with other features and colorings than those of his models Charlotte and Michele, but the essence of their souls and connectedness radiated from all the paintings.

Charlotte kept urging François to take his paintings into the town, but for a long time, he avoided the risk that they might be judged unworthy and he would have to admit his failure as an artist. He needn't have worried. His paintings sold—and at prices that surprised him. He kept at home the favorite portrait of Charlotte—which hung over the mantel—his favorite of Charlotte holding Michele, the emerald-green seascape that had brought them together, and all the nudes he'd painted of Charlotte during her pregnancy, for these were a private matter, part of their love alone. But the other paintings he took and sold and was much gratified by public response to them.

Over the next few happy months, François spent the majority of daylight hours painting, but—since his wife and child were what he painted most often—he usually shared that time with them. Charlotte concentrated on their daughter, giving her all the attention and nurturing any child could hope for. And Michele, for her part, was a perfect baby. Beyond her inherited petite beauty and her charming smiles, she was alert and sweet-natured and affection-ate, the kind of child that would melt hearts all her life. She also began sleeping through the night at a very early age, which allowed her parents to resume their wondrous lovemaking as if there'd been no interruption, yet still get a reason-able amount of sleep each night.

François could not believe his life was so sweet, and he thanked God daily for sending him such happiness and love and inner peace, such a comfortable life and accomplishment in the work he enjoyed most. And he told himself no matter what happened in the future, he would be satisfied with this life because of what he had found with Charlotte Devereaux.

As Michele grew—she walked and spoke recognizable words well before her first birthday—François began to take charge of her for an hour or two in the afternoons for little excursions to town or just down on the beach to chase the waves and feed bread scraps to the gulls and look for pretty shells to take home to *Maman*. François had never known fathers, too, could have such soul bonds with their children, and part of him ached for what he had missed in his own childhood. These afternoons also allowed Charlotte time to herself for a relaxing bubble bath or the luxury of a nap. Most times, though, she liked to lie outside on the *chaise longue* where François had once found her weeping. The terrace extended out a ways over a steep slope, affording a better view of the sea through the thick trees. She loved to read here, for she could still glance up to enjoy the sight of her husband and daughter playing on the beach far below.

On one such afternoon, François came laughing up from the beach with Michele and saw a carriage just leaving the drive. Filled with a strange sense of foreboding, he rushed into the house and found Charlotte pale-beyond-pale and visibly shaking. He made her sit and poured her a brandy; then he put Michele down for a nap and returned to find out what had happened.

Charlotte said very little. "That was ... Audric's ... parents. They'd heard I had a child. They have convinced themselves Michele is their grandchild—I told you they were crazy!—and they threatened they would take her away from me. Fortunately, I am here in Cassis where **my** family had political friends. They know they can't take her as long as I have that protection here." She turned to him with sudden intensity and fear in her green eyes. "François, promise if anything happens to me, you won't let those people have Michele."

Cold horror crept along his spine, and he protested, "Nothing's going to happen to you, Char—"

"Promise me!" she interrupted with such desperation that he could do nothing else but vow to follow her wishes.

After a few very tense weeks—in which no word came from or about the Devereaux family—they began to believe Audric's parents had come to their senses ... or at least decided not to press their case for the present. They allowed their life to return to normal with only a small amount of additional caution.

As it turned out, François and Charlotte were wise to savor every moment of their love and life together, for their union was like a candle that burns very brightly but very briefly. Somehow François was not surprised that it all ended too soon, but the surprise came in the simple and senseless way it happened. Not battling some tragic illness or struggling to protect her home and child, but because they were always too busy to deal with mundane matters such as housework and home maintenance.

On a day shortly after the child's first birthday, François was bringing Michele back from the beach. Progress was slow, because she kept crying, "Oh, look!" and stooping to capture some shell or pretty stone or piece of smoothed driftwood. François looked up toward the house and saw his Charlotte at the edge of the terrace, watching them. He waved, and even from that distance, he could see her glorious smile as she gave him a vigorous wave in return and leaned against the railing.

François saw it all in that slowed-down pace one encounters in nightmares when no matter what you do or how fast you run, there's no way to escape the inevitable. He could only stand, watching horrified, as the railing lurched and sagged beneath her hand, and Charlotte—losing her balance—pitched head-first over it and fell to the hard ground below. If anything about the incident could be called good, there was the fact that Charlotte died instantly; she could not have suffered. And thankfully, at the moment of the fall, Michele was bent down watching an interesting crab and did not see any of it happen.

François lived the next weeks in a trance. He functioned: arranging Charlotte's funeral, dealing with the executors of her estate, caring for Michele and trying to answer her questions without either alarming her or lying to her. The property reverted to a distant relative of Charlotte's father, and François was told he would have to leave before the end of the next month. Where could he go? How could he provide for Michele? He only knew two kinds of work: painting and glassmaking. He found the will to paint had totally left him; he hoped it would return one day, but in the meantime, he had to survive, and he could not force Michele to live the rigorous and risky life of a vagabond. He'd also made a promise to Charlotte to keep their daughter from the Devereaux family, and the best way to do that was to disappear from the area and never return. So he packed up clothing enough for the two of them and the few canvasses he had kept—rolled and sealed in a waterproof tube—and left Cassis for his childhood home.

In shock as he was, the plan to return to his own family's glassworks seemed reasonable, but he was only there two months before he came back to himself enough to realize it was a mistake and he would have to find another arrangement. He hated the work there as much as ever (though he did seem able to turn out exemplary glass when he applied himself); his parents treated him nearly the same except they had the additional weapon of his having sired an illegitimate child. But it was what they were doing to Michele that worried him most. Certainly they doted on her as their grandchild and gave her every luxury, but François could see them trying to implant their own seeds of selfishness and petty cruelty. They criticized her for the slightest misstep, including her own natural curiosity and penchant for asking questions. It had not begun yet, but François was sure that as she grew old enough to understand, they would use her illegitimacy to torment her.

He managed to survive there a year, time enough for his grief to ease and allow him to attend to other aspects of his life; he was able to save a small amount of money, and an anguished letter to his good friend Paul Geraud brought a tantalizing proposition.

He left his family forever and went to the Geraud Estate where he gave Michele into the care of his hosts. Hard decisions were made that wrenched his heart but would ultimately benefit Michele. Even Paul's wife did not know François was the child's father. As far as anyone knew, she was an orphan, the legitimate child of the Widow Devereaux. And as the child became more attached to the Gerauds and their young son Remi, François spent less time with her, keeping to himself in the converted barn where he made specialty bottles and glass works of art for his friend Paul.

Michele grew in this loving family and her memories began to blur so that she eventually did not remember the times with her mother and the dark times of her father's grief and her grandparents' influence. And as he'd hoped, she even forgot the times before she came to the Gerauds, and this further blurred the bonds of their relationship, and she began to call him Uncle François as her brother Remi did.

It broke François's heart to relinquish his title of Papa and hear it bestowed on his friend Paul, but this, too, had been François's choice, and it was little enough to give so that she might have a happy, secure, and untarnished life.

CHAPTER 16
Provence, France — 1879

François shifted his old bones on the bench by the pond and pulled out his pocket watch to check the time. It was even harder to read now that there were tears in his eyes, but he could see it was time to go get Michele for the ceremony. François gave a great sigh, still touched by the sadness of his memories. "**Ah**, dear Charlotte," he whispered, "I hope you are somewhere you can see our daughter this day ...."

He rose and started for the house, waving to an anxious-looking Remi to show he hadn't forgotten his task. He saw one of the Nikolaos boys over near the glasshouse. At this distance, it was impossible to tell which; Michele had made identical clothing for them so Theo and Demetri could share in the festivities, taking turns pretending to be Alexios Nikolaos. For an instant, François thought he saw both boys outside at once, but that had to be a trick of his dim old eyes. The boys wouldn't be that stupid ... to risk all they'd so carefully created.

It was cool and quiet in the big house; it had been a long time since he'd been inside. François made his way up the stairs and to the room with its door ajar. Soft laughter came from behind it, and when he knocked, it was answered by a chestnut-haired girl dressed all in lavender. He couldn't remember her name, but he knew it was Michele's friend who would serve as her attendant. The girl smiled shyly at him and—over her shoulder—called, "Monsieur Avelin—your stand-in papa—is here. I must go get my flowers. I will see you downstairs, Michele." She slipped by him and hurried downstairs in search of her bouquet.

Michele met François at the door, reaching up to pull his face down where she could shower it with kisses. François's heart seemed to stop momentarily at the image before him. Michele was every bit as beautiful as her mother, and for a brief moment, François thought it **was** Charlotte.

Amused at François's entranced expression, Michele pirouetted in her white wedding dress, saying, "It is a beautiful dress, isn't it?" Then, before he could answer, she asked, "So, Papa, have you come to give me away?"

Still half-lost in his memories, and confused by being called Papa, François murmured, "Why, Charlotte, what do you—"

"Charlotte?!" Michele interrupted with great amusement and teased, "Have you already forgotten my name?"

Embarrassed, François stammered, "You ... you ... remind me of your mother, who was a dear friend—remember?"

"I wish she were here with me now," Michele said wistfully. On another day, she might have been more curious, asked questions that could be difficult for François to answer, but it was her wedding day, and her thoughts went quickly elsewhere. She moved back to her dressing table with its array of perfumes and cosmetics, items she rarely used and never needed. She stared at herself in the mirror and added a little lip coloring. Her handmade dress was simply cut but layered in fine Alençon lace, and her hair was adorned with a halo of wildflowers. François knew there would be many a man—married or not—envying Remi Geraud today.

Turning from the mirror, Michele smiled at François affectionately and said, "Since you are acting as my father today, I will always call you Papa from now on. Do you mind?"

Startled, hoping she didn't see the quick tears that sprang up in his eyes as he struggled to regain his composure, François replied, "Of course not, Michele. I will forever be honored. Now, are you ready? I don't think your Remi can endure waiting a moment longer—and who could blame him?"

Smiling, Michele took the arm he offered and picked up her bridal bouquet from the table by the door. Then she glanced back at the room where she had grown from a child into a woman, and François knew exactly what she must be thinking: in an hour she would be a married woman, the wife of Remi Geraud. For better or for worse, her whole life was about to change forever. And no matter how well she knew him or how strong their commitment was to each other, there were no guarantees it would be what she dreamed. And there were certainly no guarantees it would last forever.

François above all others knew this. He pressed Michele's hand where it lay on his arm and tenderly reminded her of what she already knew, "God didn't make a better man than Remi Geraud."

Michele's green eyes glistened with the beginnings of tears as she nodded her agreement. She took a last look back at the room of her childhood and said, "I'm ready, Papa."

François Avelin, with Michele on his arm and a knot of tears in his throat, made his way downstairs and out to the gazebo where he would give away his daughter for the second time.

Though he was surrounded by a gaggle of admiring girls, Peter Depêche looked over the tops of their heads to check on his father. Jacques, champagne in hand, seemed right at home socializing with wine barons and other wealthy businessmen; Peter was glad he'd asked him to come. One of the girls put a glass of champagne in his hand, and he sipped from it, his first taste that day. As part of the work crew, he had to wait till late in the party to socialize or enjoy the refreshments. Only a few moments earlier, LaPorte had given him the nod that he was off duty. Almost immediately, the girls had congregated, like honeybees to a suddenly opened flower. Foremost among them were LaPorte's daughters Janaí and Odette—who had finished their serving duties and removed their white aprons—but there were several young daughters of neighboring estates or the extensive business contacts of the Geraud Vineyards. Peter enjoyed the attention and flirted with all the girls, not yet favoring one above the others. They were all trying to get him to dance with them.

The wedding ceremony had ended hours ago, and now even the reception was winding down: many guests had left or were preparing to do so, and the clean-up staff had begun its work as unobtrusively as possible. But still the musicians were playing, and a number of people were dancing on the close-clipped grass of the lawn.

Peter sipped his champagne and made an appreciative sound. "This is good," he declared. "My compliments to the Geraud Vineyards!" The girls laughed as if he'd said something exceedingly humorous and pressed closer, sensing he was about to choose someone.

There was one girl he'd been especially watching all day. She was taller than the rest, and from the way she moved in her lavender dress, Peter could guess she had long legs and an athletic build. He could also guess she spent much of her time outdoors, because her flawless skin was deeply tanned. Her chestnut brown hair, though neat, flowed loosely about her face and sometimes had to be brushed away from her eyes—candid hazel eyes he'd caught regarding him levelly on numerous occasions throughout the day. Though they'd never met, her face seemed strangely familiar to him, and he told himself that was just because she'd been so prominent in the wedding party, acting as the bride's attendant.

She stood a little back from the others, not crowding him but definitely making herself available as a dancing partner. She was also more reserved than the others, and he had yet to see her laugh. This became a challenge. Gazing into her eyes—which were exotically almond-shaped—he said, "My name is Peter Depêche. You are?"

"Cassandra Toussaint." Though her eyes danced with amusement, she kept her face solemn as she commented, "I hear you have a magic boat."

He gave her a wry smile, admitting, "I'm afraid my boat is better known—and better loved—than I am!"

Hearing this, she finally laughed aloud. And there it was—an endearing gap between her front teeth, the centerpiece of a smile that illuminated her face, and he knew who she was at last. Unable to look away from that face, he held out his champagne glass and someone took it. "Excuse me, ladies," he murmured and moved to take the hand of the girl in lavender. "Dance?" he managed to say and she nodded. The rest of the party was forgotten, except for the music playing, which gave them an excuse to move closer together and take each other's hands.

Low, under his breath so only she could hear, Peter asked her, "What would you say if I told you I have been dreaming about you since I was nine years old?"

She laughed up at him, and he could see the pink tip of her tongue peeking through the space between her upper teeth. "I'd say we don't have much time here today. Do you want to keep dancing, or would you rather go where we can talk?"

Peter was so startled, he stopped dancing and stared at her. That was all the answer Cassandra needed. She still held one of his hands, and she turned and began walking along a path which lead away from the festivities beside the pond. Utterly entranced, Peter went with her. She glanced up at him with a teasing smile. "Do you find me forward?"

"I find you delightful."

They walked without speaking into a little grove of trees and found a huge building which had once been a barn but was obviously converted for another purpose. Peter stared in fascination at the massive stonework areas of the wall which tapered up into chimneys. There was a sheltered stack of cut wood and troughs of water and a number of implements he couldn't name— everything clean and neatly arranged for a day when guests would be visiting the estate. "This is the glasshouse where François Avelin makes his bottles and other beautiful things out of glass," Cassandra explained.

She led Peter around to the far side of the barn where a small wooden bench—carved from a tree stump—stood directly below a large window. "This is my favorite place on the whole estate," Cassandra said and sat down. There was barely room for another person on the bench, so when Peter sat beside her, their bodies touched from shoulder to knee and it was less awkward when he put his arm around her along the back of the bench. She sighed and leaned against him as comfortably as if they'd known each other a lifetime.

"Do you believe in love at first sight?" she asked him.

"I do now," he replied. They sat in silence for several long minutes, gazing at the view of the sun sinking toward the grove of trees. From far away came the faint sound of music and happy laughter. Peter could never remember feeling such a sense of peace and contentment ... of completion—as if for the first time in his life he was finally whole. Then his rational mind rebelled, insisting, *This is crazy! If this is the girl you're searching for, shouldn't you be talking about it, making plans, **doing** something about it?*

"I live in a village over on the coast," he told her. "I'm a fisherman, but I have my own boat and business, and someday soon I'll be very wealthy."

Cassandra nodded. "I grew up on the estate to the east of here. Michele— the bride—was always my best friend. When my mother died two years ago, father and I moved to Fréjus, and that's where I live now."

Delighted, Peter said, "Fréjus! That's not so far from where I live."

"I know," she answered and told him how to find her house.

"Then can I come visit you next week? Start seeing you?"

She sat up a bit and looked into his eyes. "If you don't, I'll have to come looking for you." And she gave him that most wonderful of smiles.

Peter laughed aloud and bent to kiss that smile with its alluring gap between the front teeth. It was a long, soft kiss, full of passion's promise but without urgency, as if they both understood that now they'd found each other, they had only to let their life together unfold as it was meant to. After the kiss, they cuddled together as before and sat in a blissful, satisfied silence Peter had never imagined possible.

Some moments later, there was a noisy commotion around the other side of the building and the door to the glasshouse slammed shut so forcefully that it rocked the bench where Peter and Cassandra sat, making them grab each other more closely in their startlement. Loud voices could be heard inside the building—two voices that sounded very similar, though one was louder and much angrier.

"Damn you, Theo! How could you do this? You know the rules—**never** to be seen together! It was my turn to be out. You got to be at the damn wedding, and still you had to keep creeping out when it was my turn."

Peter and Cassandra stared at each other. What possible difference could it make for two people to be seen together?

"Take it easy, Demetri," the other voice said, and it was obviously slurred with drink. "No one noticed. Everyone's attention is on Remi or Michele—and with the amount of champagne consumed, everybody's seeing double anyway."

The first voice roared in anguish, "Don't you understand? We must leave here now. We cannot risk that anyone saw us both. You fool! Because of you, we are criminals and live in hiding. And now we've lost our good life here."

Frightened by what they'd heard—and afraid they'd be discovered—Peter and Cassandra quietly slid off the bench and began to hurry away, but glancing back, Peter saw a sudden movement in the window they'd hidden beneath. He pulled Cassandra after him as he ducked in among the trees beside the path. They both squatted down, clinging to each other and praying not to be noticed. Their eyes, peering between the bushes and lowest tree branches, saw another movement in the window, and then, there—framed by the window like a living portrait—were two identical faces, contorted with anger and yelling at each other. The blond heads and massive shoulders were easy to recognize. Both Peter and Cassandra had seen that fellow—except now there were **two** of him—several times during the day's celebration. The voices sounded suddenly different, and Peter realized they'd switched to another language—Italian, he guessed. As quickly as the faces appeared, they were gone.

Peter, still clutching Cassandra's hand, sprang up, and they raced down the path toward what was left of the wedding reception. The sun was about to set beyond the trees to the west and the clean-up crew was trying to finish its work before lanterns were needed. Besides that staff—and the musicians packing up their instruments—there were only a few other people lingering near the pond. Peter was relieved to see his father there, talking to LaPorte and an affluent gentleman wearing a top hat.

The three turned as Peter and Cassandra rushed up, breathless. "There you are, Cassandra!" exclaimed the man with the top hat. "Where have you—"

"Father!" she gasped, trying to get her breath.

Laughing, Henri LaPorte teased, "We'd decided the two of you must be kidnapped. We were just about to call in the *gendarmes*."

But Jacques Depêche was watching his son carefully. "What's wrong, Peter?"

"Maybe you'd **better** call the *gendarmes*," he answered. "I think there are some escaped criminals hiding in M. Geraud's glasshouse."

After the very briefest introductions, the young couple—still holding hands as if they'd never be separated again—quickly told what they'd heard and described the men they'd seen arguing. "*Mon Dieu!*" Cassandra's father interjected. "I know of these men!" He was a city official in the port of Fréjus and over a year ago had received reports of blond twins named Theodore and Demetri—Greeks who had lived in Italy—who'd killed a man in the village of Aurelia and escaped in a stolen boat. "As far as I know, they've never been seen since then," Toussaint concluded. "There was even speculation they might be lost at sea, because the boat—let me see ... it was called the *Stella*—was never found either."

Dumbstruck, Peter only half-listened to what the others were saying now as his thoughts spun dizzily around what he'd just heard. The *Stella!* So at last he knew how his *Magique* had come to him. And now wasn't this a dilemma? What should he do? Try to return his precious craft to her rightful owner? Or just keep quiet, since it was improbable anyone would find out? He was the only one who knew the *Magique*'s former name. But if the twin murderers were caught, they would tell where they'd scuttled the stolen boat. Then the trail would lead back to him, and his dishonesty would be plain to all: his parents and neighbors, Henri LaPorte, and this girl he loved and planned to marry. What was he to do?

"Peter!" someone said loudly. It was his father. "Are you paying attention?"

"I was just thinking—"

"Well, M. Toussaint wants you to accompany him to notify the authorities. You must hurry before those criminals escape or harm someone else."

LaPorte said nervously, "I'm going to tell our crew to simply leave everything and return to the Beaumont Estate. We'll come back and finish tomorrow when it's safe. We can take Mademoiselle Cassandra with us—spare her the unpleasantness of a police station. You're also staying at the Beaumonts', aren't you?"

Both Cassandra and her father nodded and agreed this was the best arrangement; then Toussaint turned to Peter and said, "We should be on our way, young man."

"Yes, sir. One moment, please?" He still held Cassandra's hand, and he drew her out of earshot of the others. "I'm sorry to leave you this way. Are you all right?"

"Yes, Peter. I'm not frightened anymore. Just excited. What a day!"

He smiled at her, wanting to leave her with a kiss, but knowing they were watched. "Yes, just think what a story this will make: meeting at a wedding and love-at-first-sight and how we helped to catch some dangerous criminals! Someday we can tell our children all about it."

"Yes," Cassandra said, giving him the lovely smile of his dreams. "And our grandchildren ...."

The kitchen door wasn't locked, and when Theo and Demetri burst in, they found Remi and Michele standing in the middle of the room, sharing a passionate kiss. Startled, the lovers moved apart, and the boys stopped short, mumbling embarrassed apologies. But François came pushing in behind them, trying to get the door closed.

Still imbued with all the heady excitement of his wedding celebration, Remi didn't at first notice the anxiety on the newcomers' faces—or the fact that the boys each carried a bundle of possessions. "What's this? What's this?" he asked, but before anyone could answer, he hoisted a half-empty bottle of champagne and declared, "Well, since you're here, let's have a toast to the happiest day of my life!"

"Remi!" François snapped in a tone that cut through both alcohol and euphoria. "There's trouble." It was he who explained for the twins—who stood shame-faced and frightened—that both of them had been out at once and had undoubtedly been seen. "And just now, there was some activity down by the pond that makes me uneasy. I know Claude Toussaint read reports about the escape, and if that's what he was discussing, he'll soon have the police here. The boys think they should flee, and I'm afraid I agree with them."

"Oh, no!" Michele cried softly.

"I'm going back to the glasshouse," François told them, "so I can pretend my own innocence and confuse the trail however I can. I know you have a plan, Remi, to get our boys safely away." Remi nodded, and the old man grabbed Demetri and then Theo, giving them both a fatherly embrace and admonishing, "Don't forget what I've taught you—or that you will always be my boys. And may you go with God—tonight and always." He was crying openly now, and in a moment, everyone was wiping tears from brimming eyes. The brothers choked out an emotional farewell, and François slipped out into the night.

"A plan?" Demetri asked now.

Remi nodded. "After you told me what happened in Aurelia, I arranged an escape route for you. Thankfully, my family has wide-ranging resources and help we can trust, even in such delicate matters. I have all the documentation and instructions you will need; I've taken the liberty of giving you a new surname: Lidakis—rearranging Kalidas a bit. Tonight, you will leave here and go four miles to the east to the home of my friend Julien Chenault—you met him today, remember? He was my best man." The boys nodded, and Remi continued, "Tomorrow he will take you by coach west to the port of Biarritz on the Atlantic coast—a journey of perhaps six days. No one will expect you to escape from such a fishing port, but from there, you will connect with a ship taking our wine to brokers in America."

"America!?" Theo and Demetri cried in unison. Never had they considered such a journey to so far and foreign a place. And a new language to learn!

Remi nodded again. "You will go with the wine, as employees of the Geraud Vineyards, and after the wine is delivered to our company in Monterey, California, there's a place for you to stay there."

The twins looked as if they were sleep-walking. They turned to each other and asked, "California?"

There was a sudden sound of hooves approaching from outside the house. "*Gendarmes!*" Michele cried, and the boys shrank together, looking more terrified than ever.

But Remi was calm. "Upstairs," he ordered. "All of you. Michele—in my bed. But first, hide them in my closet."

She nodded and shooed the boys ahead of her, making sure they had their bundles, and the three of them flew to the curving stairway and up to Remi's bedroom. There was a sudden pounding on the big mahogany front door. Remi drew a deep breath to steady himself, then mussed his hair and—dangling the champagne bottle lazily from his fingers—he slouched his way to the front door.

When he pulled it open, he saw two local *gendarmes* he knew by sight. There was also a young man of about seventeen. Remi recognized him as one of Henri LaPorte's employees, hired to cater the reception.

"A thousand pardons, M. Geraud," one of the *gendarmes* began, "but we have reason to believe there are fugitives on your property. They were seen today, hiding in the glassmaking barn."

Looking shocked and dismayed and more than a little drunk, Remi slurred, "Are you certain? I've heard no complaints from my glassman François. He would have reported strangers."

Uncomfortably, the police officer said, "They may have been your employees, helping with the glass."

"**My God!**" Remi exclaimed. "And they are fugitives? Criminals?"

"They are wanted for murder and theft in Italy. May we have permission to search your property?"

Remi had been shaking his head incredulously but now said, "Of course, of course!"

The second policeman was younger but more reserved, and he studied Remi carefully before asking, "Are you alone, sir?"

"I should hope not!" Remi laughed. "Today is my wedding day, and I have a beautiful bride waiting for me in my bed upstairs. But if you insist on searching the house...." It was a gamble, and for a moment, he thought he'd lost, because the steely-eyed young *gendarme* started to move in past him. But just then, a voice called out from behind him.

"Remi, darling! Come to bed. I'm tired of waiting for you." He turned and was perhaps more shocked than the visitors to see his bride Michele partway down the staircase. Her black hair was loose and tousled, and she'd slipped out of her wedding dress and into a white satin negligee which clung to her curves and barely contained her ripe breasts as she leaned over the stair railing. Also feigning intoxication, she called down petulantly, "Remi, you promised me things about tonight!"

Remi turned and saw the others staring past him with their mouths agape (in fact, Remi thought with amusement, the boy looked like his eyes might pop right out of his head). The younger *gendarme* recovered first and started to push his way on in for the search, but the other, who outranked him, grasped his arm and shook his head, then turned back to Remi. "Again, our apologies for disturbing your wedding night. There's no need to delay you any further with a search. Good night, sir—and congratulations!"

The last thing Remi saw as he shut the door was the back-turned face of the young *gendarme*, clearly unconvinced of his innocence. Remi leaned against the door and expelled a great sigh of relief. His hands were shaking, and he brought the champagne bottle up for a swig to ease his too-dry mouth. Michele flew down the stairs and into his arms, holding him tightly and saying, "That was close!"

He gave a shaky laugh and squeezed her appreciatively. "You minx! That was quick thinking."

"We'd better get them out of here while they're searching the glasshouse and talking to François."

Remi nodded and went quickly to his desk in the room off the foyer. From the bottom drawer, he drew a water-proofed packet fat with papers, and this he took as they went upstairs. Michele pulled on a loose peignoir of matching satin, and Remi called the twins from the closet.

Handing Demetri the packet, he picked up where he'd left off. "When you get to Monterey, find my warehouses at the harbor. The empty one is now yours; there's a transfer of title in here."

The twins had just been staring at him; now Demetri managed to mumble, "But ... what ...?"

"My thought was that you could partition off a living space—much like François has here—and use the rest of the building for a little glass factory. There's enough cash in there to get you set up, and I'll send some more later, when it's safe."

Overwhelmed by the pace of events and the continued generosity of Remi Geraud, Theo began to cry and mumble, "I'm sorry ... I've made so much trouble ... you are so kind ...."

Michele went to him and reached up to take his face in her hands. "Don't cry, dear brother. Be happy and have a good life in California. Now, you must hurry while they're searching the west side of the estate." She kissed Theo good-bye and then Demetri. By that time, all four of them were crying and squeezing the life out of each other in embraces that might have to last them for years—even decades. Then they all went quickly down to the kitchen door, and with final teary good-byes, the boys slipped out into the night and were gone.

With the door closed behind them, Remi and Michele stood holding each other and listening to make sure they didn't hear anyone setting up an alarm. When the silence held for a while, Remi began to feel Michele's hands here and there on his body in soft, teasing touches.

"Can we go upstairs now?" his bride asked in a low voice.

Remi sighed with true regret. "I don't think we'd better get involved in anything. I have a feeling those *gendarmes* will be back tonight. That's why I didn't go with the boys to help them find Julien." He smiled ruefully down at her and assured her, "This is **not** the way I hoped to spend my wedding night. I'm sorry."

"That's all right." Michele pressed temptingly against him and promised, "We'll have many, many nights to make up for it."

CHAPTER 17
SANTA CLARA VALLEY — 1885

Squinting against the sun, Luka Bogdonovich reached up and plucked one ripe apricot from the cluster hanging above his head. He told his hand to put this prize in the basket hanging from his ladder, but instead, that disobedient hand brought it up to his mouth. For an instant, he felt the soft fuzz of the skin against his lips and tongue ... then his teeth pierced through, and the sweet juices burst into his mouth. Was there anything else on God's earth that tasted like a perfect, sun-warmed apricot?

When he heard laughter, he glanced at the other pickers—Philomena and Flora, working at ground level, and Mattiza Stanich on another ladder—and found them all laughing at him.

"See, Matty?" Flora called in a teasing voice. "Just like always. Eats one for every three that go in the basket."

It was an exaggeration, but part of the ritual, and Luka basked in the warmth of his daughter's affectionate banter. He took another bite, held the half-eaten apricot aloft and proclaimed, "Perfect! What a marvelous crop this year!"

They all went quickly back to their work. The one bad thing about the apricot harvest was that all the trees—each bearing around a hundred pounds of fruit—came due in less than twenty days. That not only meant a great deal of picking for the market but also quick work preparing the fruit for their own personal drying and canning. The preserved apricots could never taste the same as the fresh, but at least he could enjoy the flavor of apricots all year round.

After a time, Luka left the picking and slipped away through the trees to where he could relieve himself in private. As his urine splashed the ground, he noticed its color with dismay. Still blood! It was over two months since he'd taken his last drink, but still there was vomiting and this blood and the pain. He knew his wife was convinced all he had to do was not drink and his body would get healthy again, and that had also been his hope. But he could see no real signs of improvement. The first week of sobriety had been sheer hell; he could never remember feeling that ill in all his life, and it'd been hard to think of anything except taking the drinks that would ease that wretchedness (though taking up his concertina once again had filled his hands and given him a concrete focus for his attention). But slowly then he had recovered, the shaking in his body diminished, and he began to be able to attend to his work properly. Over the weeks—though the craving never really went away—it became easier to resist; he felt stronger, and his thoughts were much sharper. But the pain never went away either, and he knew there was still something wrong inside him. At times, as the pain twisted in him, he would fancy he could feel forces moving inside him—like tides or winds or even tiny armies—carrying him to some future destination.

Buttoning his trousers now, Luka thought about how his life had changed in the last few weeks. He'd discovered a new awareness of everything around him and an appreciation for what he had instead of his old melancholy for what had escaped his grasp.

Instead of chiding himself for not giving his family a fine mansion like the one the Tipanovs bought, he endeavored to feel proud about their small, sturdy home and its surrounding bounty of healthy orchards providing them food and a good crop to sell.

He had wanted sons, but here was his joy of a daughter. And he was startled to realize one morning that she was no longer a little girl at all. She carried her woman's body with grace and decorum, but he felt a flicker of fear. He'd have to be on his toes from here forward, keep a sharp eye out for young bucks hanging around. Thankfully, she didn't seem that interested in boys yet. Sometimes he'd catch her daydreaming with a secretive smile, but he watched her carefully and never saw her flirting with any of the boys at church—though they were obviously trying to get her attention. He'd had hopes for Josko Tipanov's son Karsten—even if it meant having that harridan Sabina as part of their family—but the boy had left town seven weeks ago, and his parents seemed none too eager to talk about it. And though it was plain to see that Matty Stanich was more in love with her than ever, Flora still treated him like a very dear brother.

There's time, Luka thought. *She's young, but eventually she will find someone to love.* As her father, it was hard for him to think about his baby in any man's arms, sharing the pleasures of the flesh. Part of him wanted her to remain a virginal child forever, but he knew that wasn't realistic ... or fair. And certainly it wouldn't bring him the joy of grandchildren! So it was best to wish for his daughter what he hoped his Philomena had experienced with him: a loving physical union that brought her much pleasure.

For even now Philomena had healthy appetites, and as he put the drinking behind him, he realized how he'd neglected her needs. There was a new sweetness in their renewed lovemaking—even though he let her think he wasn't able to perform the way a man was supposed to. "Be patient," Philomena had told him. "It will come back when you are well again." In truth, more than the pain, he worried his wife might find out about the blood and realize something was really wrong. But in the meantime, he'd been astounded to find what pleasure he could give his wife with just kisses and caresses and closeness; ironically, he found his musical skills were put to good use here too. His fingers played Philomena's body like a fine concertina, and that body responded like a properly handled instrument surrendering beautiful music.

Trying to ignore the pain, Luka returned to his tree, climbed the ladder, and resumed picking. He glanced down at the people who were closest to his heart—winking when Philomena gave him a welcoming smile—and was glad he had found this new life before he killed himself with drink. He'd wasted too much precious time, but now he was determined to savor every moment of the rest of his life.

Philomena brushed the back of her forearm across her damp brow to keep the sweat from rolling into her eyes. Her hands were full of apricots, and she placed them carefully in the basket so they wouldn't bruise. She shifted her weight and lifted her shoulder, trying to ease the pain in her back. She'd always loved being able to help with the harvest, working beside her husband and feeling the warmth of the late-spring sun on her skin. But she tried not to think about her own work left undone in the house—and what would she put on the table tonight for this ravenous crew—much less all the fruit that needed to be cleaned and seeded and cut and cooked and poured into Mr. Mason's wonderful jars with the rubber seals so they could taste apricots in the dead of winter.

She sighed. *I shouldn't complain,* she told herself. *This is so much better than the last few years.* At those times, Luka had often been too hungover and sick to work very quickly or efficiently, and everyone else had to work twice as hard. Now he was much better. Yes, he was still pale—sometimes her eyes played tricks on her, telling her he was even paler now than before—but soon he would get his color back. Soon he would be completely well.

What a relief it was to have her old Luka back ... at least partially. She remembered only a few months ago when she'd been so desperately unhappy she'd even thought of leaving him—or making him leave. She had tried to convince herself she could survive without him, even here in this America, which could never truly be her home. But she knew it wasn't true. Without her Luka she wouldn't be able to face each morning, and how wonderful it was not to have to worry about that anymore.

Instead she could enjoy his renewed attention and the pleasures he gave her in bed at night. If it worried her a little that he still avoided intercourse, it was mostly for his sake that she was concerned. She was sure all that would come back to him when he was finally well. To her, being held was the important thing ... being stroked and kissed and cherished. Her climaxes could be nearly as good ... and occasionally were even better.

As Philomena picked two more apricots, one in each hand, she watched her daughter working at the next tree. What a woman she was becoming! Ripe and golden-pink as the apricots. *What wonderful experiences lie ahead of her,* Philomena thought wistfully. *On her wedding day, I will have much to tell her. A girl needs to be prepared for lovemaking so she doesn't expect too much ... or too little.*

Watching her daughter with pride—and some envy for the girl's youth which meant so much lay ahead of her—Philomena thought, *I bet she'll enjoy that part of marriage as much as I have.*

Yes, someday she would have a thorough talk with Flora ... but not too soon.

The leaves brushed Flora's face as she leaned farther into the tree to take its treasure. She sighed impatiently. She'd only been picking four days now, but she was ready for the harvest to be finished. Her muscles were strained from the reaching and carrying, and they ached when she lay down at night. Perhaps she wouldn't feel so tired and irritable if she'd been getting enough sleep. But during the past week and a half—when she should have gotten plenty, since Antone was away on another business trip and she could sleep the whole night—she found herself lying awake, wanting him next to her as she touched her body and pretended it was Antone's hands instead of her own.

But now he was home at last; she saw him ride in yesterday afternoon, yet the bottle still hadn't appeared in his window. Why not? Wasn't he as eager as she to lie together again in their secret hideaway?

Feeling too irritable and impatient to pick carefully, Flora decided to take a break. She emptied her hands into the basket and signaled her mother and Matty, who would think she was going to the privy. They nodded and put their attention back on the fruit. Still, Flora waited until she was out of their sight before turning her steps toward the streambed.

The grassy strip was turning golden, but wildflowers still bloomed there. Dolce's teeth had grazed it down while she waited long nights for her master to come ride her home. Flora smiled, wondering what the mare might think of all this: so many evenings saddled and packed as if for a journey, only to be ridden a short distance away and left to graze for hours. Flora went to the edge of the creekbank and stared down at the bramble-covered bower, now abloom in a riot of white blossoms that looked like a million slightly rounded stars. Beneath those sprays of flowers, Flora knew, were the knobby, green clusters of developing blackberries. She longed to be behind that thorny curtain, lying in Antone's arms and whispering her love to him. She hugged herself and murmured, *"Ja te ljubin,* Antone." And she prayed, "Please, God, send him to me tonight."

Then she hurried back to her place in the apricot grove, working beside Matty's ladder. Even as she smiled in return to her dear friend's welcome-back nod, Flora's mind was wondering whether she would see the bottle in Antone's window when she got back to the house.

Mattiza Stanich watched Flora leave the picking and then return, and his heart felt heavy as a stone inside him. He knew without a doubt that she was in love with someone else. He had seen it developing in her over the last several months, hoping against hope that something would change. But the glow that he sensed around her had only intensified. He knew parents could be blind, but how could Luka and Philomena **not** notice?

And who could it be? She'd sworn it wasn't Karsten Tipanov, and she'd never lied to him before. Besides, Karsten left town shortly after talking with Flora that day, and he hadn't been seen since. But who else was there? He'd watched her closely at church. His Slavic fellows all buzzed around her, but she hardly seemed aware of them, and she certainly never flirted with any of them. And she never went anywhere else.

Matty had been in love with Flora all his life ... ever since his mother first took him next door to visit the Bogdonovich family. He had no conscious memory of it, for he'd only been three months old—still in his mother's arms—and little Flora was barely a month old, but when she smiled at him, his fate was sealed. Nothing yet had managed to change his feelings, and he knew he could never love any other woman as much. It crushed his heart to think of Flora falling in love with someone else, but it hurt even more to think that she hadn't confided in him. If he couldn't be the one she chose as her husband and lover, he wanted at least to be loved as her brother, a confidante and friend.

From the top of his ladder, Mattiza Stanich gazed down at his beautiful Flora and made her a vow. *I promise you this: as long as I live, I will do my best to care for you and to protect you. And I will never stop loving you. No matter what.*

Late that night, Flora slipped past the grazing Dolce and gave her a soft greeting but no pat since her hands were full. Reaching the edge of the creekbank, Flora looked down at the hideaway and saw tiny sparkles of light peeking through the bramble curtain. Antone had already lighted the candles inside. These they used on nights when there was little or no moonlight, when they both were forced to carry lights of some kind to find their way. Flora's candle-lantern was a little black-metal box with glass on three sides so the candle flame wouldn't blow out. She carried it now—and a bag of ripe apricots and a folded shawl—as she made her way down the path. Often Antone would come out and meet her on the path, but not tonight.

When she pulled aside the flowering bramble canes, she found him lying asleep in their blanketed nest. He'd removed his boots but he still wore the clean shirt and trousers he'd put on to go courting Bianca. He didn't even wake when she crawled in beside him. She extinguished her lamp and set it aside with the apricots and the shawl she'd brought for her walk home. This very night marked the summer solstice and the air was plenty warm, but in the early hours of the morning she'd be glad for a wrap. Flora unpinned her hair and lay down beside Antone, not touching him yet, just watching him sleep. He was so beautiful ... and so vulnerable and so very attractive ... Flora couldn't resist any longer. She snuggled against him and kissed him awake.

They didn't speak. They'd been apart nearly two weeks, and they were hungry for each other; words simply weren't necessary. The kiss heated them up quickly on this warm night, and it was only minutes before they were helping each other out of their clothes. Within a very short time they'd loved each other to climax and then lay in each other's arms, cherishing that closeness as their breathing and heartbeats slowed to normal.

Then finally, Antone gave a little laugh and greeted her in her own language. "*Dobro veče, Gospodjica Bogdonovich* ... good evening, Miss Bogdonovich" and she returned the favor with "*Buona sera, Signore Mellini.*"

They held each other and talked awhile. Antone had much news about the progress of his various ventures, and at the end of his report, he told her, "By the last of July, I will come into a sizable amount of money." He paused for dramatic effect. "At that time I will tell my family of my intention to marry you."

Flora froze in surprise at this startling news. "Are you sure?"

"Oh, yes," he answered earnestly, kissing her hair where it curled beside her face. "I want to make love to you the way married people do. I want to lie with you all night in my bed. I want to be your husband."

Her arms around his neck hugged him so hard, he had trouble breathing for a moment, and she whispered in his ear, "I want that too."

When she loosened her hold and he could talk again, he added, "And if it's agreeable with you, we can be married at the end of summer." He grinned wryly. "Of course, it'll have to be either just before or just after the grape harvest—that's the first weeks of September."

"The sooner the better," Flora said, and Antone's grin widened.

But then he became serious again. "What of **your** parents?"

Flora's smile faded too. She sat up and found the bag with the apricots. She handed one to Antone, naming it in Croatian: "*Armelin*" and lifting her eyebrow to ask for the word in Italian.

"*Albicocca*," he supplied, sitting up to take the fruit, then thanking her, "*Grazie.*"

"*Molim* ... don't mention it."

They sat silent a few moments, no longer shy in their nudity, eating the apricots. Antone made an appreciative noise and said, "These are truly delicious. The best I've ever tasted." She handed him another and showed him a trick Papa taught her as a child: if you held the fruit in both hands and twisted in opposite directions, it would divide into two perfect halves. As Antone ate this second apricot, he watched Flora carefully. She still had not answered his question. "What of your parents?" he repeated.

Flora gazed at him, licking the juice from her fingers. Then she shrugged. "They won't like it. There will probably be a big fight ... and **many** tears. But I will marry you. And they will accept it."

Antone smiled and reached over to give her shoulder a reassuring squeeze. Then he brightened even more and said, "I have a gift for you!"

He turned, took something from the deeper shadows in the farthest corner of their little room, and handed it to her.

She took the tiny blown glass bottle and held it where she could see it better in the flickering light of the candles. "Oh!" she said in wonder. Shaped like a miniature dove, it was filled with an amber liquid, and in the middle of its back was a tiny cork stopper with a crown of glass shaped like a butterfly.

"The bottle is a gift from the Lidakis brothers, who send their love to you," Antone said. "The scent is from France. I bought it in Monterey."

"For Bianca?" she asked quietly.

He grasped her shoulders and whispered fiercely, "Forget about Bianca! I love **you**. I will never love another woman. Only you." And he kissed her just as fiercely, as if in his passion he could communicate the dimensions of his love for her and dispel her anxieties forever.

She melted against him in the kiss, and when it ended they were both breathing much more quickly. Flora lay back on the blankets, her eyes half-veiled by her lashes, the sultry look of a woman well aware of the beauty of her naked body. She tilted the bottle of perfume to make sure the cork inside was wet and then handed it up to Antone. "Here," she said. "Put it where you'd like to find it."

Taking the stopper from the bottle, he used it like a paintbrush, touching her temples, behind her ears, on either side of her neck, and in the little hollow at the base of her throat. She closed her eyes to more fully enjoy the sensation. After returning the stopper to the bottle to gather more scent, he drew a long line down the valley between her breasts, watching the way her skin tightened in response.

God, she was beautiful! In the golden glow of candlelight, her skin looked the same color as the apricots they'd just eaten. Her reddish hair spread beneath her head like a pillow, and Antone painted a line down her taut belly to that other patch of reddish hair. She opened her eyes then and gazed at him with such love and longing, it took all his will power, all his love, not to fall on her and forget about their commitment.

Flora gazed up at Antone's beautiful naked body above her, at the proof of his arousal, his desire for her. She wondered if she'd ever tire of seeing such a thing or the feeling of power it gave to watch her effect on him. She opened her thighs, and he stroked their inner whiteness with the perfumed cork. He had chosen the scent well. The fragrance that rose from her warm skin was heady and evocative but maintained somehow the freshness of innocence. It surrounded them and enwrapped them, as if they had a single aura and would forever share this mystical unity. Flora could not imagine it possible to love Antone more than in that moment, and it was certainly inconceivable that she would ever love anyone else half as much. They had taken their vows, and in a matter of months they would be properly married! She reached up her arms to him, and he was quick to stopper the bottle and set it carefully aside.

Antone lowered himself into Flora's embrace, pushing his fingers into her soft hair so that he could hold her face as he kissed her. Her mouth tasted of apricots, and her body arched up against him in a way that made it even harder to remember the promises they'd made. The kiss deepened and was impossible for either of them to end. Just the play of their tongues brought Antone to the point he knew he had to pull away from her body so they could finish in the ways they'd learned.

But Flora held him against her and whispered, "I want you to make love to me the way married people do, Antone. **Be** my husband."

Surprised and not yet daring to hope, he pulled back enough to look into her eyes. "Are you sure?" Her brown eyes looked huge and unfathomable in the dim light; Antone felt as if he could fall off the edge of the world into those eyes. But there was no hint of doubt in them. "Yes," she whispered. "Yes." And it was her hands that took hold of him and guided him inside.

It was easy at first, her body was so wet and willing, but when he met resistance and pushed harder, she gave a little cry. Horrified, he started to pull back, his mind suddenly full of Uncle Gregorio's lewd advice about "breaking virgins." But Flora would not let him withdraw. She held him to her and whispered, "Do it quickly." So Antone steeled himself and with a quick thrust, found no more obstruction. Flora gasped and clutched at him as he did this, but then her legs came up around him, holding him inside her as they rocked together in an ecstasy neither one of them had dreamed possible. And yet Antone's love for Flora allowed him to maintain a certain amount of control so he didn't finish too soon, for it was important to him that she enjoy this first time—and every time—as much as he did. It was her own climax—the sudden arching of her body and the little ripple of contractions he felt—that released him, and he exploded inside her as she cried his name in a husky voice he had never heard before.

They lay in each other's arms, spent and giddy in the wonder and terror of what they'd done. They told each other they'd never felt so exhausted or so satisfied, yet they lay awake together, talking and kissing until it was only an hour before dawn. Then they made love again, as husband and wife, for there was no going back now.

As they cleaned themselves and dressed, Flora looked ruefully at the stains on the blanket and said, "We'd better do something about this. Can you take it and get it washed—or maybe we should just burn it."

Antone, buttoning his shirt, gave her a bawdy grin and admitted, "I'd like to take it and fly it as a flag."

Flora laughed. "Yes, that would impress my family."

Antone lost his grin and looked sheepish. "I'll take care of the blanket."

Flora moved to kiss him. "Soon, *d ušo moja,* we will be able to reveal our love to all the world."

"I can't wait," he said earnestly and folded up the blanket to take with him.

They parted soon after that, with a last kiss up on the bank beside Dolce, after Antone stuffed the blanket into his saddlebag. They managed to meet on each of the next three nights, exploring new pleasures now there were no limitations on their love. Feasting on ripe apricots—"There's such a crop this year," Flora told Antone, "no one would even miss a bushel basket"—they talked about their wedding and how they would tell their families. But at last they had to admit they were physically exhausted and needed sleep. Their relatives were beginning to notice, especially Uncle Gregorio, who teased Antone about his insatiable Bianca. It seemed wisest not to meet for a few nights.

And meanwhile, the apricot harvest continued. Flora spent hours balancing on ladders, stretching to pick fruit, toting the heavy baskets to the wagon. Back at the house there was what seemed like a ton of ripe fruit to dry or put up in jars. And there were always the usual tasks of cooking, cleaning, and laundry to help Mama with. At least Papa and Matty took on all the work with the animals and the garden. Still, Flora some nights found herself even too exhausted for making love, and though Antone's bottle appeared in his window, there were days Flora found she could not answer with her own.

But then the apricot harvest moved into its final days, and as July opened itself to them with its promise of Antone's big financial rewards and the announcement of their engagement, they began to meet nightly again. As they looked forward to the time when they would be together as husband and wife, it became increasingly difficult to rise from their bed together and go alone to their own houses. They lingered as long as they could—often until the sky was dangerously streaked with dawn—and more than once, Flora barely hopped into her bed before her papa rose for his morning trek to the privy.

Pain wrenched Luka Bogdonovich from his favorite dream, and he lay trembling, trying to hold on to the images. The dream wasn't always exactly the same, but there were patterns:

It was always summer in Dubrovnik, and bright roses decorated the white-marble walls reflecting in the blue of the Adriatic. Sometimes he would be playing his concertina with young Philomena watching him, her eyes full of love and admiration; sometimes he would be strolling the city streets with his *klapa*—harmonizing on the old traditional songs; sometimes, like this time, he would be lying in his father's apricot orchard looking up at the white clouds in the blue sky as he enjoyed the most perfect fruit in the world.

Luka woke in a sweat with the taste of apricots in his mouth and a pain like a bayonet in his guts. He groaned—as softly as he could because he didn't want to wake his Philomena—and rolled out of bed, stripped off his sodden nightshirt, and pulled on his trousers. It wasn't easy to stand upright, and it was even harder to walk because of the pain, but he knew he had to get outside. He shuffled through the house, his teeth clenched as he tried to ride out the pain by putting his thoughts elsewhere. He thought of Dubrovnik and how lately he'd fantasized about returning there. Ironic, he thought. It was always Philomena who wanted to go back, but now—when she was satisfied to stay by his side—it was **he** who pined for the land of his youth.

It was still before dawn, and the air was cool outside; the sweat covering his bare torso formed a little cloud of mist around him. Even though it was agony to walk, Luka felt compelled to pass the closer outbuildings and go all the way to where his farm wagon stood at the edge of the orchard. It was barely becoming light, but he could see his dear friends, the trees, who had sustained him and his family for so many years ... had given him his best crop yet this year. The harvest was over, the trees robbed of their bounty, but here and there, a late-ripening apricot lay fallen on the ground.

Luka moaned as he leaned against the wheel of the wagon and unbuttoned his trousers. He stared at the trees, not wanting to see the color of his urine as it soaked into the earth. Suddenly the pain twisted in him like a hot knife—making him cry out—but then it immediately eased, and he gave a great sigh of relief. Ah, that was better! Hardly any pain now. He floated on this tide of surcease, noticing that little golden lights flickered all around his trees like tiny butterflies or the smallest angels in the world.

It was not until he tucked himself back in his trousers and began to button them that he felt the wetness. Disgusted, he thought, *Am I to be even less of a man now—wetting myself like a baby?* But when he looked down, he saw his trousers and hands were drenched with blood. "Ah, God," he said, as if softly chiding the one responsible.

The pain was completely gone, so it was easy to push himself away from the wagon and walk into the orchard, wiping his hands clean on the sides of his trousers. Walking was so effortless he could hardly feel his feet touching the earth. He lowered himself beneath the nearest tree and picked up the one apricot that was within his reach. His hands knew the trick well, and weak as they suddenly felt, they twisted the golden sphere until it fell apart in two perfect halves in his palms. He lay back beneath the tree, staring up at the steel-colored sky through the whispering canopy of leaves. He put the half without the seed against his dry mouth and let his teeth scrape into the sweet, honey-colored flesh. Did God ever make a better taste—or a better place than Dubrovnik?

Though the morning was still grey all around him as he swallowed the sweet bite of apricot, the sky Luka Bogdonovich was seeing shone bright blue, afloat with white clouds. The last sound he heard was that of his own mother's voice calling him home ... telling him it was time to sleep.

CHAPTER 18
SANTA CLARA VALLEY — 1885

The nails shrieked in protest as they were pulled through the boards but refused to let go entirely. Flora planted her feet more firmly and leaned harder on the crowbar. The nails shrieked again, on a different note, as they were ripped free. The cellar door snapped open with the force of Flora's determination, and before it could fall closed again, she caught it and opened it all the way. There was a rush of stale air, laden with the winy scent of fermented fruit, and Flora peered down into the darkness but could see little. She put her attention on prying up the other door, and soon they both lay back open, as they had all those years before Papa stopped drinking.

Slowly Flora went down the steps, and when she'd lighted the lantern, she stood looking around. It was all so familiar, though dustier and more cobwebbed: Papa's worktable and shelves, his notebooks and tools, the chairs where his drinking buddies had sat as they sang and told tales and sipped the best plum wine in Santa Clara. And attached to the wooden walls were forty kegs of aging wine, all labeled and dated. At least some good could come of this. And how ironic that it would come just after Papa's funeral.

Flora lowered herself into one of the chairs and sat remembering what it was like to be in here as a child, watching Papa at this hobby, back when it **was** only a hobby. Her eyes filled suddenly with tears, and she dropped her face into her hands, weeping. "Oh, Papa!" she whispered. "I miss you so much. And we need you more than ever now. I don't know what to do about Mama."

Philomena had managed to hold herself together through the days of sitting with the body, the Rosary Mass, the funeral, and all the surrounding ritual—including the expected public display of the widow's wailing and breast-beating. The rest of the time, she was like some pale, life-sized doll that sat silently staring until she was led somewhere or told pointedly to do some simple task. And all the while, tears kept sliding down her cheeks and falling onto the black fabric of her widow's clothing. Her eyes were swollen and red, and Flora was amazed that any body could keep making tears so continuously.

And then, the day after the funeral, Philomena refused to rise from bed and barely responded to anything Flora said or did. That was two days ago, and Mama had not left the house since then—not even to go to the privy. Sometimes she didn't even get out of bed to use the chamber pot. All the household tasks had fallen to Flora, who was already exhausted from these terrible days of emotional upheaval, and now there was the added chore of emptying a chamber pot—or worse yet, changing wet sheets—for someone physically capable of using the outhouse.

As onerous and repugnant as this situation was, Flora was, above all, frightened. What could she do to help her mother? What was she to do to help them both? She had decisions to make about finances and the farm, but even more worrisome was the possibility she'd have to care for an invalid. She knew how difficult this had been in the Mellini family—and Antone's mother Lucia was only physically infirm; she remained a cooperative, good-natured, and appreciative patient. *If Mama stays like this,* Flora thought, *how can I care for her and live the rest of my life, work to support us?* And what of her marriage to Antone? It would certainly have to be postponed now, but even when the time was right, what would they do about Mama?

During their wondrous nights together, they had discussed various possibilities for their life together. The Mellini house was too small to accommodate them as a couple (and Antone felt very uneasy about bringing his Flora into close proximity to Uncle Gregorio). Though she'd known there would be reluctance, Flora felt certain her parents would agree to having her husband move into her room in their house. She was aware—though he could see it was their best alternative—that Antone was uncomfortable with the arrangement. He'd finally said, "Yes, I guess we must do that. But only until I can build our own house on Mellini property."

But now Flora knew she couldn't leave her mother. Surely Antone would understand, after all the years he'd helped to care for his own mama. Antone was such a good man, but when she tried to picture what their life might be like— trying to find their way through the first tender years of a marriage full of cultural compromises, all centered around a woman who needed to be cared for as a baby—Flora shook her head in despair and pushed away the thoughts.

Oh, Antone, she cried now in her mind, *why can't you be here to hold me and talk to me?* She wanted to be held in his warm and reassuring embrace and comforted as a child. But she also wanted to be comforted as a woman. Instinctively, she knew the solace she could find in the oblivion of passion. How she longed to lose herself for a time in the purely physical and in the recognition that she herself was still alive and that—even when our loved ones die—our lives go on. But it was impossible to meet with Antone. Of course, he knew of Papa's death, but she hadn't been able to speak with him since then. How her heart constricted to see that green bottle in his window every day and not to be able to answer with the amber in her own.

Only yesterday had she been able to communicate at all. Gospodja Tesla, whom Philomena had often visited and nursed when she was ill, came to the house with a meal for the evening and told Flora, "Go take some time for yourself, child. I'll care for your mama awhile."

With grateful tears in her eyes, Flora accepted the offer, but went first to her room and penned a quick note, which she hid in the pocket of her skirt. Then she left the house, calling back, "I think I'll just take a walk in the orchard."

Outside, she stood a moment, feeling like a prisoner just released as she blinked in the glorious sunshine and inhaled lungfuls of air. Only then did she realize how musty and dark and sour the house must be. She hurried then to the edge of the orchard and in among her old friends the trees. They rustled their green leaves in greeting as she moved rapidly down the row and toward the creek. It was a hot day, and the creek itself was now barely more than a series of pools linked by a narrow ribbon of moving water.

When she reached the leafy bower, she found there were still many blossoms on the blackberry canes, but they were loaded now, too, with ripening clusters of red and purple berries. Behind that curtain, it was uncomfortably warm and still. Just being there—and longing to have Antone with her—made the tears begin to flow. She fumbled along the darkest edges, where they stashed away their treasures. When her fingers found the tiny, dove-shaped perfume bottle, she brought it out and uncorked it, breathing in the fragrance that he'd bought for her, a scent that always made her think of the night when they had first made love as if they were already married (she had not dared to use it on her body since then, for fear her parents would detect it and ask questions). Memories of that first night flooded through her and with them, more tears. It was as if some dam had broken, and she began to sob as if she would never stop, thinking of her papa, of Antone, of the fragile creature her mother had become. She cried for herself ... for what she'd lost and for what she was being deprived of in her separation from Antone.

Some time later, when she was finally empty of tears, she replaced the scent bottle, wondering where to leave the note so Antone would find it. Having sat in the dimness so long, she found her eyes had adjusted and she could see a new object hidden among the familiar.

A bottle! It was green, but it reminded her of the one Antone had used to send a note to her with the Lidakis twins. She told herself it might only have wine in it, but breathless and afraid to hope, she brought the bottle out where she could view it better. There **was** a white piece of paper rolled in the neck!

Her fingers trembled so much in anticipation, she ended up pushing the note farther into the bottle neck. "Damn!" she muttered in English and managed to wiggle the paper free. She opened it and saw his same careful printing:

My sweetheart,
I am so sorry about what has happened. I only wish I could comfort you. I understand you may not be able to meet me for a while, but I will watch for our signal. Until then, please know you and both your parents are in my prayers to the Holy Father. And remember I love you. More than anything.

How cleverly he'd written it so that it could be traced to neither of them if it was found. She had tried the same in her own note, which she now reviewed a last time before putting it into the bottle:

Dearest,

You must know why I have not been able to meet you. I only wish I could. I cannot leave Mama and I have much to think about and decide on. It is probably better if we talk before we make any announcements. Watch for the signal. I will come as soon as I can. I hope you know how much I love you and want to be with you this moment.

Flora rolled the note and pushed it most of the way into the bottle's neck and then put the bottle in a different niche so that—if he came to check this place—Antone would know **someone** had found the paper and see if the message was a new one. When she returned to the house, she put the amber bottle in her bedroom window.

Now, sitting in Papa's cellar, Flora wondered if Antone had gotten the note last night. Had he gone to the bower hoping to find her there? Had he left another note for her? Was it waiting there for her even now? What good was a note anyway? She needed to be held, to be comforted, to have her hair stroked and to hear someone she trusted tell her even though things were bad right now, everything would be all right again someday.

In the past when she was troubled, she'd always found she could share her pain or confusions with her mother or father, and they would help her think it through. And more recently, Antone had proved to be a sympathetic listener. But now she was separated from them all; she'd never felt so alone.

"Are you all right, Flora?" a familiar voice asked. She looked up at the open cellar doorway and saw Mattiza Stanich staring down at her. She nodded, tears still streaming down her face. He came down the stairs and handed a clean handkerchief to her.

"How's Mama?" she asked.

"She's still sleeping." When he'd come over a little while ago to see if there was anything he could do to help, she'd asked him to be in the house in case Mama wakened and needed something. "Gdja. Tesla came back and she offered to sit with her."

"Bless her," Flora said. "And thank **you**. I really need to get away sometimes."

He nodded and held up a little slip of paper. "Gdja. Tesla made a list of things you need at the store. Can you think of anything else?"

"No ... yes! Could you get a pencil and a package of writing paper for me?" She stood up. "I'll get some money for you ...."

He waved his hand in dismissal. "No hurry. Why don't you wait till I come back and we know exactly how much it is?"

Flora wasn't eager to go back into the house. She nodded. "Thank you."

Mattiza gave a little wave of his hand and hurried back up the stairs, calling. "I'll ride instead of walk, so I'll be back soon."

When he was gone, Flora looked around the cellar again, taking it all in. So Josko Tipanov wanted to buy this wine! He had approached the subject carefully at the wake after Papa's funeral. Quite a few people from the Slavic community had come to pay their final respects, crowding the small parlor and kitchen, spilling out onto the porch and into the yard. Gdja. Tesla had arranged the whole thing, even to donating a keg of Papa's own wine her husband had been hoarding since that source had dried up months ago. Every woman arrived at the house with some dish of food so that those gathered could eat and drink and remember Luka Bogdonovich. And everyone made it a point to speak personally to the widow and daughter. Philomena sat with a polite expression frozen on her face and nodded when guests spoke their condolences, but her eyes looked through them, and if she ever spoke a word, Flora wasn't aware of it.

At one point in the afternoon, Flora actually found herself alone for a moment, staring out the front parlor window, past the guests on the porch and across the street to where, even from here, she could see the green glass bottle in Antone's window. And then she saw Antone himself in his yard, gazing across the street ... perhaps to her own window, hoping to see the amber bottle? How she longed to have him here beside her, as a husband should be, to support her through this difficult time.

"This must be a difficult time for you," a voice said, startling her both with the sound and its parallel to her own thoughts. She turned and saw Josko Tipanov regarding her solemnly as he sipped from his wineglass. He and his wife had earlier spoken their condolences to her (the usually razor-tongued Sabina had actually given her a tender smile and patted her hand, saying, "It is hard to lose one's father") but now he was alone. "I do not mean to be indelicate," he said quietly, so that his voice wouldn't carry to those nearby, "but if finances are a problem, I'd be glad to help."

Touched, Flora told him, "Thank you, but we are fine for now. There was a good crop this year and the money is safely in the bank."

He nodded. "I understand your papa left a cellar full of this wonderful wine. I think it would distill into an excellent *slivovitz.*"

"*Slivovitz?* "Flora repeated.

"Plum brandy. I would be very pleased to buy it all from you if you'd consider selling it ...?"

"Well, I ... ah ...."

"I know this isn't the time, but I wanted to speak for the wine before anyone else, and I want you to know if you have the means to keep producing the same fine product, my distillery will buy all you can supply. You think about it at your convenience and let me know. And in the meantime, if there's anything Sabina or I can do for you, just let us know."

"Thank you. You're very kind." She fought the tears welling up in her eyes.

"Let's speak of other things, now," Tipanov said. "We have heard from Karsten. He's been back in Hvar."

"Oh, yes?" Flora responded, not revealing she herself had heard from Karsten in June. She had never received a telegram before, much less one originating half-a-world away. It contained the happy news that he had married his Ruzena and they soon would set sail back to America, which meant he was well on the way here now.

Karsten's father nodded, staring into his glass. "He got married there and is bringing his bride back here. They should arrive by the middle of next month."

"How wonderful." Seeing his subdued and fretful expression, Flora couldn't resist a small gibe. "You must be very happy." He glanced up in surprise, and she rushed on. "Karsten must have gone back to get that girl he loves so much, right?" Tipanov nodded and Flora continued, "What could make a parent happier than knowing his child has found true love and is willing to go to such great lengths—risk such dangers—to secure that love?"

Flora watched the expressions in the man's eyes as he seemed to consider the situation from this perspective for the first time. Still looking inward, he mused, "Yes, Sabina was overwrought when she learned he had gone back. She was terrified half the time we were traveling. Even after we got our feet on solid land after all those weeks on the steamship, she hated the trip. And she didn't like the train much better."

"So," Flora prompted gently, "when Karsten and his wife are both here safe and sound, you and your wife will really have something to celebrate."

"Yes," he said as if to himself. "I suppose we will." He peered into his glass a moment longer and then drank the rest of his wine and turned his full attention to Flora. "It was very good talking to you, Gospodjica Bogdonovich. And do contact me when you decide about the wine."

She nodded and thanked him again, and he went on his way looking very thoughtful.

What could make a parent happier, Flora repeated to herself, peering out the window again, gazing across Page Street to the Mellini house on the other side, *than knowing a child has found true love?* But then more guests came to greet her, pat her hand, tell her how much they would miss her father, Luka Bogdonovich.

And now, a few days later, in his cellar, Flora looked at the wine with new eyes, remembering what Josko Tipanov had said. And as she studied the labels, she realized not all had *sljiva* ... plum ... written on them. Five kegs were marked *armelin* ... apricot. Papa must have been experimenting. Flora went to Papa's bookshelves and pulled down his notebook. She sat on his stool, reading through his notes and becoming very excited. This didn't seem so difficult. After days of living in a fog, it was as if the mists suddenly cleared, and she knew exactly what she should do.

When Mattiza returned, he went first to the house to put away the groceries he'd bought and to check on Gdja. Tesla. He found her putting clean clothes on Philomena, which must mean that she had soiled herself again. At Gdja. Tesla's shooing gesture, Mattiza left them and returned to the cellar.

He found Flora reading from her Papa's book and scribbling notes. She didn't even notice that he was there. She looked much better than she had earlier. Her tears were dried and most of the redness was fading around her eyes. For days now she'd looked pale and wrung-out, but now she seemed to have some of her spark back.

Perhaps now was the time to have his talk with her ... to ask her to marry him. Now that both their fathers were gone, their lives and finances would be changing. Flora would need help, especially with her mother in such bad condition. Mattiza had almost convinced himself he must be wrong about Flora being in love with someone else. Surely any future husband worth having would have attended her papa's funeral, if not the wake afterward. And if such a man were there—even if they were still keeping their association secret—surely some careful observer would be able to see it in the couple. Mattiza had seen nothing, and he had watched her every move. And he knew now for sure that it wasn't Karsten Tipanov. He himself had overheard part of Gosp. Tipanov's conversation with Flora, and there were other rumors flying—as they will when a community gathers to celebrate its members' passages.

There was gossip that Karsten had run away and married against his parents' wishes and that Gdja. Tesla's sister was expecting a tenth child, and that it was actually Lenka Matlovich's fist and not a door that had blackened her husband's eye. Mattiza even heard whispers about his father being in prison, but he heard absolutely nothing connecting Flora with any young man.

So perhaps this **was** the time to speak, before some other fellow—someone more prosperous and handsome and educated—came offering to protect this poor fatherless girl. Mattiza stared at Flora, bent over her father's notes, and took a deep breath, gathering his courage to speak.

Flora looked up suddenly. "There you are! Matty, can you run Papa's orchard? Could you take his place in all the tasks? You've helped him with just about everything—or watched him do it—at one time or another."

Taken aback, he stammered a bit before answering, "Yes. I know how to do it all and I'm strong enough. But I couldn't give it as much time because I have to care for the pigs, and in the summer, the four of us could barely bring in the crop. Without your papa ...."

She dealt with the last part first. "We'll hire another picker, then—or two if we need them. Now, about the pigs. Could I convince you to get rid of most of them—just keep enough to feed our two households with perhaps a little extra? I want to hire you to do Papa's work."

"Hire me?" he echoed.

"Yes. I can't pay much at first, but I'll provide all your meals and take care of your laundry and sewing and such domestic matters, just as we did for Papa. And if Mama gets better, I'll work with you in the orchards as much as I can."

"It would make more sense," Matty heard himself say, "if we didn't run two houses. I could move over here and lease my house to someone else—someone who doesn't mind pigs." It was on the tip of his tongue to ask her to marry him, especially as he saw her nodding her head.

"Yes," she said slowly. "That would be a good idea. Mama could move into my room and you could have the other." She paused as if choosing just the right words, and before he could get his proposal out of his dry mouth, she spoke again. "But you see, Matty, that won't work, because in a few months I'm going to be married."

Matty's heart stopped in his chest; he dropped to the cellar steps like a steer poleaxed at the slaughterhouse and just sat there staring at her.

Flora rushed on nervously. "I don't know exactly what will happen, when. But probably my husband will move into the house with me where I can care for Mama, but he'll have his own business dealings—I intend to keep the orchard going, if you can help me ...?"

Matty nodded, but the only words in his brain were the echoing traces of *my husband ... my husband* .... "Who?" he whispered, afraid to know, afraid not to know.

She regarded him with those soft, brown eyes, and her voice was a plea for understanding. "I can't tell you now, Matty. No one can know just yet. There are too many ... complications. Please don't ask me. You're the only other person who knows this much. I promise: you will be the first I tell. Can you do this for me ... trust me ... wait until I'm ready to talk about it?"

"I will do anything for you, Flora," he said simply. She slid off the stool and came to him then, bent to put her arms around his neck and kiss his forehead. "You are the dearest friend I could ever want," she whispered, and his heart, which had merely been aching, felt as if it were tearing into tiny pieces that would wash away with his tears. If he let those tears out.

He gave her a perfunctory-seeming hug and rose quickly from the step and moved away from her as he blinked, struggling to regain control of himself. He walked to the barrels, hoping his voice wouldn't sound too strained as he said, "And yes, I'll work your orchards for you with the arrangement you mentioned. And I hear you're going to sell the wine to Gosp. Tipanov?"

"Yes." Her voice came from behind him. "And I've begun to have another idea, but I would need your help for that too." So curious he turned to face her, he could only hope she couldn't see the wetness in his eyes. He watched her as she moved back to Luka's workbench and started thumbing through his notebook. "Matty, do you think we—you and I—can make Papa's wine? To sell to Gosp. Tipanov to make into brandy. The recipes and instructions are here; they seem very straightforward; we have all the equipment we need. What do you think?"

It was a very new idea to Matty, but he found he felt uncharacteristically confident. There was something about the strength he sensed in Flora that made him feel he could succeed at anything he did for her. So he nodded and said, "Where do we start?"

Her smile was like the sun coming from behind the clouds, and she gestured toward the notebook. "You don't read Croatian, do you?"

Matty shook his head and reminded her, "They didn't teach us that in school." They both knew neither of his parents could read or write, so who was there to teach him their cultural language as her parents had taught her?

She nodded and beckoned him closer. "Time for your first lesson."

Two mornings later, Flora rose feeling exhausted and cranky and uneasy in her stomach. She knew she'd had bad dreams all night ... vague images of doom and danger. Near the end, though, she'd dreamed she was walking in the apricot orchard, and she saw her father coming toward her. She ran to him, feeling as light on her feet as a child of six. He smiled his most wonderful smile and stooped with his arms wide, ready to scoop her up as he had when she was young. She came right up to him, felt herself leave the ground as she leapt up, knowing he would catch her—

And then she woke, full of the realization that her father was dead—that he'd never again lift her up in his secure embrace, that she would never see that smile again except in her dreams. As this reality crashed in on her, she lay in her bed and cried, hugging her pillow to herself and burying her face in it to muffle her sobs.

Her mood only blackened when she looked out her window for the security of the green glass bottle in Antone's window. Not only was it missing, but there stood Dolce in the yard, saddled for a journey, and she remembered that Antone was going off on one of his damn business trips. The last days had been bad enough—not being able to see him or to lie with him for a few hours— but at least she knew he was so near, wanting to be with her, and there was the possibility of communicating by notes left in the bottle in the bower. Flora had managed one more trip there yesterday and had taken the paper and pencil she'd had Mattiza buy so that notes could be written on the spot in response to what was found.

There was a new note from Antone, so she knew he had gotten hers, but there was little they could say to each other if they wished to protect their secrecy.

He did write, "I will wait to tell my family anything about our plans until you tell me it is time. I must be gone for a while but I will carry you in my heart wherever I am."

Flora wrote a note welcoming him back and wondered how long it would be before he read it ... before he held her again and whispered her name and touched her in ways her own hands could never imitate.

As she dressed now and brushed her hair, she kept watch on the window so she saw when Dolce stepped out into the road. She ran to her window and pressed her face against it, straining for a glimpse of his handsome face and lithe form. He looked right at her, and their eyes met. She wanted to wave, but someone might be watching. This time of year he wore a hat for protection from the hot July sunlight, and he touched the brim as if he were merely tugging it on more securely, but she knew he was saluting her as he rode away and left her there alone with what her life had become. A life without Papa but with plenty of worries and too many chores and with Mama.

Flora sighed. Mama. Something had to be done. Maybe she could get her up out of bed today, get her to eat a real breakfast—though the thought of cooking something was quite repugnant. Steeling herself, Flora buttoned her last buttons and took a deep breath, telling herself she was ready for whatever she had to deal with this day.

Philomena Bogdonovich was in Dubrovnik. It was spring, and the hills near the town were covered with blooming lavender-colored irises; their subtle perfume filled her nostrils as she lay in the grass listening to Luka play his concertina and sing love songs to her. She was young and vibrant, and her body longed for the caresses of her new husband, but she resisted the temptation to entice him there in the field. After all, there was tonight. There was the rest of their lives to love each other.

But part of her knew it was 1885, and her husband was dead and there was nothing to be done about it.

Philomena wanted to die. In that moment, she could think of no good reason to go on living. Her Luka was dead. Her daughter was just about grown. Her own life was practically ended. There was no reason to even move her body. That would be too difficult anyway. She could feel herself sinking deeper and deeper into her mattress. Her limbs were too heavy to lift. The easiest thing was to just give up, let go of everything within her power, and let Death take her. Surely he would come do that, wouldn't he, if she were such a willing subject?

But Death didn't come to take her, and Philomena lay inert, feeling the weight of her every atom and regretting her whole life. *If I hadn't married Luka, I probably never would have left Dalmatia. And my husband would be satisfied with his life and only drink in moderation, and we would get to spend all our years together.* So what if she couldn't imagine loving any man as she loved Luka?

Perhaps that would have been better. Loving so intensely only produced unbearable intensity in grief. And wasn't it ironic that only months ago she had considered ending her marriage to Luka? Why couldn't he have just died then, when she thought she felt so much less for him?

A voice inside her asked, *So you would rather not have had these last weeks of tenderness and renewed passion and closeness?* But that question, too, was just too hard. She was bone-weary of everything in her life: of the physical work of farm life; of the emotional strain of being tossed between joy and sorrow, bitterness and near-contentment, hope and despair; of the spiritual battles she'd fought with her God over the death of her first two children and, now, the death of Luka—after he had given up drinking and reclaimed his life. *It isn't fair!* she thought. *I've been a good woman. I have lived my life the best I could. Why do You keep punishing me?*

But no answer came to her, and Philomena lay like a corpse in her bad, feeling abandoned by both God, who would not answer her, and Death, who would not take her.

The smell got stronger the closer Flora got to Mama's room. She'd been in the kitchen, heating water for a bath and brewing coffee, which filled the room with a rich aroma that had momentarily overpowered the other odors in the house. Now, holding her breath to keep from gagging, Flora moved to the bedside. It struck terror to her core to see her mother lying so pale and lifeless-looking. If it were not for the tears sliding out of the corners of the eyes, Flora would have believed her dead. And she knew that was the road her mother was trying to take.

The fear of losing this parent too overwhelmed her. *No!* she vowed, filled with new determination. "Mama!" she said sharply. "It's time for you to get up."

There was no response at all, almost as if the woman had not even heard her.

Flora tried again. "I miss Papa, and I know you must miss him far more, but you can't go on like this. I can't go on with you like this. Now, open your eyes and let me help you get dressed."

Feebly, with eyes still closed, her mother's head moved from side to side signaling a negative.

"Then I'll have to help you," Flora said and pulled back the covers. The appalling mess assaulted her eyes and her nose, grabbed Flora in her belly and wrenched. Before she could try to prevent it or even turn away, Flora's vomit spewed out of her and went everywhere: across the floor and bed, on her mother and on her own clothes. "No-o-o-o!" This time she screamed it, and it ended in the howling sound of an animal in anguish. "I will not have it, Mama! Do you hear me!?" And Philomena's eyes opened. They only stared blankly at her daughter, but they were open.

Quickly, Flora got out of her splattered dress and threw it down on the floor. Clad only in her cotton shift, she grabbed her mother's arms, commanding, "Get up!" as she pulled her out of the bed and to her feet. For a terrifying moment, Flora wondered what she would do if her mother would not stay standing and simply sank to the floor and refused to move. But Philomena stood, shaky and shivering, despite the warmth of the morning, her gown plastered to her body with human waste and her daughter's vomit.

Gagging behind clenched teeth, Flora pulled the gown from her mother's body and tossed it over among the soiled bedclothes. Then she led the woman out of the room, into the kitchen, and helped her into the steaming bathtub that waited there.

Philomena leaned back in the water with a sigh that sounded as if it came from the center of her soul and closed her eyes. "That's it, Mama," Flora said. "Just have a good soak. I'll be back shortly."

Knowing the tub was too small for her mother to slide down in and drown, Flora hurried to her bedroom and slipped her robe on over her shift ..She went to the window and threw up the shade and then pulled up the lower sash of the double-hung window, filling her lungs with sweet fresh air. Leaning out, she saw Mattiza coming to the kitchen door with a full pail of milk. For years now he'd been milking the Bogdonovich cow in exchange for a portion of the milk—a good arrangement for both households, and more peaceful since he was the only person who could go into the Bogdonovich barn without setting off *Vučak's* barking.

Flora called to him to set the milk on the step by the kitchen door. "Mama's bathing."

He nodded and did as she asked and then came to stand beneath the window. "Is she any better?"

"She will be," Flora answered grimly. Then she asked, "Do you have an extra mattress at your house?"

He shrugged. "I only need one now that Father's ... gone. Do you want the other?"

"Please. And could you help me for a few minutes?"

"Of course."

Flora asked him to come around to the front door so he wouldn't disturb Mama in the kitchen. When he came in the room, his face showed his horror at the mess, but neither of them spoke of it. Together they managed to fold the mattress on itself and all the soiled bedclothing—and then squeeze it out through the window. Looking out after it, panting from the exertion and the stench, Mattiza asked, "What will you do with it now?"

"Burn it."

"The sheets and gown too?"

"They're old," she answered. "Mended many times and wearing thin.

Not worth the hard work it would take to clean them." She picked up her own dress. "This isn't so bad. I'll put it in to soak."

Mattiza nodded and gestured out toward the mattress. "I'll take care of that. Do you want the other one?"

"Not just yet," she said. "I want to finish cleaning up in here and let it air out some. I'll let you know. Thanks, Matty."

He nodded and went out to burn the mattress.

Flora returned to the kitchen and found her mother still lying, eyes closed, in the same position in the tub, but her face looked different, more peaceful somehow. Flora asked, "Would you like some more hot water?"

Philomena opened her eyes and said, "Yes. Please." The first words she'd spoken since the day of the funeral.

Flora dipped out some of the cooling tub water and replaced it with more from the pot simmering on the stove, careful not to let any splash on her mother's skin. She put more water on to boil and filled a mug with hot, black coffee. This she handed to her mother and told her to drink it. Mama was sipping from the mug as Flora left the kitchen carrying a bucket of soapy water and a scrubbrush. In Mama's bedroom, she cleaned the floor, thankful her vomit had missed the rug there. By the time she'd finished—and had selected a complete set of clothes for her mother—the room smelled fresh again, and she left it to air for a few hours longer.

Mama's eyes followed her as she came into the kitchen and put her dress to soak in another bucket. A comfortable kind of silence enwrapped the room as Flora washed her mother's hair and put down a towel for her to step out on. She dried Philomena's body and dressed her, and by the time she was finished, Mama's hands were helping with the buttons. Then Philomena sat at the kitchen table and had a second cup of coffee while her daughter made breakfast for her.

First Flora brought in the milk and strained it and set two tall glasses on the table, setting the rest aside to make butter a little later in the day. But the cooking itself was not an easy task for Flora; her stomach was still sensitive from its earlier turmoil, and the smell of cooking bacon made her decidedly queasy.

When she put the plate on the table in front of her mother, Flora was afraid the woman would refuse to eat as she had so many times over the last few days, but Mama picked up her fork and began to feed herself. Knowing she, too, must have nourishment to keep her strength up for all that lay ahead of her, Flora found some crackers and sat down to eat those with her milk.

Philomena ate slowly, but she ate every bite prepared for her, and Flora praised her for it. When they were finished, she took Mama's hands in hers and said, "I do not want to be unkind. And I mean to show you no disrespect as my parent, but you simply must find a way to grieve for Papa without giving up on life." Her mother's eyes misted up again, and Flora hurried on, "I need your help, Mama. There is so much to do if we are to keep this farm." Quickly she told the plan she'd worked out with Mattiza, and it was clear how much help was needed running the house and helping with the trees. "So you see, Matty and I must have Mama back to help us."

"I don't know if I can ...." Mama whispered, new tears springing up and flowing down her cheeks. "How can I be **me** without my Luka? I was crazy to ever think I could live without him. It feels like my whole life is finished ...."

There was so much misery in that voice, it touched all the pain which was still so raw in Flora, and the tears started from her eyes too. She slid out of her chair and down onto the floor, pillowing her head and arms on her mother's lap. "Are you alive now ... today ... Mama?"

There was a long, puzzled hesitation and then Philomena answered, "Yes ...."

Flora sat upright, holding her mother's arms at the elbows and looking deep into her eyes. "Then God must not think your life is finished yet, don't you think? He must have some reason for you to still be here, right?"

"Perhaps," Mama conceded. "But living is simply too much to bear. It's too hard and I'm too tired and I can't believe I will ever feel happy again. I just want to give up, and I wish you'd let me."

Flora gave her a little shake. "Mama! What's the greatest sin? What would the priest say if I asked him?" Philomena tried to wave away the question; it was too much work to talk about such things. "Think!" Flora demanded. "What would he say is the greatest sin?"

Still shaking her head, trying to get out of it, Philomena found she could not deflect her daughter's intensity, and the answer came to her: "Sin against the Holy Spirit."

"Yes! And isn't that the sin against hope? Isn't that why it's a sin to take one's life—because it's a sin against hope? It's saying 'There is no hope.' Isn't that right?"

Philomena thought about it and saw the truth in it. If she gave up hope and committed such a terrible sin, then she might not get to heaven and she might never see her Luka again at all. Realizing this, she began to weep in earnest. It wasn't fair! Now even the solace of an easy death was taken from her. "Oh, Flora!" she sobbed. "I loved him so much. I don't know how I could have ever loved him any more than that, and I could never love anyone else half as much ...."

Flora now freed her own grief in tears, her head on her mother's lap. They held each other and cried together for a long time and at the end, Philomena's voice asked, "Then how can I also hate him so much for doing what he did? For poisoning his body and dying ... leaving me here without him?"

Flora, too, felt this anger. It made no sense for her to feel so angry at him for leaving her while she was still so young, for forcing her to take such responsibility, for making it necessary to delay her wedding plans, for denying her future children his presence as a grandfather. How could she be so selfish and unreasonable herself?

She raised her head and gazed at her mother with streaming eyes. "Oh, Mama," she whispered, "I don't know. I don't know ...."

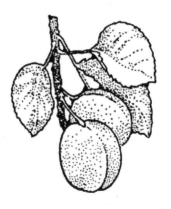

CHAPTER 19
SANTA CLARA VALLEY — 1885

Flora rushed into Antone's arms, her embrace so tight, her kiss so hungry, for a moment it was difficult for him to draw breath. He returned the kiss with all the emotion of lovers separated so long, and when they drew back, he could see that she was crying.

"Oh, Antone," she said with a catch in her throat, "I don't ever want to be apart from you that long again. Not ever!"

He felt the same, but he was so moved by her intensity, he found himself trying to lighten the moment. "I promise then," he said with a little laugh, hoping it was a promise he could keep. "We won't ever be apart that long again."

She pulled his mouth back to hers, and it was only moments before they were sinking down to the blanketed floor of the bower, their fingers feverishly unbuttoning each other's clothes. They made love quickly and without words, both lost in the frenzy of more than three weeks' separation. Afterward, they lay for a long time in each other's arms, still silent, each needing more than anything the great comfort of the other's presence instead of an image in memory or dream.

"I missed you so much," she sighed at last, tracing the black curve of his eyebrow with her finger.

"I missed you more," he teased. But then he became serious. "How did you manage to get away?"

"Gdja. Tesla has another bout of fever from her malaria, and the rest of her family is away at a funeral, so Mama is staying the whole time with her."

"How **is** your Mother?"

"Much better! Oh, Antone, I can't tell you how horrible it was.... I never expected the loss of my father to affect her so terribly." She gave him a brief account of her mother's behavior in the days after the funeral, then concluded, "But over the last two weeks, she's gotten to be more herself. And nothing makes her stronger than taking care of someone else—especially since Gdja. Tesla took such good care of her."

Antone nodded. "And how are **you**?"

Flora sighed. "I miss Papa. I think about him every day...I cry..." Antone stroked her hair back from her temple and kissed her there. She snuggled closer against him, despite the heat of the evening, and continued, "But I have made some important decisions about the farm." She told him how Gosp. Tipanov had bought all Papa's wine—and wanted any she could produce—and of her plans to keep the orchard and winemaking going with Mattiza's help.

Antone was surprised to find himself a little uneasy with her new business sense and strength of purpose...and there was something more. He tried to joke about it, laughing as he asked, "Should I be jealous?"

"What?" Flora answered as if he were out of his mind. "Of whom?"

"That Mattiza fellow."

"Jealous of Matty?!" she said incredulously. "Whatever for? He's my **friend**."

"He's in love with you," Antone pointed out, and as Flora continued to stare at him in disbelief, Antone assured her. "It's plain as day. I've watched him watching you when you're not looking…"

Flora sat up suddenly, as if she couldn't puzzle over this while lying next to him. "Oh dear!" she said softly. "We've always loved each other, but as brother and sister."

Moonlight fell through the opening of the bower where he'd tied back the curtain of brambles, and Antone reached up to touch one of her bare breasts—so beautiful in that pale light and even fuller than he remembered. "He doesn't look at you as if you are a sister. And who can blame him?" Antone asked, wanting her again.

But Flora was concerned and vowed to herself to try to be more aware and sensitive to Matty. She couldn't imagine what it would be like to feel as she did about Antone and have to listen to him talk about being in love with someone else. Then she turned her attention to Antone and told him, "You need never be jealous of my love. I can never love anyone else as I love you."

He pulled her down against him, his lips near her ear as he whispered that he loved her in Italian, "*Io ti voglio bene*" then added "*per sempre*…that means 'for ever.'"

"*Ja te ljubin.*" She said the familiar Croatian words first, then, "*Volim te zauvijek*…I love you forever."

"*Eternamente,*" he swore. "For ever and ever."

She kissed him instead of speaking, and they made love again, more slowly this time and even more lovingly, whispering endearments in Italian and Croatian and English. And then they ate their fill of ripe blackberries picked from the curtain wall of their nest as they talked of his most recent trip to the coast where he'd received not only the expected share of profits from the Fortunallo Company, but also some good advice from his friend Dante about his new business venture with the Lidakis brothers.

"Dante said a glass shop such as we envision would be more successful in San Francisco than in Monterey. Since none of us wants to move there just now, Dante suggested we hire someone else to run it. As it turns out, he has a widowed daughter, Isabella, who would be perfect in the role for the time being…until she remarries or until the twins—or you and I—want to move there and take it over."

"San Francisco!" Flora breathed, her eyes shining as she imagined what it would be like to visit—to live in!—such a bustling, cultured, cosmopolitan place…someday.

"Theo and Demetri were in agreement," Antone continued, smiling at her dreamy expression. "So all is progressing well." He told her he'd spent two days with the glassmakers, attending to the last legalities and—as he admitted with a rueful grin—"doing quite a bit of celebrating." Then, looking very sheepish, he confessed, "I'm afraid I told them we planned to marry as soon as we can after a proper period of mourning has passed. Oh! I forgot—they send their condolences in the loss of your father."

Flora nodded. She could see no harm in the twins knowing about their intended marriage (they were already well aware of the love they shared); she'd told Mattiza she would marry, and that was much more dangerous.

Antone mused, "They seemed quite affected by the news about your father. At any rate, I feel sure we can trust them to keep our secret. I've always had the impression they had a few big secrets of their own. And they say very little about their parents."

In pensive silence, they ate more blackberries (*kupina*, she called them and he, *mora*). After a time, sated and licking the last sweet juice from her fingers, Flora asked Antone, "What are you thinking?"

"About my parents. My mother has been much worse lately. Sometimes she seems so near the end…she may not live to see our wedding. But I have been prepared a long time for her passing and know that in some ways it will be a blessing for her." It was painful to think of his mother—once a proud Sicilian beauty—now deteriorated into a frail ghost so often gasping for breath and racked by coughing that brought up foul-smelling sputum. "But it's my father I worry about. He works himself too hard taking care of her—won't let us help him. And what will he do when she's gone? I worry he'll react the way your mother did. I couldn't bear to see him like that."

They embraced, each trying to comfort the other, and soon turned the conversation to happier topics: their business adventures, their wedding, their life together. As the hours slipped by and Flora made no move to leave, Antone began to feel apprehensive and asked in jest, "Have you decided to stay all night with me?"

"Yes," Flora said, as if this were the most natural thing in the world. "I've decided that I will. And tomorrow night too. My mother won't be home until the middle of the next day. I've told Matty I won't need his help until noon both of those days. That way we can stay here together until after dawn. Then I can go sleep for a few hours."

He laughed. "Lucky you! I have to go home and get right to work."

"Well, if it's **inconvenient**," she teased, sitting up and pretending to gather her scattered clothing, "I can just go home now and—"

Growling like a playful bear, he grabbed her, and she squealed—until his mouth found hers, and the sound became something quite different. They made love another time and then lay comfortably together, watching the sun rise beyond the bramble curtain and looking forward to all the mornings they would welcome together once they were married.

Later, after they were dressed, Flora helped Antone tidy away their belongings. "What did you ever do with that blanket?" she asked him. "Burn it?"

"No. That would have drawn too much attention," he answered. "I buried it out at the edge of our plum orchard. Don't worry...no one will ever find it."

"Unless coyotes or someone's dog digs it up."

"I didn't think of that," he admitted. "I'll check on it when I can."

They parted with a kiss and the delightful knowledge they would spend the whole next night together. And knowing this ahead of time, they were able to further enhance their time together. Antone brought a bottle of the Bella Flora wine and some *caciotta* cheese, and Flora brought bread and smoked ham called *dalmatinski pršut*. They laughed when they realized they'd both brought ripe plums—though different varieties—from their trees at home. And there were all the succulent blackberries they could hope to eat. It was a feast, and they ate before making love, savoring both the food and the anticipation of the pleasure they would share. They drank enough of the wine to feel intoxicated but not enough to interfere with that pleasure.

And when they finally lay together, Flora asked Antone to scent her body with the French perfume from the dove-shaped glass bottle. "Are you sure?" he asked.

She nodded and said, "I will have time to bathe before Mama returns—and before Matty comes to help pick plums. This may be my last chance to wear your wonderful gift before we're married."

Antone was quick to oblige, stroking her skin with the butterfly-topped cork stopper. So they rode the waves of rapture bathed in that heavenly fragrance and with the taste of wild blackberries on their tongues.

Antone slumped down on the bedside—resting his head on his mother's breast—and wept as if he were a child. Her thin hand came up and stroked his hair, calling him her "precious boy" and then saying, "I know...it isn't fair. It should have been me. I am ready and all of you are ready to let me go. I trust the Holy Father will take me when He's ready."

How can God be so cruel? Antone wondered. To let Mama continue to suffer but to take Papa in a moment—like breath taking a candle flame. *Shouldn't I have seen it coming? Were there signs in Papa I didn't see because I was so worried about Mama's deteriorating condition?*

They had all been in the vineyards working together—Antone and Bruno, their papa Gian and Gregorio—walking between the rows and scrutinizing the bunches of grapes as they began to ripen. Antone was experiencing a rare sense of peace, despite the fact his Flora had been unable to meet with him since her mother returned from the Teslas'—and that was nearly a week and a half now. "When I'm sure my mother will sleep through the night," Flora's last note in the bottle had said, "then I will be able to meet with you again." At night, though he was certainly tired from the day's work and from worry about his mother, still Antone often lay restlessly awake thinking of Flora.

But at that moment, on a sunny early-August morning—only two days after his nineteenth birthday—he had found a moment's respite in the beauty and abundance of what looked to be a record crop for them. How he loved these grapes and the way the plump, oval berries lost their green and darkened as they filled with sugars. In a week they'd be a dusky blue-black, and in two more, each berry in the heavy clusters would be large and black as jet.

"Papa," he called happily to his father, who was walking the next row, "these will make the best wine yet!" There was a sound in response, and Antone glanced up in time to watch his father die: For the space of one heartbeat, Gian Mellini stood bolt upright with a startled look on his face, one hand clutching his chest, and then he dropped to the earth and was gone.

Comforted now by his mother, Antone pushed the rest of the memories away. He wanted to forget the panic he'd felt—though on the surface he'd been exceptionally calm while Bruno and Gregorio both worked frantically trying to revive a man they all knew was well beyond their reach. He blocked out, too, the funeral and the burial in the plot beside the church in Santa Clara. How ironic that from where he stood, half-listening to the priest's words, he could see past this section of Italian graves—and the next of Irish—to the area where those of Slavic origins were buried; and there he could see the new white marble marker recently added to Luka Bogdonovich's grave.

And perhaps even worse than losing Papa—and getting through the funeral and those most painful days of grieving—was what happened afterward. Papa was barely in the ground before Gregorio started trying to take over—bringing up all the old arguments about how he was the eldest and so, should be in charge. Antone was in no mood for it. He had no energy for such struggles over power or thinking about anything except how to deal with his grief.

But Gregorio kept pushing and Antone lost his temper, and the next thing he knew, they were in a fistfight, and he remembered—too late—that his uncle was never one to be concerned about fighting fair. Antone ended up doubled over in the dust with a split lip, a black eye, and such a pain in his groin he wondered if he'd ever get the chance to sire children. And above him, coming at him fast with a wild light in his eyes, was Gregorio.

Just when Antone was sure he was about to die—or be crippled for life—Bruno came upon them and grabbed Gregorio. Bruno was big enough to control his uncle, and the fight ended there—for the present at least.

That was two days ago, and the strain in the family had been terrible.

Antone knew he had to come up with a strategy to protect himself and the business. If Gregorio were given free rein, he'd certainly ruin everything Antone had so carefully built on his good nature and good business sense. But he found it impossible to think while in his own house. It was almost as if some malevolent force—once held in check by the presence of Gian Mellini, Gregorio's older brother—was now released and creating a miasma of fear and dread in their household. And it was focused on him, because Gregorio saw him as his major rival, perhaps even an enemy.

Only an hour ago, Antone had announced he was taking an unexpected trip to the coast and that it might be for an extended period of time.

"That's it," taunted Uncle Gregorio. "Run away to your little business friends and cook up some new schemes to put money in your pocket instead of benefiting the family."

Antone shrugged helplessly. There was no sense in repeating yet again his explanations about how the different ventures were structured and just how well the family-owned Mellini Vineyards were doing—thanks to the sales of all the Bella Flora wine they had already bottled.

They were in Mama's bedroom where Antone would say good-bye to her. Bruno tried to smooth things over. "It's a good idea for you to go now," he said. "Uncle and I can take care of the vines. Just make sure you're back for the harvest."

"But I hate to leave you, Mama," Antone told her, sitting down on the edge of her bed.

"Don't worry about me," she chided. "I have Concetta to take care of me." It had been a stroke of genius on Mama's part. Donati Podesta's sister shone when it came to caring for the sick, and on many occasions, the Mellinis had had the girl keep Mama company when Papa was needed in the fields. She knew what Mama needed and when; she'd learned to help Mama through the coughing spells and how to hold her and thump her back to help her lungs drain. Now she had been hired to stay with Mama full time and also help with the cooking and household tasks, which freed the men entirely. The only drawback to this arrangement was that Concetta still seemed bent on adding Antone to her list of conquests. He avoided her as he could and hoped she'd be discouraged. Perhaps if he were gone, she'd see that Bruno's fondness for her was genuine—not like that of other boys she'd dallied with.

Suddenly strong in her voice and manner, Lucia Mellini told those gathered, "I want to speak to Antone—alone—if you'll excuse yourselves."

Bruno was quick to agree and went off to the kitchen to see Concetta—who was preparing Mama's medications—but Gregorio took the opportunity to sneer and say, "It's always Mama's Boy, isn't it?" before he stalked from the room.

When they were alone, Antone said, "I don't want to leave you, Mama."

She nodded. They both knew he feared he'd never see her alive again. "I know, but you must. Give that hothead Gregorio time to cool down. Give yourself time to grieve enough for your papa that you can think about other things. A little time will help all the situations."

He looked down into her eyes—which were dark Sicilian blue—thinking how much he loved her. He wanted to hope she would still be alive when he returned, but that was a selfish wish, to postpone his pain at losing her too.

Perhaps she could read this in his eyes, for she said, "Remember that I'm ready to go—even more so, now I know Gian is waiting for me."

That was when Antone slumped down and rested his head on her breast, weeping like a child. She stroked his hair, calling him her "precious boy" and tried to comfort him. When his crying quieted, Mama patted his back and said, "You'd best be on your way—before Gregorio can think up some other way to torment you."

They said their good-byes as if they might be their last, and Antone was soon out in the yard, swinging into Dolce's saddle. Gregorio had disappeared, and Antone felt great relief as he leaned down to squeeze Bruno's shoulder in farewell. "Take care of Mama."

"You know I will," Bruno said. "Concetta and I." Antone turned Dolce onto Page Street. He thought he could see his Flora watching from behind her lace curtains, but he couldn't wave or acknowledge her in any way. "You'll stop in and see Bianca on your way?" Bruno called. "Let her know you won't be visiting for a while?"

Antone—whose first stop would be the creekbed bower to leave a note explaining and apologizing for his absence—told Bruno, "I'll make sure my sweetheart knows."

SANTA CRUZ MOUNTAINS AND
BIG SUR COAST, CALIFORNIA — 1885

Antone's first visit was with Sven Heglund, where he got roaring drunk and spilled out much of his troubles to the Norwegian woodsman: his father's death, his mother's illness; his conflicts with Gregorio; the fact that he was desperately in love with a girl from another culture and was being kept not only from marrying her, but also from spending very much time with her. Throughout the evening, Sven's only answer seemed to be a gruff "Tsk-tsking" and a hearty "Have another drink, Antone!"

But the next morning, in the sober light of day, Sven told him, "It sounds like you have much to think about. To—how they say?—sort out. A man needs a special place to do that."

Antone nodded, but even that made his head ache.

"I know such a place," Sven said, sparking Antone's interest. "Down the coast a long day's ride south of Monterey…and about a mile east of the road, there is a hermitage. All men are welcome to go there and spend time peacefully—the hermits themselves are sworn to silence—while seeking the answers they need…and perhaps to renew their connection with God. You'll find some surprising things there—like real stained glass windows in the chapel; I'll let you discover the other surprises yourself."

Antone didn't need any more convincing. Within the hour he was waving good-bye to Sven, and he rode out of the redwoods and down to the Pacific coast, following it south, not even stopping in to see the Lidakis brothers. He let Dolce carry him quickly past Monterey and the Carmel mission and into the wilder country that lay beyond, not resting until he made camp for the night on a small beach at the mouth of a creek. He rose early the next morning and continued on his way. The road twisted and turned and dipped into deep arroyos as it clung to the side of chaparral-covered mountains rising steeply on his left and falling away even more steeply on his right into the crashing waves of the Pacific. He was accompanied by soaring eagles and numerous seabirds, his ears full of the sounds of the surf and wind and crying gulls.

When the road dipped into a deep ravine, he looked up into its canyon and glimpsed the huge white cross that Sven said marked the location of the hermitage. He continued along the road to the next turn-off, a smaller dirt road—flanked at the entrance by simple stonework—which went sharply uphill. Fit as Dolce was, she was blowing when she reached the gate at the top of the road, about a mile inland.

Antone dismounted and led the mare through the gate and past the stand of trees to where he could better view the location. Here, on the side of the mountain, was nestled a little plateau of perhaps three acres. The white-painted cross towered well over fifty feet above the grouping of buildings. Sven had told Antone a bit about the place, so he knew the building straight ahead included the kitchen, communal dining hall, and a room for receiving visitors and displaying the products they offered for sale. To the left, facing the sea, was a single long building divided into individual, private rooms where visitors such as he could stay.

On the other side of the open central area was the imposing stone chapel with its row of tall stained glass windows. Antone could hardly believe there were such things in this wild place, and he could hardly wait to get inside to see what they looked like with sunlight streaming through them as Sven had described. Clustered around the back and sides of the church were the hermits' tiny, individual cabins, each with an equally tiny garden plot beside it. Beyond this area were the barns, orchard, and communal garden.

It was quiet here, though there was work going on (Antone could discern several brown-robed figures moving among the distant fruit trees)—a quiet not of silence but of serenity, and Antone could feel the tension of his worries and his long ride washing out of him. It was as if here, beneath the outstretched arms of the great white cross, all was safe and sure. The troubles of the outside world could not intrude on those sheltered here; he could not ever remember feeling so secure.

A sound made him turn, and he watched a figure emerge from the reception building and come toward him. With a shock, he realized it was a woman, dressed in a pale-blue hooded habit, her hands clasped in front of her, her head lowered humbly so it was impossible to see her face. What was a woman doing here?

Then she looked up at him and it took his breath away. Her face radiated a purity and serene confidence surpassing anything he'd ever seen in life—rivaling the finest artistic renditions of the Virgin Mary—and her eyes, which seemed both blue and green at the same time, were huge and luminous with a mixture of curiosity, compassion, and great wisdom. Though there was an ageless quality about her, Antone guessed she was only a few years older than he was. With envy, he wondered, *How can anyone so young be so wise and self-confident?* He was stunned by her beauty, but there was nothing physical in the feeling, any more than if he found himself in the presence of the Blessed Virgin—or any lesser saint, for that matter.

"Welcome," she said in Italian and when he didn't respond, she tried again in English and in French.

Antone shook himself and answered in Italian, "A thousand pardons for staring. My name is Antone Mellini. A friend told me men come here to think and pray when they are troubled, when they need to sort things out and make decisions." She nodded, smiling gently. and Antone continued, "I wonder if I might stay here awhile and see if I can find some ease in my spirit."

"Of course," she answered. "You are welcome." When he began to reach into his pocket as if to get his money, she held up a hand and told him, "We will accept no payment. We only ask that you help with the chores…and obey the rules."

"Of course," he echoed her own words.

"Tie your horse to that post—Father Rodrigo will tend to her when he returns from the garden—and follow me. I am Sister Antoinette."

He hitched Dolce, gave her a pat on the flank as he untied his saddlebags and threw them across one shoulder. Then he walked toward the visitors' quarters with that intriguing young woman in blue, listening and nodding as she told him, "While you are here, you may communicate only with me or with Father Rodrigo. The hermits are vowed to silence; please do not speak to them or distract them in any way and do not go into the areas where they work. You are free to use the chapel at any time. Tomorrow when you come to the main building, Father Rodrigo or I will tell you what chores need doing. Your meals will be delivered to your room. Are you hungry now?"

He shook his head. He felt too elated to think of food. They stopped at the long building with about a dozen doors along its length. She opened the first door and said, "This will be your room. You are welcome to stay as long as you like. And may you find the peace you seek while you are here."

Antone thanked her and returned her parting smile, then watched her walk back the way they'd come. She moved so lightly and gracefully, he could fancy that she floated across the ground. Then he laughed at himself and went inside.

The room was very small. On one side was a cot with a folded blanket and on the other, a table bearing a lamp, a drinking cup, a book and writing materials. A single chair stood against the wall with a towel draped across its back; and on the seat, a pitcher of water set in a basin. There were no windows, but the opposite wall of the room had another door, and near the one he'd entered there was a strange box with a door fitted into the wall. It puzzled Antone until he realized this was how his food tray would be delivered into his room. Wishing there was a window—the view must be incredible from here— he dropped his saddlebags near the cot and went to open the door in the back wall. What he found, like his first sight of Sister Antoinette, took his breath.

He walked out on the tiny balcony and gazed at the most magnificent view he'd ever beheld. This edge of the plateau fell away steeply, so that even though he had come over a mile inland, it seemed as if his balcony were directly above the blue ocean currents pounding against the craggy shoreline. Other cathedral-like rock formations rose from the waters farther out at sea, crowned with haloes of seabirds circling above their nests. The sun was low now, painting the horizon with orange and yellow.

Antone slumped down on his little porch and leaned tiredly against the wall, his spirit breathing in the colors and sounds and fragrances of the place along with the good salt air. In moments he was asleep.

He awoke some hours later, shivering from the night mist that had rolled in and with his muscles protesting the long ride and the position he'd slept in. It was very dark and still, but he could hear a strange sound like distant humming. With a groan, he rose and went inside. He used the towel to dry his hair and changed into a drier shirt. He found a tray had been pushed into the receptacle by the door. Ravenously he ate the bread and cheese and then took a bite of the perfectly ripe pear, which melted like sweet butter in his mouth.

Opening his door and looking out across the compound, he could see little more than the now-ghostly white cross and the sparkling jewels of the chapel's stained glass windows, which were ablaze with light. He could hear the humming sound more clearly now and knew it must be the monks chanting. He quickly finished the pear and headed for the chapel. He fixed his eyes on one of the windows—a beautiful scene of St. Francis with a blue bird on his shoulder and a deer at his feet—and let that guide him across the dark courtyard.

He opened the big redwood door carefully, not wanting to intrude upon anyone and ready to withdraw if it seemed he would be disturbing the hermits. But the room was empty. The wonderful chanting was much stronger here, but its source was obscured by an ornately carved wooden screen, through which one could catch little more than flickers of movement. Candles were lit everywhere, and life-size statues of saints lined the walls. He moved closer, impressed with the workmanship, which made them seem so lifelike he felt as if at any moment one might step down and touch his shoulder. Yet it was not an eerie feeling, but one of peace and companionship.

The statue of the Virgin Mary graced the left side of the altar, which was covered with a pristine white cloth and a number of objects wrought of pure gold gleaming in the flicker of candlelight.

And above the altar, in the center of the back wall, hung an equally impressive figure of Christ on the cross. It drew Antone irresistibly, and as he moved closer, he saw that, though blood dripped from the wounds on the hands and feet and beneath the crown of thorns, still the face showed a tranquility that transcended the pain. Antone moved to the steps in front of the chancel rail in front of the altar, gazing up at the face of Jesus Christ, so pale yet calm and reassuring, and it seemed to Antone that the eyes looked directly into his own, asking him to find that same peace within himself. He fell to his knees on the top step, crossing himself before he clasped his hands and rested his elbows on the rail, staring into those eyes as the chanting wrapped him in a mantle of otherworldliness.

The next conscious thought Antone had was that the chanting had stopped, and as he pulled his gaze away from the eyes of Christ, he saw that it was morning. The candles had all burned out and the stained glass windows were now lit from the sunlight outside. He felt as if he had been somewhere else, as if he'd been dreaming, yet he felt as rested as if he'd slept ten hours. There was no sense of hurry in him either, and before leaving the chapel, he studied each and every one of the statues and the windows, all of them exquisitely crafted.

At last, Antone returned to his room where he found last night's tray had been replaced with another holding a breakfast of cooked oats and cream and the largest peach he had ever seen. He opened the door facing the sea and ate on his tiny balcony, watching the waves play in the swirling remnants of fog and deep morning shadows in the canyon below. Then he washed up and went in search of someone to tell him which chores most needed doing.

He went directly to the visitors' reception room, where he found a sort of store with honey and jams and wine for sale. He wondered briefly what their wine tasted like, and then his attention shifted to the artwork: small carved statues and rosaries and other items crafted of wood and ceramic. And there were paintings on the wall, mostly on religious topics and all as fine as any Antone had seen in San Francisco galleries. One drew Antone's eyes especially.

In a variation of a classic tale, it showed a kind-hearted man removing a thorn from a sad-faced lion's paw. Only in this case, the man was a monk, seated in his cell and surrounded by his books. Something in the picture touched Antone in a special way. *I feel like that lion,* he thought. *I came here with a thorn in my paw, but somehow it was removed last night, and now all I have to do is take care of the wound until it's healed.*

Just then a monk came into the room, wiping his hands on his apron. "There you are!" he said in Italian. "I saw you leaving your room. You must be Antone; I'm Father Rodrigo."

Antone nodded and returned the greetings. He gestured around the room. "These are truly beautiful works of art. Were they created by the monks who live here?" When Father Rodrigo nodded, Antone asked him, "Did you do any of these?"

The monk laughed heartily and shook his tonsured head. "No, no, no! I've known mules more artistic than I am!" It was hard to tell his age from his round, flushed face and lively dark eyes, but his hands were those of a man past sixty. "But I can teach, I can say the masses, I like to talk to visitors—and that's what the hermits really need me for. I also cook, and if you're looking for chores, I can use some help with the bread."

"Of course," Antone said and followed the man into the back part of the building and into a large, immaculate kitchen. Everything was simple, but the utensils and cooking implements were well-kept and of the best quality. There was no sign anywhere of Sister Antoinette.

Father Rodrigo, chattering on, set him to kneading bread dough. As they worked together—when Antone could finally get a word in—he remarked, "You said you are a teacher. Whom do you teach here?"

"Sometimes men come here wanting to join the order or study with the hermits. Understand, with the vow of silence, all work with the others must be done in writing. I assist with education which cannot be handled that way. And, of course, I have been Antoinette's only teacher."

Antone glanced quickly at the older man, his curiosity warring with his fear of prying or asking the wrong question. "I was quite surprised to find her here," Antone said carefully.

Rodrigo laughed merrily. "I'll wager that's true! And I'll bet you'd like to know how she came to be here, wouldn't you?" Antone looked embarrassed as he nodded. "Everyone wants to know," the monk said. "And it's a story worth telling." As they made the bread and Rodrigo gave Antone other things to do around the kitchen, he told Antoinette's story, and he proved to have an enviable flair for the dramatic.

"Some people call her Antoinette of the Lightning," he began. "One night—some twenty-two years ago—there was a terrible storm along the coast here. Great bolts of lightning flashing from the sky and thunder so loud everyone had trouble hearing for days afterward. It made the monks so uneasy they gathered in the chapel to pray together. That tall cross out there has drawn electricity to it before in storms."

Antone nodded he understood how this worked, and Rodrigo continued. "There was one tremendous bolt of lightning outside the chapel and then dead silence for a moment, and then the brothers thought they heard a knocking on the door. When no one went to answer it, the knocking came again, and one brave soul—a Brother Gaspard—went and opened the door, fully prepared to see old Lucifer himself and all his minions. You can imagine how shocked he was to find a little girl! And as he stared at her, another great bolt of lightning sliced down into the yard behind her, so he grabbed her hand and pulled her safely into the church. She didn't seem afraid at all; she just smiled at all the brothers, pointed to herself, and said, 'Antoinette.' In fact, though she was probably almost two years old, that was the only word she seemed to know.

"Truth is, she's a real mystery. No one knows anything about her or how she got here. Some people believe the Blessed Virgin sent her here on a lightning bolt and this is where she's intended to be. The brothers certainly tried to get her housed somewhere else, but every time they made some kind of plans to have her removed, there were all kinds of disasters to delay their plans: earthquakes blocking the road with rockslides, washouts, broken wagon wheels—and this coast never saw as many lightning storms as it did those weeks they were trying to move Antoinette to what they thought was a more suitable home. Finally Brother Gaspard had a vision in which the Holy Mother spoke to him, telling him that this was where Antoinette belonged and that she must stay, so the brothers started trying to figure out how it could be arranged to house and educate a young girl here under the rules of the order. After that, the weather settled down and everything began to run smoothly around here again."

Antone was staring at him incredulously. "This is all true?"

The monk shrugged. "I was not here, but this is the testimony of the brothers who were here then, and I hardly think they'd lie. You see, I was brought in to take care of her when it was clear she had to stay." Father Rodrigo looked suddenly older and sorrowful as he told his own story: how he was a young teacher in San Francisco whose wife and daughter were killed in a fire for which he felt responsible; he'd withdrawn from the world he knew and become a monk—though he could never quite bring himself to a vow of silence. Still he grieved especially for his lost daughter, and it interfered with his performance in the service of God. He was chosen to go to the hermitage and raise the mysterious Antoinette, who turned out to be a splendid pupil, especially adept at languages. Father Rodrigo taught her Latin, of course, and that made the French and Italian much easier, but she also learned English so that she could receive almost any visitors.

"My work with Antoinette healed my life," Father Rodrigo said simply, "and she has helped countless others to overcome their pain and confusion. Some even hold her in such reverence they call her Mother Antoinette. Many people come here…we turn no one away as long as they abide by the rules. Some heal themselves and return to their lives; some choose to join the hermits permanently. I have no doubt there are men here who have suffered greater losses than I myself…some undoubtedly have committed crimes, but here we are all the same in God's eyes…and in Antoinette's."

And so it was for Antone Mellini. In the week and a half he spent at the hermitage, he found a new sense of himself and an inner peace he had not imagined possible. He spent part of his days outdoors chopping wood and cleaning the barns. He liked working outside because sometimes he caught glimpses of the bearded hermits who seemed indistinguishable since they all had full beards and wore identical brown habits with the hoods up and only sandals on their feet. But he also enjoyed helping with cooking and cleaning chores inside the main building because this gave him an opportunity to talk with Rodrigo and Antoinette. He usually ate his evening meal on the little balcony where he could watch the miracle of every sunset, for no two were ever alike over the Pacific. He would sleep a few hours on his simple cot and then go to mass, after which he would linger in the chapel where he could pray and study the statues and look deep into the eyes of Jesus as he listened to the numinous chanting of the hermits on the other side of the wall. He read the Bible and other writings Rodrigo and Antoinette suggested, and in their talks together, they asked him questions which helped him organize his thoughts and decide what was most important, and what actions to take.

After a time, there was an easing of the grief for his father—and for his mother, who he was sure would follow her Gian before long. He was able to review his business and marital plans from a more objective perspective and was pleased to find them still sound. He saved the most difficult decision till the end: what to do about Gregorio?

It was Antoinette who helped him the most with this, and many of her questions guided him to new awarenesses and possibilities. He saw a way to give Gregorio more power in the company, without putting him in a position where he could damage the venture too much. The main key was leaving the wine production to Bruno and Gregorio, now that it was set up and running smoothly. That left him free to concentrate on his other ventures, which would make it possible for him assure his family would accept his marriage to Flora.

Ah, Flora! A day did not go by when he did not think of her a dozen times or more. He missed her companionship and their lovemaking, but he found himself reluctant to leave this peace and security behind. *If only,* he thought wistfully, *I could just go back and have it all changed already. To have the businesses running smoothly and paying well; to already be married to Flora and in our fine home, with both families giving their blessing.* But no, he had much work to do yet to make these things come about. When he found himself thinking too strongly of how good it would be simply to stay on at the hermitage, he knew it was time to leave, to face these new challenges like a man. Besides, with Papa gone, his hands were desperately needed for the grape harvest if the Mellini Vineyards were to survive and prosper.

On the morning of his departure, Father Rodrigo embraced him and stuffed his saddlebags with bread and cheese and fresh fruit. Then he said, "It was a pleasure, young man. May our Lord God bless you wherever you go, whatever you do. Now, I must excuse myself. I tend to weep over good-byes. Do come and see us again." Then he hurried away, and Antone turned his attention to Antoinette.

How beautiful she was with her sweet face and huge, soulful eyes. "Are your spirits more at ease now, Antone Mellini?" she asked quietly.

He smiled. "Yes, thanks to you." He reached out and took her hands in his and told her earnestly, "There's no way I can ever thank you for all the help you've given me, and a simple thank-you seems insignificant." He raised her hands to his lips and kissed them. "Thank you, Mother Antoinette." He squeezed the hands gently as he released them.

"You are very welcome," she responded. As he mounted the honey-colored mare, she added, "And, of course, you are welcome to return here any time and stay as long as you like."

Antone smiled down at her and touched the brim of his hat and rode away. She followed him to the gate so she could close it behind him. He turned to wave once before he was out of sight, and she waved back, but he was too far away to see the tears streaming down her face.

Antoinette of the Lightning stood waving, feeling Antone's kisses still burning on the backs of her hands, hoping he had not seen her tears. Why did he have to leave? Why did he ever have to come here?

Her life had always been so simple. She knew her place was here where she could help troubled men find the truths in their lives and heal their spiritual wounds. This the Holy Mother had told her from the very beginning. In all her years she had been surrounded by men, and though most of them were like the hermits—old enough to be her parent or grandparent—many had been young and handsome. A few had even been as beautiful to look at as this newest visitor. But never had she felt an attraction to any of them. Never had her physical body and her emotions been stirred as they had been by this Antone Mellini. And to what purpose? It was obvious Antone was in love with someone else, had been unaware of his effect on her, and certainly nothing could be allowed to interfere with her solitary work here at the hermitage.

Blessed Mother, Antoinette prayed now, staring down the wild canyon where the honey-colored mare had disappeared, *why have you sent me this challenge? And is it a test that is completed now... Or will I see Antone Mellini again someday?*

CHAPTER 20
SANTA CLARA VALLEY — 1885

Flora nodded, slapped her hand on the wooden cask, and said aloud, "That's it!" She was alone in the cellar and had just gotten the last of this year's plum wine kegged for the aging process. There was a sense of accomplishment in how smoothly this first attempt had gone, thanks to Papa's detailed notes and Mattiza's dedicated assistance. Confident this wine would be as good as any Papa ever made, she was sure it would please Josko Tipanov, who was determined to honor Luka Bogdonovich.

The last time Flora spoke with Tipanov, he'd told her he was having custom bottles made in San Francisco. The glass would be blown into special carved molds, so that the finished *slivovitz* bottle would be embossed with the words "Bogdonovich Plum."

Flora let her fantasies carry her a moment, imagining money flowing in for this wine, allowing her extra luxuries she would not usually envision: pretty silk dresses for Mama and herself, gifts for her soon-to-be husband—perhaps even a carriage for going into town. And travel. Antone had promised once they were married he would take her traveling with him, and they would journey to faraway places for pleasure, not just business. Perhaps someday they'd even get to Dubrovnik and take Mama with them for a visit.

Such a daydream—traveling with her husband Antone and her mother—was so thrilling, Flora actually felt lightheaded for a moment and sat herself down in one of Papa's chairs to catch her breath and equilibrium.

A shadow fell into the cellar as someone blocked the doorway, and a voice called, "There you are! Your mother told us we could find you here."

Still a little dizzy, Flora squinted at the figure, black against the hot August sunlight, trying to identify the familiar-sounding voice. "**Karsten?**" she ventured.

"Yes, Flora, and I have someone I want you to meet. Shall we come down?"

"No, no, I'll come up there!" She hurried up the steps, blinking in the brightness, and took the hand. "How wonderful to see you!"

He looked handsomer somehow, as if the happiness radiating from his face had made his features less plain, and his hazel eyes were certainly alight. His other arm was around the waist of a dark-haired young woman. "This is Ruzena," Karsten said, "my wife." There was such love and pride in his voice, it brought tears to Flora's eyes, inspiring hope that someday she might hear Antone introduce her in just this tone.

Ruzena Tipanov was also plain of face but radiant with her love and enhanced by the beauty of her clothing. She wore a lovely dress of change-

213

able taffeta that shifted between rose and pale green as it moved against the light, and the matching beribboned hat was adorned with plumes dyed in the two colors. Flora gave a thought to what it would be like to be married to a wealthy man—especially if one came from poverty as Karsten had said Ruzena did. Of course there were many things more important than pretty clothes, but Flora hoped that someday she would have a dress much like this.

Karsten's new wife reached to take Flora's hand and told her shyly, "We had to come right away and thank you."

"**Me?**" Flora said with a laugh.

"Oh, yes! My Karsten told me how you encouraged him to go back to Hvar and marry me and bring me here to a new life. It was you who gave him the courage to stand up for himself, to make the life he wants rather than what his parents want for him."

"And even better," Karsten chuckled, "you said something to my father that made him see everything in a new light. Why, he's even got my mother to accept our marriage, and when they get to know Ruzena better, they'll love her for herself. We've only been here two days and already they're starting to—as the Americans say—come around."

"I'm so happy for you," Flora told them, squeezing their hands. "Would you like to come inside and have a cool drink of cider—or some wine to celebrate?"

"Cider would be very nice, thank you," Ruzena answered in such a way that Flora knew she'd been getting lessons in etiquette. As if reading Flora's thoughts, Ruzena smiled and said, "I've also been learning to read and to speak some English words."

"Yes," Karsten affirmed, giving her an affectionate squeeze. "And she's even quicker to learn than I thought she'd be. Soon she'll be translating English for me."

They had turned toward the house, and Flora was thinking it might be very helpful for Mama to see such a happy young couple whose parents hadn't initially approved but were now accepting the marriage.

As they neared the kitchen door, Karsten touched Flora's arm to detain her a moment. "Before we go inside," he said in a barely audible voice, "what news in your secret love?"

Flora shrugged. "There have been ... complications ... and delays...."

"Ah, yes," Karsten said with some embarrassment. "Forgive me for not extending our condolences sooner. Your father was a very likeable and generous man."

"Thank you. My sweetheart and I had planned to marry within the next few weeks, but with all that's happened—there have been similar difficulties in his life—we have postponed any announcement, and my mother still has no idea."

The newlywed Tipanovs nodded their understanding and sympathy. Karsten put one hand on Flora's shoulder and spoke with grave sincerity. "We give you our support and good wishes to as happy an outcome as ours. And if you **ever** need **anything**, you let me know."

"Yes, please," said Ruzena. "Even if it's just to talk."

Touched, Flora felt her eyes dampen, and she nodded wordlessly, but Karsten wanted to make sure she understood this was no empty courtesy.

He gripped her shoulder and said, "I mean it, Flora Bogdonovich. We owe our marriage and our happiness to you. It is a debt that can never be fully repaid, so will you promise me you'll tell me if there is ever anything you need?"

Still speechless, Flora nodded again, but he would not let her go until she said it aloud. "I promise, Karsten. Thank you."

Then the three of them laughed, feeling the bond of their friendship—knowing it was something that would last—no matter what the future brought, and they went into the kitchen to chat with Flora's mother and cool their August thirsts with cider kept cool in the well.

On the way home from his extended stay at the hermitage, Antone stopped at the bower and retrieved Flora's "welcome back; I missed you; hope you had a good trip" note and left one of his own: "I hope we can meet soon, but I don't know what the situation will be at my house, and the next two weeks will be very busy. I love you more than ever."

When he rode into his yard, his brother Bruno came rushing out of the house to give him a hearty welcome. "I'm sure glad to see you. Thought I was going to have to pick your share of the grapes too."

But seeing anxiety as well as happiness in Bruno's eyes, Antone's first question was, "How's Mama?"

"The same," Bruno said, and he, too, seemed surprised. "No better, but certainly no worse."

Relieved, Antone nodded and asked, "Then what are you so nervous about?"

Bruno glanced over where the edge of the vineyard began, and looking that way, Antone could see their Uncle Gregorio there, walking among the vines. Bruno said, "I'll help you put your horse away" and walked off toward the barn.

Baffled but apprehensive, Antone followed, leading Dolce. Inside the barn's dimness, Bruno stayed close to the door where he could keep an eye out for Gregorio. Antone began to unsaddle the mare. "What's going on?"

"It's Gregorio," Bruno began in a low voice. "He's gotten worse since you've been gone. He's always been crazy and dangerous. You remember what he's like ... what he did."

It was a memory Antone tried to avoid calling up. He had been seven years old; Bruno was nine and Gregorio fourteen. There was another boy, Franco, who was Antone's age. The four of them had gone fishing in the part of the creek that ran through the Mellini property. There was one place where a deep depression kept a year-round swimming hole sizable enough to maintain a small population of fish. They'd caught a few tiny fish, but the shimmering water in the summer heat called to the boys, and the three youngest were soon stripped of their clothes and into the water.

Gregorio never went skinny-dipping—he always said he was older and more mature, but in truth, he took great pains that no one would ever see him naked. In fact, he would never even show enough of himself to take a pee where anyone could see him. (Privately, the brothers used to joke about this, for what was more natural or satisfying than a good pee while enjoying the beauty of nature? Especially when there were rocks to splash and toads to spray and contests to be won! But, of course, they never dared let Gregorio know they laughed at him.)

And it was not that he was shy about such matters, for he had much to say—most of it lewd and repulsive and frightening to the younger boys. Neither was he shy about watching others, often laughing at them or making disparaging remarks, so that most of the boys who were friends with Antone and Bruno didn't want to be around Gregorio, even when they had their clothes on.

That summer day at the swimming hole, Franco was in the deepest part when he was seized by a cramp and cried out for help. Watching his panic, both Antone and Bruno were too petrified to help him. Their Papa had impressed them with a story of how he'd almost been drowned trying to save someone who'd then pulled him under. So the brothers were still trying to figure out what to do when their Uncle Gregorio simply dove in and went after Franco.

At first they'd been relieved and had even cheered Gregorio on, but when he got to Franco, the older boy began to tread water just beyond Franco's reach, telling him to "Calm down so I can help you." But the desperate youngster began to cry plaintively, "Help me! Help me!" and the two boys on shore witnessed a strange and horrifying event unfolding before them. As Franco screamed and pleaded and clutched at Gregorio, the older boy stayed just out of his reach. From the shore, it was difficult to hear what Gregorio was saying, but it seemed he was mocking the drowning boy—and there was no mistaking the sneering smile on his face.

Antone knew he wanted to scream at Gregorio to help their friend, but he stood frozen, unable to look away. It must have been the same for Bruno, for he made no move either.

Slowly, the thrashing of Franco's arms weakened, and he gasped and spluttered as it became more difficult to keep his face above the water. And then the worst thing—the most unbelievable—happened: Gregorio reached out a hand, grasped Franco's head and pushed it under water, holding it there.

Now Antone screamed—and Gregorio let go. But Franco had stopped thrashing, and he slipped away beneath the water. Bruno suddenly thought to run for help, but had to take the time to pull on his trousers before he went tearing up the creekbank toward the house. Antone watched as Gregorio now tried to find Franco: taking a deep breath and then diving down into the dark, cold water for as long as the air in his lungs would sustain him. On the third dive, he brought up the pale and lifeless-looking body of Franco and dragged it up on the bank next to Antone.

At that moment, Bruno returned, out of breath but managing to gasp, "Papa's coming!"

Gregorio, his clothes soaked, gasping for breath himself, reached out and grabbed each of his nephews by a wrist and clutched them so tightly Antone could feel his hand going numb. He glared into their eyes and said in a low, tight voice, "It was an accident. And if either of you **ever** says otherwise, I'll cut off something of yours you'd hate to be without. **Understand?**"

They didn't answer right away, and Gregorio wrenched their arms so that they both cried out. "**Understand?**"

There was nothing to do except to nod agreement. Secretly, Antone hoped that Franco would be alive and he would tell on Gregorio. But he never recovered that much. For, though Papa arrived only moments later and was able to get the boy breathing again, Franco was never the same. The doctor said his brain was damaged, and he was never able to walk or speak again. Adults praised Gregorio for saving the boy's life, and he basked in this unaccustomed acclaim, and it seemed to Antone that he even derived some twisted sort of satisfaction in the irony. No one ever told the truth.

Even today, Antone thought now as he brushed his mare in the barn, *Franco sits in a chair on his front porch and stares without seeming to see anything or anyone.* Antone shivered and then switched his attention to the present, telling Bruno about how he'd reflected on what might be done with their uncle when it came to the business dealings he was so determined to direct. "I came up with a plan that might ease my trouble with Gregorio some. But it means you'll have to take a more active part, brother, so you can guide the transactions in ways he'd resist from me."

Bruno, still keeping watch at the door, glanced over at his baby brother and grinned. "Time for me to grow up ... settle down ... get to work?

I knew it would come someday. So tell me…." Then he listened to the plan Antone had devised in the peaceful atmosphere of the hermitage. Afterwards, Bruno nodded in satisfaction and pronounced it "a good plan—and fair."

"Let's hope it works," Antone said, putting Dolce in her box stall and giving her a measure of grain.

Bruno left his post at the door and came right up to Antone and said gravely, "The best plan in the world won't be enough if we're not careful." His voice dropped even lower. "Antone, he has a gun!"

"**What!?**"

"I don't know where he got it," Bruno said. "Or when or how—or who he got it from—but he has a gun, and he won't be afraid to use it. You must take great care. His hatred for you is beyond reason."

Antone gave his older brother an affectionate grin and tried to make it more cheerful than he felt. "Thanks for the warning. Believe me, I intend to be careful. I have much to live for."

Flora and Antone managed a single night together before the Mellini grape harvest consumed the next two weeks of Antone's life. Mama Bogdonovich was beginning to sleep better now, and Flora was desperate enough to see her lover that she would risk being missed during the night. As she said to Antone, "We'll be announcing our intentions soon." But it was less than two months since the death of her papa and only a month since he'd lost his father, and they decided they must wait longer. Secretly, they both worried that Lucia Mellini would finally pass away and further delay their plans, but neither spoke of this and both felt guilty for entertaining such selfish thoughts.

Their night together reaffirmed their love; being separated put no distance between them. As soon as they touched or looked into each other's eyes, it was as if they had never parted. Except they had much to tell each other. Though he couldn't have said why, Antone did not tell Flora about the hermitage. Perhaps the experience was still too profound to share with anyone, though he would tell her all about it when he had truly assimilated its many elements. He simply said he'd gone to the redwoods and he'd found a peaceful place to think things through and make some plans.

She told him all about the visit from Karsten and Ruzena, saying, "I know you'll like them when you meet them, and they will help us be better-accepted in my community. It never hurts to have rich people on your side." She described the bottles for the Bogdonovich Plum wine, and then there was the latest news: "Josko Tipanov says Papa's apricot wine makes even better brandy than the plum, and he wants to bottle it separately and let me name it. I've decided to call it Armelin—let the Americans learn the

Croatian word for apricot! I've talked him into buying amber bottles from the Lidakis brothers and using labels, which Mama will design. I got my idea from your Bella Flora wine. Only ours will have a drawing of an apricot sprig."

"I will never eat another apricot," Antone told her, "without thinking of that night when we truly became husband and wife."

"Nor I," Flora murmured. "That's exactly what I was thinking of when I named the brandy." And then they kissed, and that was the end of any conversation for quite some time.

It was good they made the most of their time together, for it was impossible to meet during the grape harvest. The work was exhausting enough but Antone also had to spend much of his evenings on legal and professional matters, preparing everything so that the reorganization went smoothly with his uncle. Gregorio had agreed to Antone's proposals about the new business arrangements with such uncharacteristic alacrity that it made Antone uneasy. After the grapes were in and sorted for the table or for wine, the winemaking process had to begin, so it was past the middle of September before Antone could steal another night with his Flora.

He brought beautiful black clusters of grapes—uva in Italian and grožde in Croatian—and they feasted on them throughout the evening. When they talked, it was mostly about the wine. Antone was in one of his best storytelling moods and made her double over with laughter describing the scene of Concetta and Bruno with their bare legs and feet stained purple from crushing grapes in the huge redwood tubs. "Don't laugh," he told her. "Next year at this time my wife will be up to her knees in Mellini grapes."

She kissed him and vowed, "Certainly, if my husband will help with the Bogdonovich apricots and plums."

Late in their time together, after making love, they dozed off for a short time in each other's arms. But they both came awake in the same harsh instant, wrenched from sleep wide-eyed and gasping. They stared at each other fearfully. "I had a bad dream," Flora whispered.

"I did too," Antone answered, equally subdued.

But they did not tell their dreams or ask about the other's, as if afraid of what they would hear. Instead, they began to make love one last time before parting. They moved like reverent mountain climbers—slowly and with great awareness of the beauty all around them, every tiny flower and stone and dewdrop. They ascended together, with the utmost tenderness, open-eyed and gazing at each other as if memorizing the sight. They whispered their love for each other, and when they'd reached that last quivering pinnacle together, they lay holding each other very tightly, and Flora found she was suddenly crying.

"What's wrong?" Antone asked, but he felt sure he really didn't want to hear.

She shook her head and whispered, "I don't know," and he chose to believe it, though he thought it was probably not true, that she must have felt the same cold finger of premonition along **her** spine too.

They parted with a last kiss and the promise to meet again as soon as they possibly could.

Flora woke the next morning not only weary from so little sleep but also feeling lightheaded and sick to her stomach. Her mother had just called her to breakfast, but eating was the last thing she wanted to do. Dutifully, she dressed and went into the kitchen, where the floor was still damp and shiny from a good scrubbing. Mama was dishing up a plate of food at the stove, humming and looking more at peace than she had in months. "Sit down, Flora," she said. "I've made your favorite...."

Flora sat and realized she'd been holding her breath in hopes that it would ease her stomach, but it only made her feel more dizzy, so she let out that breath and took another deep one, but it brought in the cooking odors as well as the air. And at that very moment, Mama set the plate in front of her, and Flora saw the eggs staring up at her ... and the spicy sausages glistening with fat. "...*Kobasica!*" Mama said, pleased with herself for this small act of preparing—without one tear— a food which had also been a favorite of Luka's.

The response was immediate and explosive. Flora barely had time to turn away from the table and her mother before vomiting forcefully onto the freshly scrubbed floor. Coughing and gasping, Flora continued to retch, even though there was nothing to expel.

"Oh, my sweet *janje!* " Mama cried, stroking her daughter's temple. "Are you all right?"

Flora nodded and said miserably, "Oh, Mama, I'm sorry about your clean floor."

Philomena actually laughed just a little and went to get the rags and bucket of wash water still sitting next to the back door. "Don't worry, child. I seem to remember when you did some cleaning up after me." She began to clear away the mess. "Are you feeling all right now? Do you think you're getting some kind of illness?"

Flora didn't know which question to answer first. "I'm afraid it's the sausages. There are just some smells that have been bothering me lately—cooking meat is one."

Her mother looked up sharply. "For how long?"

Flora shrugged. "Weeks. But it can't be some kind of illness because I usually feel better later in the day."

Leaving the clean-up, Philomena sat herself in another of the chairs at the table. "Has there been anything else unusual in your health?"

Flora shrugged again. "Some dizziness...."

Philomena scrutinized her daughter's body, the look of her skin and the way her breasts strained the fabric of her bodice as if they'd recently grown larger. *No, this can't be true!* she told herself. **Not Flora!** There was a question that had to be asked. "What about your..." She looked away in her own embarrassment and her voice dropped lower, even though there was no one else to hear, "monthly cycles?"

Flora was startled. This was a topic her mother avoided. There was that one talk they'd had when the onset of menarche had sent her running, terrified, to her mother. Mama was obviously uncomfortable but had managed an explanation and given enough information that Flora hadn't had to ask any more questions ... until now.

"What does that have to do with being sick?"

"Answer me," she said with such intensity that Flora blinked in surprise.

She thought back. So much had happened in the past weeks. "The last time was before Papa died." Seeing the look on Mama's face, she said, "That time we talked ... you told me things can make it not happen. Like being sick ... or being very upset. You told me how when you were on the ship coming to America you were so upset they stopped."

Yes, Philomena thought. *And I was sure I must be pregnant.* With her elbows on the table, she dropped her face into her hands, and her voice came out a little muffled and full of regret. "There's something else that makes them stop, but I didn't think I needed to tell you yet ... I thought you were too young."

Suddenly frightened, Flora leaned toward her mother and cried, "What's wrong, Mama? Do I have an illness?"

Philomena lifted her head and reached across the table to take her daughter's hands. "No, Flora. Not an illness. These things you have been experiencing are the signs that you are pregnant."

"**Pregnant?!**" Flora spoke the word as if she had never heard it before. She knew that babies were made by making love, but she **couldn't** be pregnant. When Mama explained it all to her, she'd said, *When you grow up and get married and make love with your husband, then you can have babies.* This didn't make sense. "But Mama," she said patiently, "**I can't** be pregnant. I'm not married!"

Philomena gave a short, startled laugh, and then her eyes filled up with tears. "Yes," she said wryly, "that **is** a problem. I probably should have explained things better ... told you more: it's the ... intercourse ... not the being married that makes the babies."

"Oh," Flora said in a little voice, like a child who had made a mistake in her lessons, and then the enormity of the situation hit her, and the bottom seemed to fall out of her stomach. She balled her hands into fists and pressed them against her belly, feeling as if she would throw up again. What would happen now?

"Who is the father?" Philomena asked with a calm she did not feel. When Flora looked away and bit her lip but did not answer, Mama asked, "Is it Mattiza?" After all, who else **could** it be?

But her daughter looked startled. "**No! Not Matty….**"

"Who then?" Philomena waited for an answer, steeling herself.

Instead, Flora told her in a pleading tone, "I love him, Mama. He loves me. We'd planned to already be married by now. But Papa died and then … other things happened, and we thought we'd better wait."

There must be a reason the girl was so reticent. Mentally, Philomena scanned the congregation of their church. Which of these young boys would Flora be reluctant to name? Surely not a married man? "**Who?!**" Philomena demanded, afraid now to hear the answer.

Flora stared down at her hands clenched in her lap, and her voice was soft and full of love. "His name is Antone…."

Antone! Philomena thought, baffled. She knew no one in any Slav community with that name. She repeated the name: "Antone?"

Flora nodded. "Antone Mellini."

It took a moment to sink in. "**Mellini!** Not that guinea boy across the street?!" This was almost more shocking than a married man. But Philomena remembered the day the boy had come about repairing the fence. If she tried to see him as a Slav instead of an Italian, she supposed she could understand how an impressionable young girl could find such a face and lithe body attractive … perhaps even beautiful. But he was not Slavic. He was Italian, and what good woman would want her daughter to marry out of the community, much less an Italian? Everyone knew they were dirty and lazy and much too loud and boisterous. She dismissed her memory of the Mellini boy—clean, neatly dressed, and courteous—taking responsibility for what his horse had done and fixing the fence the very next day.

Flora had nodded to confirm the boy's identity. Already guessing the answer, Philomena asked, "He didn't force you?"

"**No, Mama!**" She leaned toward her mother as if to better impress her with her sincerity. "If anything, it was **my** choice. **I love him.**" She paused. "But what do I do now?"

Philomena sighed. "You must get married." She pondered a moment. "How long ago did this happen?"

Flora realized now that she could've gotten pregnant any of the times she had intercourse, and she was wise enough not to tell her mother how many times that had occurred. Flora decided it was safest to say the earliest occasion, and suddenly in that moment—with some new-found, retrospective intuition born of her womanhood—she knew with certainty it **had** been that first time ... that magical night of perfumed skin and ripe apricots. "The night of the summer solstice," she answered.

"That will make it a very early baby, but some people might still believe it. You must get married as soon as possible."

"Yes, Mama," Flora said dutifully, her heart suddenly singing. Perhaps this was working out for the best anyway.

Then she heard her mother saying, almost to herself: "Mattiza is a good boy, but it wouldn't be good to marry the son of a criminal living his life out in prison. Many boys at church have shown interest in you; it should not be difficult to get one of them to propose to you in a matter of days."

"**What!?**" Flora came up out of her chair so quickly, it fell over behind her with a crash. Her face was both incredulous and outraged. Startled by the transformation, Philomena fell back in her chair. "What are you talking about?! I tell you, I love Antone. He is the only man I will marry. Do you understand? He is already my husband—as long as we live—and this," she cupped her rounding belly with her hands, "is his child. I will not have anyone else!"

Even Flora's actions when she pulled her mother back to sanity had not prepared Mama for this defiance, this total self-assurance, this determination. "What if he won't marry you?"

"He **will**," Flora said with some exasperation. "Haven't you been listening? He loves me too. He asked me to marry him months ago, and it is only observing periods of mourning in both our families that has kept us apart."

Philomena saw very clearly that she must tread carefully: she was in danger of losing her daughter, and she couldn't afford that. With her Luka gone, what else did she have to live for? Only her daughter and —wonder of wonders—a **grandchild!**

So she was forced to ask herself which was more important: her daughter marrying within the Slavic community or having a daughter and grandchild at all. Could she not accept an Italian son-in-law if he turned out to be a good Catholic, a good husband and father? Would it be easier to hold her head up in the community if her son-in-law was a good Italian man or if he was a Croatian who treated his wife as Vlach Stanich used to treat Matty's mother Eliska?

"I will not have any other husband," Flora said again. "Not ever."

Philomena sighed. "Then you'd better tell your Antone about this baby as soon as possible, and we'll arrange for a wedding right away."

The dark defiance on Flora's face broke apart like storm clouds chased by the sun. She beamed at her mother and rushed to embrace her and give her a noisy kiss on her cheek. "I love you, Mama!" She held tightly to this woman who had carried her in her womb, given her life, nursed her and nurtured her. *I hope I can be half as good a mother to my child.* But aloud, she said, "And you will love Antone when you get to know him." *And I'd better go put that amber bottle in my window, so he'll come meet me tonight.*

When Flora released her—her thoughts obviously on that Antone fellow—Philomena felt the loss, wanted to hold onto her child a moment longer ... if not forever.

Turning away, Flora said, as if to herself, "I will arrange to meet with him tonight and tell him the news."

Philomena watched her daughter turn and rush excitedly out of the room, but she still sat at the table where the plate of eggs and sausage had grown cold and unappetizing. There on the floor was the evidence of Flora's morning sickness, still to be cleansed away. With her daughter so happy and herself resigned to the indignity of an Italian son-in-law as a lesser-of-evils, why should she feel such a cold sense of dread? But she could not shake the feeling that more heartbreak was hurtling toward them. "Hasn't enough happened in this family?" she whispered. "What will happen to us now?" Suddenly overwhelmed, she dropped her face into her hands again as the tears began, and she prayed, "God help us all."

CHAPTER 21
SANTA CLARA VALLEY — 1885

Flora wasn't used to being the first at the bower. Usually Antone could get away earlier, and he would have their place prepared: blankets spread, candles lit, perhaps the bramble curtain pulled back if the night was hot. It had been a warm day, but it was cooling off fast. Flora could hardly believe it was so late in September ... the autumn equinox already! Only a little over half a year ago, she'd first fallen in love with the boy across the street, and now she would be marrying him, and she carried their child.

She reflected it was good that their secret meetings were coming to an end. The nights would soon be uncomfortably cool, and the bramble canes would not be enough to shelter them from the cold and rain of winter; there would even be times when the creek flowed bank to bank, flooding the bower completely.

When she had prepared their little room—including a jar of apple cider and some ripe figs for the evening's refreshments—she readied herself: brushing out her loosened hair and —now that secrecy was no longer needed—she applied some of the wonderful scent from the little dove bottle. Soon all was ready, but Antone still did not come. Flora had always hated waiting for anything, even the most delightful rewards. It gave her a new appreciation for all the nights Antone had waited here for her.

All day she'd been practicing how to tell him about the child growing inside her—their child. And she'd also fantasized how he would respond. Most of the time, she pictured him overjoyed—even grateful that this situation would allow them to marry before they'd observed a more proper period of mourning for the losses in their families.

But now, as the waiting increased her nervousness, she began to worry he wouldn't be pleased. She knew a baby was a great deal of work, and she had so looked forward to the time they could spend alone together once they were married. A child would alter that drastically and her own amount of work would have to change. But surely they had love enough to share it with a third person, one they had created together, a life that bonded their two lives together for all time.

And what will our child be like? Flora wondered, spreading her hands across the slight swell of her lower abdomen. For the first time, she thought to speak directly to that child. "Hello, little one," she whispered. "Are you a little boy or a little girl? And what shall we name you?"

Flora lost herself in dreams of what the child could look like. Sometimes she would envision a girl, sometimes a boy. She saw Antone with a son nestled in front of him in Dolce's saddle as he rode along the edge of prosperous vineyards. She saw herself with a daughter in the orchards, showing her how to twist open an apricot. She saw a child—boy or girl—who was bright and daring, humorous and kind, could ride and cook and draw and play Luka's concertina, could speak Croatian and Italian and English. A child admired on both sides of Page Street, helping to bring those two cultures together in understanding and acceptance.

In the peaceful haven of the blackberry bower—where all things were possible—Flora smiled and lay back waiting for Antone.

On his way, at last, to meet Flora, Antone touched Dolce with his heels and lifted her to a trot. He'd been surprised—and delighted—to see the amber bottle appear in Flora's window this morning and had eagerly awaited the time he could pretend to ride off to Bianca's. He was especially anxious to hold Flora in his arms again so that he could banish the vague sense of dread he'd felt since that bit of nightmare they'd shared the night before. He'd felt so restless and uneasy all day, he'd even walked out to the edge of the plum orchard to look at the place where he'd buried the blanket, but there was nothing amiss. He scuffed his boot across the spot, which had sunken a little and had newer vegetation, but he was satisfied the casual observer would never notice the difference. Yet the feeling of imminent disaster lingered. Soon, though, he would hold his Flora, and all would be right with the world.

The moon was only a day or two short of full, so there was plenty of light. Dolce was so used to the routine, she slowed automatically and turned off the road onto the slight path she'd created taking Antone to the bower. Eagerly, she moved toward the rich grazing that awaited her. She had no reason to be watching for danger.

With a sudden, inhuman roar, a black shape leapt up out of the grass at her, clutching at her bridle. She squealed in fright and shied violently away, feeling her rider losing balance and her head being jerked around, caught by the beast that had attacked her. Then his scent hit her, and—recognizing who it was—she snorted warily but lost her terror.

"You bastard!" Gregorio roared. "So it's true!" and before Antone could regain his seat on the mare, his uncle had grabbed him and was dragging him down to the ground, raining blows on his unprotected head.

Antone yelled, trying to make sense of what was happening. Tasting blood in his mouth from a cut lip, he was smothered by the stench of his uncle's unwashed clothes and the sharp smell of whiskey. Gregorio could drink great quantities of wine, but Antone had learned whiskey could make him crazy.

All the while Gregorio was pounding Antone with his fists, he was bellowing at him in a voice so full of pain, it sounded near tears. "You always had everything, didn't you, you bastard? You can do anything you want—break the rules, ignore what's right in a family."

Bruised and gasping, Antone managed to land a blow that hurt Gregorio enough to make him loosen his hold. Antone slipped from his grasp and backed warily away from his attacker. The best thing would be to get on the mare and get the hell out of here ... try to deal with this when his uncle sobered up. But Dolce had stepped out of reach as soon as she was freed, taking herself several yards away where she stood—head high, ears pricked attentively—waiting for her rider to find her when this bizarre drama ended and her world got back to normal.

Panting and keeping out of Gregorio's reach, Antone circled and tried to talk to the man in reasonable tones. "I have no idea what you're talking about, Uncle Gregorio. What are you upset about?"

"Upset!" Gregorio roared. "Don't you know how much I hate you? Do you know how many times I've wished you dead ... thought about killing you myself? I have dreams where I'm pushing your head under the water and holding it there!"

Chilled by these words, Antone said, "Uncle, what is this about?" Gregorio lunged at him, but he sidestepped easily. They stood then, facing each other in the moonlight. Gregorio, his shirttails loose and hair disheveled, swayed with the effects of strong drink and bitter hatred; Antone kept himself ready to spring away at any moment. This man could hurt him, and he was determined not to let that happen again.

Gregorio snarled, "It's about that bitch of yours. Don't act so innocent. But that's the way you are, isn't it? The perfect son ... the perfect businessman: so personable and generous. But underneath it all, you're always scheming to get what you want, stealing away what is rightfully mine." He thumped his chest. "I am the eldest now—it is **my** place to run this family and the business. Not you—you aren't even fit to be part of a good Italian family anymore."

It still wasn't making sense to Antone, but he didn't like the drift. "Look, Uncle, why don't we go back to the house and talk about this—have a little wine and straighten things out?"

"Go back to the house? I don't want you in my house ever again. I want you to get on your horse and ride out of this valley. You don't belong here anymore. And you can take her with you."

"Who?" Antone's voice was barely above a whisper.

"That Croat whore you've been having."

Cold poured down Antone's spine; he felt as if he were walking along the edge of a steep precipice. "Who are you talking about?"

Gregorio laughed—a cruel, humorless sound that made the hairs on Antone's body stand on end, covering him with goose flesh. "Did you think I wouldn't figure it out? I'm not as stupid and trusting as your brother, you know. I was always suspicious about that Bianca tale. I wasn't sure what you were hiding." He sneered. "It occurred to me you might have a boy for a sweetheart instead of a girl, so I've been watching you. And today you tipped your hand."

The chill grew in Antone as he listened. It was hard to hear because the pounding of his heart seemed so loud in his ears. His mouth was full of the brassy taste of blood.

"I followed you down to the plum orchard," Gregorio said. "Watched you kicking dirt in a certain spot, and after you left, I took a closer look and saw that something had been buried there. So I got a shovel and dug it up and what do you suppose I found?"

Antone's patience and sense of caution were wearing thin. This was, after all, no more than an overgrown bully, and Antone was no longer a scared little seven-year-old. "I'm sure you'll tell me."

Gregorio grinned coldly at this indication he was getting through Antone's pretenses. "Why, I found a blanket, and I wondered, *Why would anyone bury a blanket?* So I unfolded it and found the most interesting stains ... semen and blood. It surprised me, but I thought, *Well, good—that pup Antone is finally getting some from his Bianca.*"

Antone felt himself begin to relax a little. Maybe this would be all right after all.

"And then," Gregorio said slowly, drawing out the moment,. "I unfolded the thing all the way and what do you think I found?"

Antone was afraid to even guess. His heart pounded in his ears and his jaws ached from clenching, but he didn't speak.

Obviously enjoying the drama and Antone's discomfort, Gregorio said, "There was an apricot pit! Stuck to the blanketcloth where a little bit of the sticky fruit had dried. So I was picturing you with your black-haired beauty Bianca— remember you described her to your parents?—eating apricots after your big moment. But then you know what else I found?"

Antone felt suddenly sick, and it was more than simply his revulsion picturing his uncle so carefully scrutinizing that stained blanket. He felt now as if he were caught up in some inexorable whirlpool which would spin him around and around until he lost all sense of direction and then suck him down into black oblivion.

When he could no longer resist revealing what he'd found, Gregorio crowed, "A long red hair! Not from Bianca, I'll wager. So it set me thinking— why would my little nephew lie about who he's seeing? Who might he be ashamed of? Then I remembered what a ripe little apricot our Slavic neighbor has gotten to be. Flora. That's her name, isn't it? She has hair just that color, and she's a tasty-looking thing at that ... if you don't mind stooping so low. Amazing that she was a virgin.... Handy having her so close here. I walked down the road till I found this little path you ride in on. Meet somewhere in the orchard, do you?"

Antone stood with his fists so tightly clenched, his fingernails were digging into his palms. It was like holding his hand in a flame to stand there and not rise to the bait as his uncle spoke Flora's name in that cold, threatening tone and insulted her decency. But he knew he must not lose control of himself. He decided the best action—now his uncle had calmed down—was to dispassionately tell the truth. It hardly mattered now that Gregorio knew. After all, what could his uncle do to him here, now, without the element of surprise? All he had to do was keep an arm's length between them.

"Well?" Gregorio demanded as if he were a father calling a young son to task over some shameful transgression.

Antone shrugged as if Gregorio's findings—and opinion—meant nothing to him. "Well, what?" he said. "Flora and I are getting married, so if you can't stand being around Croatians, you might want to move somewhere else, because Flora and her mother are going to be part of our family."

"No!" Gregorio bellowed. "I will not have her in my house! It's **you** that's leaving, Antone! I'm the one that's in charge now!"

Antone couldn't help snorting—it was all so ridiculous. "What makes you think that?"

Gregorio reached under his loose shirt, pulled something out of his belt, and pointed it at Antone. "This does!"

Seeing the gun glint with deadly menace in the moonlight reminded Antone this was not a simple boys' game to be won with defiance and braggadocio. It had suddenly become a very serious situation and called for a cool, reasonable head. "Put the gun away, Uncle. There's no reason for anyone to get hurt."

"Hurt?" Gregorio snarled. "You don't know the meaning of the word. You've never been hurt in your life! You had parents to love and protect you and give you everything you wanted!"

This was too much for Antone. "Yes," he snapped, "and my parents took you in and gave to you exactly as they gave to Bruno and me. They offered you love and protection, but you always turned it away."

"Don't you see…" Gregorio said in an agonized voice, "by then it was too late!" Lost in some black memory, he lifted the gun toward Antone's head and fired.

Antone felt the bullet strike his temple at the same moment he saw the barrel flash and heard the loud report; it knocked him back like the blow from a fist, and he fell crashing to the earth.

In the bower, Flora was jerked upright by the sound of the shot, and she sat a moment—ears straining, heart jolting in her chest. She told herself there was danger and the wisest thing was to stay exactly where she was—there was more than her own life to consider now—but in the next moment, she was outside and scrambling up the path to the top of the creekbank. She knew with absolute certainty that Antone was involved. So she ran barefooted through the dry grass, praying, "Please, God ... please, God...."

She saw Gregorio first because he was standing, and she saw he was holding a gun pointed at something lying at his feet, as if preparing to take a second shot. There was movement on the ground, and she saw it was Antone, trying to rise with one hand pressed to his head.

Before she could stop herself, she screamed and—as Gregorio turned, startled—saw the muzzle of the gun swing around to point at her like a malevolent eye. There was no time to even think of moving before it went off. She felt the bullet whip past her like a little puff of wind against her cheek, and she dropped to the earth, biting her lip to keep from screaming again.

Still dazed but suddenly galvanized by seeing Flora in danger, Antone leapt up and threw his body against Gregorio's gun arm. They both staggered and fell, the gun flying out of Gregorio's hand and into the grass. Rolling around, they struck out blindly with their fists, trying to get the advantage, and grunted as they landed blows or received them. Antone knew he was in trouble. In the best of times, Gregorio was bigger and more powerful than he was and delighted in the most savage of strategies. Antone could feel himself weakening as blood poured from his scalp, blinding his left eye. There was no way he could win this as a fistfight. He knew his only hope was getting hold of the gun.

Marshalling all his will and energies, Antone struck upward with the heel of his hand, smashing his uncle's nose and splattering them both with new blood. Gregorio howled, let go of Antone, and fell back, clutching his bloodied face. Antone scrambled out from under him and half-crawled in the direction the gun had gone, his hands searching frantically in the grass.

"Look out, Antone!" Flora's voice cried just as his hand closed around the butt of the gun. He turned over quickly and aimed it up at the dark shape suddenly looming over him. "Get back!" he cried. "I'll shoot you."

"No, you won't," Gregorio said confidently, but he backed a step just to keep from crowding Antone too much. He laughed. "You're a good boy, Antone. You'd never shoot an unarmed man."

Antone had never held a gun before. It was heavier than he thought it would be, and he was feeling dizzy again. "I don't want to shoot, Uncle, but believe me, I will protect myself."

Gregorio rocked back on his heels and mopped his streaming nose on the sleeve of his shirt as he watched Flora rise from the ground, holding something in her hand. She looked fierce and beautiful in the moonlight with her hair loose and wild and her eyes huge with fear. She was breathing hard in her excitement and the upper swell of her breasts was very noticeable where her bodice had torn when she fell.

"And what about her, pup? Will you protect her, too?" He made as if to move toward her, and she hefted the rock in her hand; Antone cocked the gun. Gregorio halted, grinning at them both and switched from Italian to English.

"I've never had a piece of that Croatian meat. What's it like, Antone? Worth the trouble to get past the smell?"

"I'm warning you, Uncle. Back off." He hoped Flora would be wise enough not to let Gregorio provoke her into a reaction.

"Relax, Antone," the older man said, but his eyes never left Flora. "Can't you share with your old uncle? And you, little lady, seems like you'd enjoy being filled up by a real man, not some puny—" the rock caught him on the ear and dropped to the ground behind him. Flora had cocked her arm and thrown with such speed and skill neither of the men had seen it coming. Gregorio yelped and clapped a hand to his damaged ear, and when he pulled the hand away to inspect it, there was blood. "Bitch!" he yelled. "You're gonna regret that."

"Leave her alone, Uncle," Antone warned in a tight voice. The gun was very heavy in his hands; his arms were beginning to quiver. Careful not to let the gun point anywhere except at his uncle, he dragged himself to his feet, but that only made him feel dizzier. "It's time for you to go home and leave us alone."

With a flash of anger, Gregorio growled, "Don't tell me what to do. I'll go where I want and do what I want." He stared at Flora's heaving bosom. "**Take** what I want."

"If you make one move toward her, I will shoot you."

"Don't threaten me!" Gregorio shouted. "If you're going to shoot me, better do it now, because if you don't, you won't live to get another chance. See, I've decided I want my rightful place as head of the Mellini family, and make no mistake: I plan to kill you, Antone—tonight if I can—and when you're dead, I'll enjoy your little piece here."

Antone realized the man was trying to get him to shoot the gun, to waste the remaining bullets. *He knows I've never fired a gun; he knows I don't want to shoot him, and I'll probably miss him every time. I've got to be smarter, not let him stampede me.* Even though he fought his dizziness, he wavered, his legs like jelly, his head spinning out of control. *I can't faint!* he thought desperately. *Not now.*

"Oh, yes, I'll enjoy her," Gregorio promised. "But she may not enjoy it so much. That's all right. I like it when they scream—and I'll give her plenty to scream about, Antone. I'll take her so many times we'll both lose track of the number. I'll take her as you've never dared to—in ways you've never dreamed of. And when I've had enough, I'll throw her away like the garbage she is."

It all happened so fast, everything seemed to occur in the same moment: Flora's composure slipped enough that a sob of horror escaped her and her attention wavered. Gregorio made as if to lunge and grab her. Antone rushed to intercept him, prepared to shoot if he needed to, but aiming low to catch him in the legs and stop him that way. It was his body that betrayed him. He staggered with his dizziness, caught his foot against some obstruction on the ground, and began to fall. His fingers clutched as if to catch himself, and the gun went off in his hand, kicking back with surprising force and deafening sound.

The bullet might have passed Gregorio completely or hit his legs as intended, but at that moment Gregorio outsmarted himself, stooping and turning away to grab up the rock Flora'd thrown at him so he could use it as his own weapon. The bullet caught Gregorio in the back of his head, splattering brains and blood in all directions. Flora screamed. Gregorio fell into the grass without a sound. Antone continued to fall in stunned disbelief, the gun dropping from his fingers, and he hit the earth hard enough to knock the breath from him.

Antone lay, sliding in and out of consciousness, hearing only the echo of the deafening gunshot. He could feel the stiff, dry grass beneath his cheek and the trickle of blood still oozing from the cut on his head. Distantly, he heard someone calling his name, and then everything went black.

When he opened his eyes again several minutes later, it felt as if he'd been out for hours. He was still on the ground but lying on his back, and someone was holding him and rocking; his head was pillowed on something soft and yielding, and his nostrils were full of the fragrance from the little dove bottle. He realized it was Flora who held his head against her breast, and one of her hands was pressing the wound on his temple. He could feel her tears dripping down onto his face as she rocked him and sobbed, "*Molim vas... molim vas... molim vas....*"

"Please what?" he asked in a feeble attempt at humor, but when he spoke, she gasped in joy and began to shower the top of his head and forehead with kisses. "Please be alive," she answered with a shaky laugh. "Oh, Antone, I was so frightened!"

He found his arms—many parts of his body still seemed strangely distant—and brought them up to hold her as tightly as she was holding him. He didn't want to think about how frightened he had been for her ... and for himself.

"Gregorio?" he asked.

"Dead," she answered. "But what about you? How does your head feel? Where else are you hurt? I see bruises on your face, and a cut on your lip."

"My head is starting to hurt now," he realized. "And I'm still dizzy. How does the wound look?" He knew she would have inspected it.

"Not deep. It looks like the bullet only grazed your skull, but there's so much blood...."

"Scalp wounds always bleed like that," he said to reassure her.

"You're not shot anywhere else?"

"Not that I know of," he joked, wishing he had some water to wash out his mouth and take a long, cool drink. Ruefully he told her, "This was not my plan for our time together."

"Nor mine," she murmured, deciding her news about their expected child could wait until he had recovered a little more. "We should get you cleaned up. Are you thirsty?"

They discussed the situation briefly and decided against going to either house just yet. There would be too much excitement, too many questions in either household. They wanted to be alone a little longer, to catch their breath and assess the situation. They decided to go to the bower to collect themselves.

But before they did, Antone knew he had to go see Gregorio's body. His uncle lay very still in the grass; part of the back of his head was gone and in the moonlight where colors are indistinguishable, the blood all over him looked black. The sight was like a fist slamming into Antone's gut; he turned away and was violently ill. When he'd finished retching and coughing, he looked back again and was surprised to notice that—despite the terrible gunshot wound and the shattered nose and lacerated ear—somehow Gregorio's face looked truly at peace, and it was the first time he had ever seen such an expression on his uncle's countenance.

Flora came up beside Antone and took his hand, drew him away from the horrific scene in the grass. "Did you have Dolce with you?" she asked.

He nodded. "She was over there last I saw her. Gregorio gave her a pretty bad scare, but she was still standing. I guess the shots were too much for her and she took off."

Holding hands, they began to walk toward their little safe haven, not an easy task for Antone with his head spinning the way it was. After a few moments, Flora released his hand, put her arm around his waist and said, "Lean on me" in a voice that invited no argument. He obeyed her with a sigh of relief and they were soon at their destination.

Flora brought a little water from the creek so he could rinse his mouth and she could bathe away all the blood on their skin. There was nothing that could be done about their clothes. Antone drank a good deal of the cider, and together, but in silence, they ate all the figs. At first they felt elated and then shaky, and—as their heartbeats, breathing, and adrenalin fell to normal levels—they became more and more frightened. As the night paled toward dawn beyond the bramble curtain, they sat staring blankly, lost in horrifying memories of the evening's events.

After a very long silence, Antone whispered, "I killed a man. I killed my uncle." He squeezed his eyes shut, but still he saw the image of Gregorio's shattered skull.

Flora touched his face below the bullet wound, which had finally stopped bleeding, and reminded him, "He was an evil man; you were defending our lives."

Antone shook his head. "But I didn't have to kill him. I should have found another way…. I have broken one of God's laws, committed a mortal sin."

"Not a **mortal** sin. It was an accident. God gave you a way to save our lives."

"God gave me a test and I failed."

It was difficult not to feel impatient with him, but Flora tried. "Go to confession today, and the priest will absolve you. It was not your fault."

"Who will believe that? And what will the law say? It looks like murder. He was shot in the back of the head, and you are the only witness. When people know we are to marry, they will say you are only lying to protect me."

Flora realized that might be true, especially when they learned she was his lover and bearing his child. It crossed her mind to finally share this news with Antone but then decided to wait until he was less upset. "What will you do about reporting the death to the authorities?"

"I don't know," Antone said miserably. "I'm afraid, Flora. What if they put me in jail? What if someone has already found the body and they are looking for me?"

"Oh, my darling," Flora whispered, putting her arms around Antone to reassure him. She felt him lean gratefully into her comfort. *He is wounded and confused and overwrought,* she realized. *I must be strong for him and help him through this terrible time.*

She opened her mouth to speak, but then both of them froze, hearing a sound outside the bower. They sat, clutching each other and not daring to breathe, staring at their concealing drape of brambles and straining their ears to interpret the sounds.

Oh, my God, Flora thought with panic rising in her, *someone is walking around out there!* Heart pounding like that of a rabbit trapped and hiding in a hollow log, she could detect a figure beyond the canes, moving close to inspect the curtain. *Maybe he'll just pick a few of the last blackberries and be gone.*

A hand reached inside their hideaway and pulled the curtain open. The intruder stooped and poked his head inside.

"Matty!" Flora gasped with relief and some embarrassment, watching her friend's solemn grey eyes study her embracing Antone—who pulled her even closer as if to protect her from some new danger ... or perhaps to emphasize his claim on her.

But there was no surprise in Matty's eyes or in his voice as he said, "Your mama was worried when you didn't come home. I thought I'd find you two here." He reached into one dark corner and pulled out a rope which he used, as they did, to tie back the brambles. Then he hunkered down in the opening of the bower and answered the question in Flora's incredulous eyes. "We used to play house here, remember? After you told me you were in love, I wanted to know who you were seeing. There was that time you were staying alone—your mama was taking care of Gdja. Tesla—and I was watching over your house while she was away. I saw you come back in the early morning, and I knew you had been somewhere all night. The next evening, I followed you here. I saw his mare grazing on the bank; I heard your voices from inside, and I knew who it was you were in love with."

Flora felt the hot color in her face, but her voice was indignant. "You spied on me?"

Matty regarded her with a slightly wounded look. "No. I went home. Later I came back here to see what it was like inside, how you had made a secret place to be alone together. Very clever."

She could see that he was sincere, but she wondered if it had hurt him even more to learn she was meeting her lover in a hideaway she had once shared with him. "Matty," she said in a rather formal tone, "this is Antone Mellini, the man I will marry. Antone, this is Mattiza Stanich, my dearest friend." The men shook hands with grave courtesy, and Flora watched them take each other's measure.

As if a question had been asked, Matty told Antone, "What Flora wants is what I want for Flora, and I respect her judgment." Antone nodded his thanks. Then Matty got to the point. "Looks like you are in a bunch of trouble."

In his laconic way, he told how Dolce had gone straight home, and was found by Bruno when he went looking for his missing brother and uncle. He'd mounted up and ridden her south, the direction Antone had gone, but the mare turned off on the path to her favorite pasture and took him straight to Gregorio's body. That was only an hour ago, and Matty found out when Bruno came looking for information at the Bogdonovich house, because what appeared to be a murder had happened on Bogdonovich property.

"It was an accident," Flora interrupted. "Gregorio threatened us both. See this wound on Antone's head? His uncle tried to kill him and had ... other plans ... for me. Antone was protecting us, but it was still an accident."

Matty looked at them a long moment and then said, "I believe you. But others won't. It's too bad your brother didn't think something like that might've happened before he set up an alarm. He's got everyone pretty stirred up, convinced there's a murderer on the loose that's kidnapped you."

Antone spoke for the first time since the other man had arrived. His voice was heavy with the painful irony of it. "He probably can't imagine that anyone or anything could push me to murder."

"It wasn't murder!" Flora cried, becoming more agitated.

"Everyone thinks it is," Matty pointed out. "And even though no one liked Gregorio, feeling is running high, and I don't know how wise it would be to turn yourself in just yet ... not until everyone comes to their senses. Men have been hanged for less in this town."

"Hanged!" Flora whispered with sick dread. "What can we do?"

"Well, you can't hide here. They'll be searching everywhere. I told them I'd take this section, but when no one's found they'll go back over the whole area."

"May I beg a favor?" Antone asked and when Matty nodded, he elaborated. "Could you get my brother alone and tell him what's happened, get him to come here with you?"

Matty considered, then nodded and rose to his feet. "I'd better hurry. Time is running short." Before he left, he untied the cord and let the bramble curtain fall to conceal them again.

Antone and Flora clung to each other. How could things get any worse? And it was hardly the time to tell Antone he had a son or daughter on the way. Antone said, "I may have to go into hiding for a while. We may have to be apart ... not be married for quite some time."

She thought of the life growing in her womb—of all the disgrace and hardship that might fall to her if the marriage was delayed—and assured Antone, "We will do what is best for you. You are more important to me than anything else, and above all, I want you to be safe."

He held her close and asked, "How can I bear to be apart from you?"

Before she could give him any answer, they heard voices coming their way and fell silent in case it was not the men they awaited. But it was. Matty swept back the bramble curtain and Bruno stared in incredulously. "Antone! What's going on?" He stared at Flora as if she were from another planet. "What's she doing here?"

Much as Flora had done in introducing him to Matty, Antone said in English, "Flora, this is my brother Bruno. Brother, this is Flora—the woman I love."

Frowning in confusion, Bruno asked in Italian, "What will Bianca say?"

Antone gave an snort of surprised laughter and shook his head. To Flora and Matty, he said, "If you'll pardon me, I can explain all this much more quickly and easily in Italian." He turned to his brother and began to explain, "There is no Bianca. Well, there is, but none of that matters now. This is the girl I'm going to marry when we get this mess straightened out. Now, did Mattiza explain what happened?"

"Not the details. I can't believe you shot anyone, Antone, not even accidentally."

Very quickly and concisely, Antone described the events of the evening, while his brother listened in near disbelief. At the end, Bruno said, "He was even crazier than we thought. I warned you he had that gun. Do you know what Mama said when she heard he was dead?" Antone shook his head. Their mother had compassion—a good word—for everyone. "She said, *That's a relief. Now I can stop worrying about what he will do.*"

Shocked, Antone only stared, wondering what their parents had known but had never told.

"I don't mean to hurry you," Matty interrupted. "But you'd better decide what to do."

The three men talked together then, weighing plans and trying to see the pitfalls. None of them had any faith in the good sense of a crowd whipped to a frenzy, and every community has its personalities that delight in such mischief, especially when power or political rewards could be involved. Nor had any of them much faith in the local justice system. People on both sides of Page Street knew the law could work very differently for immigrants and their children. And they aloud all agreed there was no safe place to hide in the community.

Flora had been listening to all this conversation, appreciating the way a Croatian and two Italians were working together to solve a problem and help someone who didn't deserve to be in trouble. But then she became aware of the direction the conversation was going. "But if he runs away," she pointed out, "they'll be convinced he's guilty!" The men conceded the point, but they were all so convinced he had a better chance protecting his neck first and working things out later that it began to make sense to Flora too.

A short time after that, Bruno went back to the Mellini house and collected a number of things Antone asked him to get. Then he sneaked back, leading Dolce, whose saddlebags were stuffed to bursting. Separately, Bruno carried a clean change of clothes for Antone and—embracing him—said, "I'd better get back to keep the search party away from here as long as I can. I didn't have time to tell Mama the whole story, but she understands you have done nothing wrong but must go away. She sends her love."

"Take care of her—and the vineyards and winery," Antone implored. "The entire business will be in your hands as long as I'm away." Bruno swore he would take very good care of their mother and their flourishing new business. Antone told him, "I'll send any messages through the Lidakis brothers, and if you need to contact me, they will know where to find me." They parted with a great show of emotion; Bruno was openly crying, and Flora could see Antone's eyes were wet too.

When Bruno was gone, Matty said, "I'll walk up to the road and make sure it's clear for you. Don't be long saying good-bye."

Antone nodded. "Thank you. I'll see you there in a few minutes."

When Matty was gone, Antone quickly changed into the clean clothes, leaving the ones stained with blood for Flora to dispose of. To keep herself busy, Flora swept her hair back up into the customary bun and pinned it in place, a more formal touch in striking contrast to her torn and blood-spattered dress.

Then Antone pulled Flora into his arms, and though they assured each other they'd meet again before long, each clung to the other as if they might never be reunited. Then they climbed the path to where Dolce waited. Antone took up the trailing rein and—as if suddenly echoing her own thoughts of only a few moments before—Antone said, "I don't even want to think it, Flora, but we must face the possibility we might not be together for a very long time. Is there anything we should tell each other?"

We have a child. She almost said the words also, but then she knew he would not go—he'd never leave her simply to protect himself. If he stayed they might still be separated and something far worse would likely befall him. "Only this," she whispered, "that you are the only man I will ever love and that no matter what happens, *volim te zauvijek*... I will love you forever."

He crushed her against him and choked out the words in Italian, "*Io ti voglio bene ... per sempre ... eternamente.*"

Determined not to cry lest that delay him or make him decide to stay, Flora kissed him with all she felt in her heart and felt every nuance of that love returned in his kiss. Then she broke away from him, saying, "Now go! And be safe."

She saw the tears on Antone's cheeks and understood why he remained silent; she herself could not say another word without breaking down and begging him to stay. He swung up into the saddle and looked one last time at her, and the love that she saw there in his dark eyes was enough to sustain her to her dying day, if need be. Then he turned the mare and cantered her away toward the road where Mattiza Stanich would be acting as look-out.

The sobs broke from Flora as soon as he was out of earshot. She could not bear to return to their bower, so she went, instead, to the edge of the orchard and dropped down beneath the green canopy and hugged her knees to her and put her head down on her arms and wept as one who has learned there will be no happy ending and that there is grief that can never be healed.

Some minutes later, Matty came to find her and sat silently beside her with an arm around her shoulders. She leaned against him and cried until she thought she had no more tears. When the sobbing gave way to small sniffling sounds, Matty hugged her against his side and said, "I'm sorry ...." A few moments later, he gently suggested, "We'd better go clean everything out of your little room and get you home to change clothes."

She nodded but did not move to leave. Slowly, she sat upright, and her arms dropped into her lap so that they cradled her belly. "Oh, Matty, I have this most terrible feeling I won't ever see him again." *And what is to become of me and our child?*

Matty Stanich studied her face a long moment and then asked, "There's something else, isn't there?"

Flora looked away from his eyes and nodded.

"Tell me," he said and she did.

CHAPTER 22
Monterey — 1885

By the time Antone got to his friends in Monterey, he was thoroughly terrified, convinced the authorities were close on his heels. The wound on his temple, never properly cleaned, was festering, and the aching in his head made it impossible to think clearly. He said only that he was in trouble and needed help. The Greek brothers asked no questions. They hid his exhausted mare in the barn, cleaned and dressed his wound as he ate the soup they pressed on him, and then put him to bed behind the partition in their living quarters. They let him sleep the clock around. When he awoke, he was agitated about the time he'd lost, though admittedly feeling better on other counts. They made him sit to another meal before letting him talk.

As he sat eating a plate of rice and the little meatballs they called keftédes, he told the brothers, "It's only fair I tell you I'm in a great deal of trouble. I killed my Uncle Gregorio. It was an accident, but the authorities think I murdered him, so I have to get away."

He saw the twins turn to stare at each other for a long moment, and the guilt which hung like a weight on his heart got even heavier. He rushed to explain, "It really was an accident. I would never intentionally hurt anyone—"

Theo reached out to grasp Antone's shoulder in a sympathetic gesture, and his brother Demetri said soothingly, "We know, we know. Accidents happen. Men die. We also know it will help you to talk about it, if you can. You know you can trust us, and you will feel better."

He found it was true. When he'd described that terrible night to them, he did feel somehow straighter inside, but his culpability was still as clear as ever, and nothing could erase the vision of what his carelessness had caused: his father's brother lying dead. "Have you been to confession?" Demetri asked, sensing the turmoil in the younger man's soul.

"Not yet," Antone admitted. "I'm on my way there, but I need your help first." Between Page Street and Monterey, he'd managed to lay out a plan in his head. Now he brought out legal papers Bruno had packed for him, and—with writing materials Theo provided—Antone made it clear what he wanted done. Everything involving the Mellini Vineyards and Bella Flora wines—including future contracts for Lidakis wine bottles—was now the province of his brother Bruno. The benefits of all his other business dealings were to go to Flora Bogdonovich. "I stopped in to see the fellow I've bought redwood from to let him know I'm out of that business for a while, but the San Francisco glass shop is coming along, isn't it?"

The twins nodded enthusiastically. It was Demetri, of course, who elaborated. "Dante Fortunallo's daughter Isabella is doing a good job and enjoying herself. The location is proving ideal."

"Good," Antone said. "And if you have any questions about all these legalities, take them to our friend Dante, and his lawyer will help you."

In the dim hours before dawn the next morning, Antone parted from his friends in an emotional moment full of embraces and backslapping and moist eyes and gruff voices. Antone had refused to say where he was going, insisting that would be safer for everyone. He would send a letter when he could and tell them how to contact him.

"Above all," he stressed, "I'm asking the two of you to take care of my Flora. It may be a very long time before I can see her again. Perhaps I will never be free to marry her."

Distressed, the Greeks protested, assuring Antone the whole matter would soon be cleared up, and he could be with his Bella Flora.

"I hope so," Antone said, swinging up into Dolce's saddle and settling himself for a long, fast ride. "Till then, God be with you, dear friends."

"And with you," they echoed, waving forlornly as the honey-colored mare took him quickly away into the dim September dawn.

Antone had acted as if he wasn't sure where to go, but he knew exactly where he most wanted to be at this moment. There was only one place that could offer the sanctuary and spiritual counsel he needed. Like a wounded lion, who knew where to heal his paw, Antone rode quickly through Carmel and into the remote stretches of the Big Sur Coast.

Two weeks later, Demetri returned from a shopping foray in the main part of the city and told his brother excitedly, "There were two letters for us at the post office!"

"From Antone?" Theo asked hopefully.

"No. Not yet. But one from Flora and one from Michele! Which first?"

"Michele!" Theo declared, hurrying to fetch the glasses and oúzo. "It's been longer since we heard from her."

They settled comfortably in their chairs, raised their glasses to each other and sipped. Then Demetri began to read aloud a letter that was written in English, as usual, and it began as they always did:

My Darlings,

Remi and I are very well. Young Charles is healthier than the two of us together and just celebrated his third birthday. I know you will be pleased to hear François finally agreed to move into the main house with us. Unfortunately, he is too blind now to do any glass work at all, but he spends a great deal of time keeping Charles company, which allows me to help Remi more (all our business matters continue to prosper and increase). We have asked François if Charles could call him Grand-*père* and act as his honorary grandfather, and that dear man seemed very moved to do so, easing my fears we might be imposing on him too much. François (who knew my mother Charlotte) says she would be very proud to know she has such a bright and capable grandson named in her honor.

I hope my English is more readable after these years of practice. By the time we come to America, I will be able to write it very well. If only I can speak it enough to make myself understood! I am so thrilled to think of seeing you two again. Be forewarned! I will cry, and so might Remi, for that matter. He has such a soft heart (and a special corner of that for you). We are both so happy all has worked out well for you in California. How terrible were those last, fearful hours when we were together.

And I must tell you the irony of it. Do you remember that it was a young couple who discovered you? I think you know the girl was my best friend Cassandra. I must tell you that she and that boy Peter Depêche fell in love at our wedding and were married soon after. They, too, have children now: twin daughters two years old! Since our marriages, our families have become even closer and the Depêches have heard us speak so often about our plans to visit you in California that they have now decided to consider joining us.

Is it not amazing that in a few short years you will meet as friends the very people who caused you to flee Provence? But do not fear. They now know the truth of your situation—how you were not in the truest sense criminals in need of apprehension. They were most sympathetic to your plight and chagrined to learn they had caused you such trepidation and hardship.

However, my dear ones, it is also worth noting that they say they owe you a sizable debt because of a boat called the Stella which was the catalyst for Peter's fortunes and eventually brought them together at our wedding. And I suppose you could consider that any good fortune, adventures, and new friendships you have found in California are due to their unwitting betrayal of you. We are constantly reminded that the Lord moves in very mysterious ways, and I am sure you will treasure the friendship of these people as much as we do.

I must close now. Remi is calling that the horses are saddled. We are taking Charles for a trip to the coast to visit the Depêches. Peter will give Charles a ride in the boat he calls Magique. We wish you could join us, but we look forward to seeing the great Pacific Ocean at your California doorstep.

Remember, you are always in our hearts, and we send you our love till we can be with you again.
Your loving sister, Michele

Theo and Demetri talked awhile about the contents of the letter and the strange turns of fate that affected their lives and led them to affect others. They were as eager as ever to have Remi and Michele come visit—to finally see their son. And what of this new element, of meeting and becoming friends with the very people who had forced them to leave France?

They'd finished their oúzo, so Theo poured some more and urged, "Now read the other letter!" It was always Demetri who read aloud, and if the letter was in French or English, he would often read a paragraph silently first to make sure he didn't stumble over any of the words.

Flora's letter was also in English but more formal, for her contact with them had been much more brief. It thanked them for helping Antone and executing his wishes for his property. She noted that Bruno was doing well handling the winery and was well-liked by the people he hired to help. His wedding to Concetta had been a small, quiet affair, at the bedside of Lucia Mellini, who still confounded her doctors by continuing to breathe.

Flora then placed an order for a shipment of the amber bottles, which she said would be filled with an apricot brandy distilled from wine made by her papa's recipe.

Theo waited patiently as his brother scanned the next paragraph, but then Demetri made a shocked sound as if someone had hit him in the stomach. Theo raised his eyebrows. Little surprised his brother that much. "Listen to this!" Demetri commanded incredulously and read aloud:

This next matter is of utmost delicacy and I entreat you to keep it confidential. I know from your last letter that you still have not heard from Antone. Nor have I. I must ask for your solemn word you will not divulge the following even to Antone, should he contact you. I am with child.

"Dio!" Theodore cried, equally shocked, and leaned forward as if that would make his hearing better. Demetri continued with the letter:

My mother and I have decided it would be better if I leave here before it becomes too obvious. She can stay and run the orchard and winemaking with the help of our business partners Mattiza Stanich and Karsten Tipanov (who was kind enough to help us a great deal financially because of a debt he felt he owed me).

I, of course, have no plan to marry anyone but Antone, should he ever return, but I do not want this child to be a factor causing him to return to a dangerous situation. If he cannot return, I intend to bear and raise this child by myself, and I wish to do so where there will be no stigma. Perhaps you can help me find a comfortable place and a way to support us?

Please contact me at your earliest convenience if you can assist me. I expect the child to arrive in mid-March and I will not be able to conceal it much longer.

And please do remember the promise not to tell Antone.
I send my heartfelt thanks and my love, Flora Bogdonovich

"Of course we will help her!" Theo fairly exploded. They hated the idea of withholding such information from the child's father, their friend Antone, but—though they hadn't been given the chance to decline the promise—they felt bound to honor it. The way time was passing without word from Antone, they might never have occasion to test the vow.

Theo and Demetri talked well into the night, discussing different possibilities for Flora and her child, and when they fell asleep at dawn, they had a plan.

SAN FRANCISCO, CALIFORNIA — 1886

The spray of apricot blossoms Mama had brought from Page Street looked striking displayed in one of the fine Lidakis amber glass vases. Though grateful for the thoughtful gift, Flora couldn't help feeling a little sad that she wasn't at home to see all the orchards in bloom.

Last year at this time... she mused and then realized with a start that it was March 11, and exactly a year ago today, she had stood in her garden falling in love with Antone Mellini. She took her eyes from the white blossoms, and looked down beside her. *And now, today, this ....*

Beautiful as any Madonna in her loose morning gown of cornflower blue, Flora sat rocking the wooden cradle and humming a lullaby from the coast of Dalmatia. Her hair had not been confined again into a bun but was pulled over one shoulder in a thick auburn braid. Her face was tired yet radiant as she gazed into the cradle at the child Antone had given her.

"Christena Armelin Bogdonovich," she whispered, rolling the name on her tongue, feeling its rightness. The first name had come in a dream—and it was Antone who gave it. She dreamed they stood facing each other across a bottomless abyss with wind roaring all around them in a storm wild with bolts of blue lightning and deafening thunder. They wanted to hold each other, to kiss, to talk of all that was in their hearts, but neither found it possible to touch—or even to hear—the other. Then Antone pulled a piece of paper from his pocket and held it up to show her, but it was too far away. Then the wind snatched the paper from his hands and whirled it across the abyss to fall at her feet. She picked it up and read the one word printed there: "Christena."

Looking into the cradle now, Flora reflected what a lovely name it was, one she never would have thought of. She reached down and cupped her palm around her baby's head and smiled. "Armelin" had been easy. The child was conceived on a night she could never remember without thinking of apricots. In the long months Flora carried this babe, she had dreamed of how it might look. She was torn between the wish for a child that showed a blend of ethnic cultures—one dark, one fair—and the more pragmatic wish for a child who would not raise much comment when contrasted to her.

This child was golden as an apricot at birth, not ivory-skinned like her mother nor dusky like her father, but tawny as one perfectly tanned by the sun.

It was impossible to tell yet what color her eyes and hair would be. The eyes—
which appeared dark blue as they gazed up at Flora and seemed to focus on her
only hours after the birth—could stay that color or darken to brown or lighten
to any number of shades of blue. Christena had no hair to speak of yet, but when
Flora caressed the head, it had a velvety covering and reminded her of nothing
more than the skin of an apricot—if one could be found as large as this little pate.
"Will your hair be dark like his?" Flora whispered. "Or reddish like mine? Or
blond like Papa's parents? Or will you choose to be different from us all?"

Christena stirred in her sleep, squinting her eyes more tightly as if in
concentration, and her arms stretched out as if raising her little fists to make a
point. "Oh, oh!" Flora said the favorite expression of her new friend Isabella and
then laughed. "What have I gotten myself into?"

Flora could not seem to look away from the child, who was, in her eyes,
absolutely perfect. "You are so beautiful," she whispered. "Your father ... " she
paused until the sudden knot in her throat could ease, but her voice was huskier
and her eyes were wet when she completed the thought, " ... would be very proud
to see you."

Flora's hand touched the letter in her pocket. There was no need to take
it out and read it; she'd memorized it long ago.

Postmarked in Monterey, it was accompanied by a short note from the
Lidakis brothers saying three letters (one each to them, to her, to Bruno) had
been slipped under their door, all from Antone and delivered by some obliging
traveler, no doubt. (They had received one other such letter at the end of
October, asking them to pass on its news to Flora until he could manage another
letter: he'd been gravely ill for a number of weeks due to his infected head
wound, but he was now on the mend; he had spent a good deal of time thinking
and praying about his situation, but as yet he did not know what he should do;
he still didn't feel safe revealing his whereabouts, but would send another
message when he could.)

That first letter to the Lidakis brothers had arrived just at the time Flora
moved to San Francisco and into the arrangement they had prepared for her
here. The letter she held in her pocket arrived nearly a week before Christmas.
It was in English and in his familiar, carefully printed hand, but quite different
from the short and cryptic notes he'd written to her in the past. It was as if, Flora
thought, he had told someone what he wanted to say—perhaps even in his more
comfortable Italian—then that person had written the words in English and he
had copied them. By the time she finished reading it—and at the end of many
other readings—she was weeping, not only for her own situation, but for the
tortured spirit living now in Antone's body.

My Dearest Bella Flora,

I apologize for this unforgivable delay in contacting you, and I will not
try to dignify it with excuses. My wound is entirely well at last, and I am

otherwise in good physical health.

You undoubtedly expected that I would act before now to clear my name so that I might return. But I have come to understand that what the law thinks is of little consequence. This is a matter between me and my God. I have sinned against Him, and that must be rectified.

I know that you and my other relatives and dear friends all believe I was justified in what I did ... that it was an accident. But the truth is, I should have protected us in another way. I took a human life. No matter how Gregorio treated us, he was also God's child, and I have come to believe there were reasons for his behavior. Grown men and women can be haunted by events in their pasts. This, of course, does not excuse their acts against others. Similarly, I can never excuse what I did.

Please believe me, Flora, that I intended to return to you as soon as I could. But now I realize I am not worthy of your love, and it is better if I free you from your commitments to me so that you can find the husband that you deserve. Do not for a moment think I have found another woman to love. I will never love anyone as I loved you—as I still love you. But I see now that the only way I can save my soul is to give it into the keeping of our Holy Father ... to dedicate my life to God.

As a child, there were two mysteries which puzzled me. I used to wonder what would be my purpose in life and why my parents chose to name me Antone instead of the traditional Antonio (when I asked, they only shrugged and said they liked the sound, but this has never satisfied me).

I realize now that my true purpose is to "atone" for my many sins—most especially the killing of my father's brother—and perhaps in this, I can help others to find a righteous path ... perhaps even prevent their falling from grace.

I do not expect to write to you again, hoping that this will help you put me from your life. (I am forced to confess there is still a part of me that selfishly hopes you won't forget me, but perhaps someday I will rise above such weaknesses.) As you know by now, I have arranged for a portion of my worldly goods to assist you as you move on in life and to prove I still hold you in the highest esteem. I never meant to hurt you or to abandon your love, but you deserve a better person than I can ever be. I hope you find him soon and have a happy life. And I hope that someday you can forgive me.

Io ti voglio bene ... eternamente, Antone

There were tears in Flora's eyes, remembering the content of his letter. She ached to hold him, to put her arms around him and comfort him as if he were a frightened child ... help him see the truth. And how unfair it was that she had no way to find him, no way to tell him her beliefs and opinions. No way to tell him he had a daughter, if she decided it was time for him to know.

I must simply trust God, Flora told herself. *I must believe it is all part of some great plan that will come right in the end. Even if I never see Antone again, I must believe that this is the right thing to happen. And I must accept it because I cannot change it.*

There was much in her life now that was within her power to guide or change—most especially the shaping of this new life she had created with Antone—and she resolved to focus her efforts on those matters and leave the rest to God.

Looking down at the sleeping child, Flora spoke to Antone in her mind, as if she could send a message that way: *You have a beautiful daughter, Antone, and I will raise her to be strong and intelligent, compassionate and generous and bold. And I will make sure she loves and honors the memory of her father.* Then she spoke aloud, whispering one last time, "*Volim te zauvijek.*"

Christena stirred and opened her eyes, looking up at her mother with such an aware expression that Flora found it hard to believe what Mama had told her: that newborns cannot see well enough to distinguish figures or faces. Flora reached down into the cradle and lifted Christena out, carefully bracing the head as she'd been instructed. "Well, my little apricot," Flora said softly. "You know who I am, don't you?"

Flora sat again in the rocking chair and cradled her daughter against her breast. "Not hungry yet, are you? That's how Mama—your *baka*—said it would be. Well, shall I tell you a story? Your father was a wonderful storyteller, but I know a few stories too. Shall I tell you about Dubrovnik, the beautiful place your grandparents came from? Listen now! On the edge of the blue sea, there's a city of white marble covered with sweet-smelling roses. And once long ago there lived near that city a handsome boy named Luka and a beautiful girl called Philomena ...."

Philomena Bogdonovich paused, unseen, in the doorway to watch her daughter, rocking her own child and telling of life in Dubrovnik. A wave of emotion swept up through Philomena. To see her own child grown and a mother herself was piercingly bittersweet. Especially since it appeared the babe would remain fatherless. Mama knew now Flora's strength and determination to do things her own way, and if Antone did not come back, she would remain unmarried.

Philomena was very proud of how her daughter had dealt with the situation. She had arranged to leave Santa Clara before the pregnancy became apparent. The Greek twins, whom Philomena now treated as nephews, had brought her to this house, which was big enough to have their glass shop on the ground floor and room for three households in the three storeys above. Just now the lowest floor was shared by Flora and Isabella Ribisi, the widowed daughter of Dante and Teresa Fortunallo. Isa—as she liked to be called—ran the glass shop and would be helping Flora with the baby as Flora prepared to take over the shop herself at the end of the year.

The top floor was reserved for the twins when they came up from Monterey. The rooms of the middle floor were available for other guests such as parents when they visited, as Philomena did now. It was a safe and comfortable home for Flora with plenty of companionship.

Philomena still missed her daughter immensely, but she knew this was the best arrangement of all, and she had plenty to keep her busy with the Bogdonovich apricot orchards and preparing the wines for Tipanov's distillery. She also had plenty of help from Matty Stanich and the younger Tipanovs. Visits from that sweet Ruzena helped ease the pain of living away from her daughter.

Yes, Philomena decided, she was very proud. Flora had kept herself healthy and active, weathering well her pregnancy and her intense seven-hour labor. And here she was, a mere twelve hours later, a beautiful seventeen-year-old mother rocking her child.

And my Luka would *be proud,* Philomena thought. *Of course he'd want to find that boy and hang him up by his heels, but all of that with the uncle's death is a mess best left alone for now at least.*

Reflecting a moment on the events over the past year, Philomena thought ruefully how only eight months ago she lay in her reeking bed, hoping—trying—to die so that she could follow her departed husband. *Ah, Luka,* she thought now, *I still miss you so much, and I look forward to the time when I will be beside you again, but look what I would have missed if I had joined you then! Look at our beautiful Flora, all grown with her own daughter—our grandchild! Just looking at them fills my heart, and I hope you can see them too.*

Flora glanced up then and smiled at her mama, and Philomena's eyes prickled with sudden tears as she smiled back and went into the room to embrace what was now most precious in her life.

CHAPTER 23
SAN FRANCISCO — 1890

"Don't **worry**!" Isabella said with an exasperated laugh. "We'll do just fine while you're away." She was trying to herd her parents and Flora and Christena toward the door of the shop.

Flora still lingered, gazing back into the room where she passed so many hours—a specialty shop that was now called Flora's. Theo and Demetri had told her the idea originally came from Antone Mellini: a spacious shop like a box of light. Three walls were made up of window panes, and the floor-to-ceiling tiers of glass shelves in front of them were crowded with Lidakis creations so that the sunlight streaming through illuminated the colored glass objects as if the whole room were formed of stained glass windows. "My jewel box," four-year-old Christena called it.

The north wall was of polished bird's eye redwood burl, lined with more shelves displaying wines from the Mellini Vineyards—including a hearty red called Bella Flora—and a number of specialty spirits from the Tipanov distillery, the most sought-after being Bogdonovich Plum *slivovitz* and the much renowned Armelin, which some considered the best apricot brandy available in California. Some status-conscious citizens soaked off the distinctive labels—which had an exquisite drawing of an apricot bough bearing both blossoms and fruit—to save as collector's items. The empty Lidakis amber glass bottles could then be used as vases.

Surveying the room, crowded with richly dressed men and women eager to buy something from such a famous shop (and willing to pay a little more to get the finest quality), Flora found herself still amazed at how the shop drew people. And—though Isabella was actually a more accomplished shop manager and salesperson—receipts were always higher on days when Flora was present. (And twice that if Christena was there with her, but that was understandable. As Isa once said, rather indelicately, "That child could charm the miter off a cardinal." And already the child had begun to make astute observations about the shoppers and ask questions which proved she had an innate sense for business, which Flora was quick to foster.)

Flora noted with satisfaction the wealth of roses Isabella had gathered to finish the room's decor and perfume the air. They tried always to keep the room full of whatever fresh flowers were in season, some—like the spring irises—grown in her own garden out back from slips and bulbs and cuttings Mama provided. The roses reminded Flora that—since spring was about to turn to summer—the same kind would now be covering the bay window of Mama's house on Page Street, and that brought her back to the matter at hand.

She turned toward the door and saw Isa motioning vigorously for her to come along. Outside the door she could hear Christena yelling, "Hurry, Mama!

Hurry up! I want to see Page Street!" Yet Flora lingered, wondering, *Why should I feel so reluctant to go home?*

This would be her first trip back to Page Street…Christena's first visit ever. Flora wondered what it would be like to see her first home again. To sleep in her childhood bed and touch the silver lamps in the parlor and eat *kobasica* and *ajvar* with Mama in the kitchen. She kept herself from wondering what it would be like to see Antone's house across the road or anything else that had to do with him.

His fate was still a mystery to her…to all of them. No one Flora or Theo or Demetri or the Fortunallos knew had ever heard from him again. On the rare occasions she allowed herself to think about him in ways that touched the depth of the love she still held for him, she felt she could still sense the connection she had shared with him. As illogical as it sounded, she was convinced she would know if he had died. She was still unmarried (though she had numerous and frequent proposals and a standing offer from Mattiza Stanich). At one time she had thought she would never marry, but now she wasn't so sure. In her heart, she would always be married to Antone, but someday, perhaps, she would meet someone she could love nearly as much…someone who would be a good father to Christena.

Flora was only twenty-one, and the thought of never again making love—having her body delighted by a loving man's touch—was sometimes more than she could bear. But for now she was content enough. And she had all the loving companions a person could hope for—and a child who radiated love and happiness like a beacon.

Am I feeling nervous about returning to Page Street with the child? she wondered. Here in San Francisco she was known as Widow Bogdonovich, a polite fiction she was willing to use to protect her daughter. But it would be more complicated back home where people knew her birth name—and how long she'd been gone—and when they saw her four-year-old daughter, she knew certain ones of them would be counting on their fingers. But she hadn't wanted to give up her father's name, and so she and her mother and Karsten and Ruzena had concocted a story that she had married a third cousin twice removed—or some such distant relation—with the same name. Most people would see through it, but would go along with the fabricated identity. She was a rich and powerful woman now, and no one of integrity could say a word against her business practices or her character.

And if there was one woman in her old community who might have started gossip and made her return uncomfortable, it would probably have been Sabina Tipanov, but she had died three years ago, finally succumbing to a cancer eating away at her spine.

Flora shook her head, marveling at how strangely things work out. For now she was on her way home to attend a party celebrating the announcement that Mama Philomena would marry Josko Tipanov in December. Flora knew her mother could never love Josko as she had Luka—and he knew this too—but as the two did business together during the past five years, a genuine respect and affection had grown between them. Flora was delighted to accept Josko as a stepfather—and Karsten and Ruzena as stepbrother and stepsister-in-law!

"Dante and Teresa," a laughing voice said, "are about to take your child and leave without you."

"Demetri!" Flora exclaimed and laughed. "Don't even joke about someone taking my Christena. I'll go now, but I wish you were coming with us."

Her Greek friend got that evasive look in his eyes and started mumbling. Smiling at his discomfort, she waved a dismissive hand and said, "I know, I know. You and Theo have this mysterious errand. Well, I'm warning you, Christena thinks you're planning some splendid gift for her—like the pony she's been asking for."

Flora gazed affectionately at this dear man who, with his more reserved brother, had been her salvation, supporting and guiding her through all that had happened since Antone left. The brothers lived here permanently now on the top floor of the San Francisco house, and they ran a small glass company nearby with employees to do most of the bottle work, freeing them to create the works of art which were so rewarding—both artistically and financially.

Almost overwhelmed by the sudden tide of gratitude she felt, Flora reached up and kissed Demetri on the cheek, and he turned bright red and beaming. But before Flora could say any of the things in her heart, a great commotion could be heard from outside the shop's front door. Christena's clear, sweet voice had set up a chant: "Page Street! Page Street! Page Street!"

Flora laughed and patted Demetri's chest good-bye. "Have a safe trip, and we'll see you back here in three weeks." She started for the door then, murmuring, "I guess it's time to go home…"

BIG SUR COAST — 1890

Antone Mellini knelt before the altar, praying, lost in the visions he could see while looking deep into the eyes of the Christ figure. He did not hear the chapel door open and in any case would not have heard the silent approach of the figure in blue.

"Brother Ambrose," a voice said softly. "I'm sorry to disturb you, but you have guests."

Antone ended his prayer and left the altar, saying, "Thank you, Sister Antoinette. That should be the men with the grape slips I asked for. Are they in the reception area?"

She nodded, and he smiled at her and hurried away. Curious, she followed at a distance. He crossed the yard with his long strides, unimpeded by the heavy brown skirts of his habit. He passed the freight wagon in the yard and entered the building.

Antone started speaking as he entered the room. "I want to thank you for going to all this trouble—" He froze, speechless, when he saw who was waiting for him.

The Lidakis brothers turned, as one, from viewing the painting of the monk and the lion with the wounded paw and stared at him. They blinked, taking in his habit and sandals, his full beard and the length of his wavy black hair. They noticed, too, the silvery little scar on his left temple and the tiny streak of white hairs that traced the path the bullet had taken past his hairline, and that helped them see beyond the other externals. "Antone!" they cried in unison, rushing to embrace him, but they stopped just short of him, waiting to see some sign of recognition or welcome.

He stared at them, letting the shock fade, and then his eyes misted up, and in a voice choked with tears, he said their names and reached for them. Then the three of them were all crying and hugging and kissing cheeks and trying to talk.

After a few moments, Antone said, "Let's go into the dining room, and I'll see if I can't get us some refreshment." He walked between the two, with an arm around each, saying softly, "My name is Brother Ambrose now. Partly for my protection, but also because this is a new life." They nodded that they understood, but it was clear this worried them.

He introduced the twins to Father Rodrigo as his "dearest friends from the outside world," and the good father served the weary travelers bread and cheese and some of the wine made there at the hermitage. Antone told them, "Yes, we make this here, and it's one of the areas where I can contribute the most to our community. In fact, you took me by surprise, because I've been waiting for a shipment of cuttings from some vineyards in the Napa Valley. Now, tell me, how long can you stay?"

Theo and Demetri spent three days with Antone at the hermitage. They each got one of the visitor's rooms near Antone's. Though he was obligated to discharge his duties, he was still able to give the brothers a good portion of his time. But because conversations had to be worked in here and there, everything couldn't be covered at once.

The first thing he wanted to know was: "How did you find me? Is it likely anyone else would be able to follow the same trail?"

Theo shook his head and Demetri answered, "I doubt it. When we hadn't heard from you in so long, we started questioning everyone we knew who had business dealings with you. It took us awhile to find out about Sven Heglund, and when we first went there, he had returned to Norway for an extended visit. He only arrived back two months ago. When we finally met with him and asked him if he had any ideas where you might be hiding, he remembered telling you about this hermitage. He said you had come here after your father died and had found great solace."

Antone nodded. "But Sven is unlikely to tell this to anyone else?"

"Yes, we impressed upon him the need for utmost secrecy. We will all protect you. But now, tell us about your life here and your plans to clear your name."

Briefly, Antone described the workings of the hermitage and explained that he was not called to be a hermit himself or to take a vow of silence, but he told them, "I am studying to become a priest, and might perhaps take Father Rodrigo's place when that time comes. But that is a distant dream—I have much to learn and to overcome in myself before I could attain such an honor." It was apparent he felt much the same as when he had written those letters so long ago: that he was atoning for sins which could never be forgiven and that he was following the only path he could. "As for clearing my name," he said, "I only care about doing that with my Holy Father."

Though her image was foremost in the thoughts of all three men, not one of them mentioned Flora's name. Theo and Demetri sensed that in some ways, Antone felt like a fox run to ground, and they wanted to do nothing that would make him feel further threatened.

They didn't offer information about anyone except themselves—telling him they lived in San Francisco now and had a prosperous glass business, and that the shop he had envisioned was now a reality—and even more successful than he had predicted. He grinned at this, having at least one of his dreams come true and people benefiting from it.

He asked first about his family and was saddened but relieved to learn his mother had finally breathed her last—two years after his departure. But he couldn't stop grinning when they told him about Bruno's happy marriage to Concetta and the three little bambinos they already had—with another on the way. He said he had heard from other sources that the Mellini Vineyards were doing well and selling a respected product at a reasonable price.

It was not until the second day—when he could suddenly think of nothing else to ask—that he broached the one topic that was most important. "So," he said in an overly casual voice, "what of Flora Bogdonovich?" He saw the twins look at each other in that familiar way when they were sharing a single thought, especially a secret. Antone blurted, "Did she marry?"

Those two pairs of blue eyes swung back to study him, not fooled by the tone of voice he had intended to sound hopeful. Antone shifted uncomfortably beneath their scrutiny. As one, the brothers shook their heads to signify "No" and Antone felt the surge of relief and joy, even as he was saying, "That's too bad. I had hoped she would marry and live happily."

Demetri told how she lived in their house in San Francisco now and was in charge of the glass shop—which was called Flora's. Antone asked about her mama and Mattiza, and learned all the new developments in their lives and their thriving businesses. "So Mattiza has never married either. Is he still in love with her?"

"Oh, yes," Theo said. "Everyone's in love with Flora."

As if he hadn't heard those last words, Antone rushed on: "He impressed me as a very decent man. Why doesn't Flora marry him?"

There was a long silence as Demetri tried to decide how best to answer. Finally, he just said very softly, "I think you know why." Antone looked away from those piercing blue eyes and asked some questions about if and how his business ventures had benefited Flora.

And all the while, both brothers were bursting to tell him about Christena. Knowing he was the father of such a remarkable creature—and that he was unaware of her very existence—seemed a terrible irony to the Lidakis brothers, but even more tragic was the fact that Flora trusted them not to tell Antone he even had a child.

And at the end of the conversation about Flora, Antone said, "Now I must ask a favor. I want you both to promise you won't tell her that you've seen me…where I am. I want her to forget me."

Their protests were quick and lively, but Antone held up his hand in a gesture that made them fall silent. "If you are truly my friends," he reminded them, "you will respect my wishes and my privacy. Now promise me not to tell her. In fact, you'd better promise not to tell **anyone**." Reluctantly, Theo and Demetri gave their word, but they were most unhappy. They knew now that Antone was still in love with Flora and certainly the reverse was true, yet both had barred the brothers from revealing anything which might bring the two together again. It was an intolerable double-bind, and in the twins' minds, the one who lost the most was young Christena, who was being deprived of her father—however unwittingly—by two very proud and hardheaded young parents.

But Theo and Demetri did enjoy their time at the hermitage. It was the most beautifully peaceful spot they could ever remember finding—and a refreshing change from the bustle of city life in San Francisco. They took their meals in the dining hall with Antone, Father Rodrigo, and Sister Antoinette, who ate after the hermits had finished their meal and returned to their quarters. There was fresh ocean fish of some kind every night with rice and vegetables straight from the garden. In exchange, they worked alongside Antone and were called upon to do some heavier chores that none of the men there could manage, even with the use of their draft animals—such as uprooting three huge, old redwood tree stumps impeding expansion of the vineyard. They were delighted when Dolce whickered a hello from her pasture and came over to show off her leggy young colt—her second, according to Antone.

They admired the chapel's colored glass and statues as they listened in rapture to the chanting of the monks. More than once they observed Antone at his prayers and were incredulous to note how long he could kneel, immobile and in total silence.

They were pleased to find what good company Antone had in Father Rodrigo and Sister Antoinette, two exceedingly intelligent and likeable beings. Though most impressed with the spiritual nature of the woman in blue—and fascinated by Antone's tale of how mysteriously Antoinette came to be there—they were also very aware that she had a special fondness for Antone.

It was equally obvious Antone was completely unaware of this and probably would have scoffed if they'd brought it to his attention, but they were well-acquainted with unrequited love—in their own lives and in the lives of those around them.

Their parting after the three days was more emotional than any of them had expected. Father Rodrigo and Antoinette withdrew after a short time to give Antone more privacy.

"I hope you will come back to visit again," Antone said quite sincerely. "I do miss spending time with you." The brothers promised they would, joking that they'd come more often if it weren't a week's journey on the wooden seat of a freight wagon.

As they were embracing at the final good-bye, Antone repeated, "Now, remember your promise. Don't tell anyone about Brother Ambrose—especially…her."

The brothers nodded with resignation, noticing he could not even utter Flora's name. Not the sign of a man who no longer loves a woman!

They all waved and yelled more good-byes as the freight wagon rumbled down the road toward the coast road, and Antone swung the gate closed behind them.

The Lidakis brothers rode in silent thought for a long while, almost oblivious to the wild beauty of the sea and chaparral as they followed the road clinging to the cliffside. Finally it was Theo who voiced a conclusion they'd both come to: "Brother, I fear if we return here, I may not be able to keep my promise to Flora."

Demetri nodded and sighed in relief to hear his brother felt the same as he did. "Yes. That child deserves to have her father know she exists. Then he can decide whether or not to see her…or do anything more."

"But a promise is a promise, and I'll keep it as long as I can."

"Yes, as long as we can…"

Antoinette of the Lightning paused outside the chapel, watching Brother Ambrose stand at the gate and stare down the empty road. *What will happen now?* she wondered. *He has been so happy here. Is he thinking of going back?* That possibility dragged in her like a heavy weight. How could she stand to be apart from him now? She had managed to convince herself that what she had with Antone was enough. To have his company and admiration, to be able to instruct him on his spiritual path, to be able to see every day the beauty of his face and graceful movement. For these pleasures she could forgo wanting more, deny herself the dreams other women might have looking at him.

Antoinette went into the chapel and knelt before the statue of the Virgin Mary and prayed for a very long time. *Immaculate Mother,* she said at one point, *God has given me life and a purpose to fulfill. Please help me receive His guidance to follow this sometimes-difficult path you have shown me, and please give me the strength to accept and embrace what He says I must do.*

Antone leaned heavily against the gate for support, and his hand went up to his temple—fingertips pressing the furrow where Gregorio's bullet had gouged his skull—but it didn't ease the aching. How could God do this to him? After all these years trying to put that other life—other people—behind him so that he could devote his life to healing his soul! How discouraging to have it all rush back so clearly ... what it was like that last year in Santa Clara. And worst of all was remembering Flora. He'd kept telling himself he was past needing her or wanting her, that all he had left was the purest kind of love, sifted free of the physical aspects, which he then discarded. But it simply wasn't true.

For here he was, in this most holy of places, and all he could think of was how her body and her spirit had filled his senses as well as his soul. He remembered all too well what it was like to kiss her, to hold her close against him. Suddenly, he could smell that French perfume on her skin and hear her say his name with that certain throaty catch in her voice. God help him, he could even feel her legs wrapped around him and taste her mouth, sweet with apricots.

Antone clung to the gate and put his head down on the top rail and wept. *Dear Jesus,* he prayed, *I tried so hard... But it's all for nothing. I love her more than ever, and I am still unworthy...unforgiven...and a fugitive. I am lost, and I beseech you to show me what I must do to serve you best.*

As always when he prayed, he was filled with the sense that his Savior was near and comforting him, so when his tears were finished and he felt in control again, Antone whispered to reassure himself, "It's over now. They're gone, and maybe they'll never come back." Like a child who had built a castle of blocks only to have them scattered by a careless friend, he set himself to picking up and beginning anew.

But what if they **did** come back and opened these wounds again? Antone wondered. Would he be strong enough and dedicated enough to stay here and follow God's plan for him? And then another question came in, more terrifying than the others: *What if the life I'm living isn't really God's plan for my future? What if my true purpose asks me to show even more strength and courage by going back to Page Street someday?*

SANTA CLARA VALLEY — 1890

The party had been going on for hours, and it was obvious the guests were enjoying themselves immensely. So many old faces remembered from church and community functions when she was growing up. So many new faces—not only children born to these families but also new immigrants come to the valley. There was much laughter and lively conversation. The food and beverages disappeared almost as quickly as they appeared, but there was always more to take their place. Philomena was radiant, looking younger than she had in years, out of her widow's black and with brilliant coral-colored roses pinned in her hair. Josko Tipanov said little but Flora could not think of a moment all day when she had not seen him beaming.

"You think this is a party?" Karsten whispered in Flora's ear. "Just wait till their wedding!"

Flora laughed and declined the plate of food Ruzena was offering her. How wonderful it was to see these dear friends—and Matty—for the three could only rarely get away to visit her in San Francisco. Matty was looking very dapper and prosperous in his fine suit, and a number of young ladies had noticed his blond and square-jawed good looks, enhanced by those solemn grey eyes and the tiny scar that made him seem more daring and mysterious. Flora could tell several young ladies were trying to flirt with him, but his attention was on the girl who gripped his hand as if she would never let go. Christena towed him from place to place in the room, asking, "What's this, Uncle Matty? Who made these, Uncle Matty? How does this work, Uncle Matty?"

Flora noticed with a touch of annoyance—but no surprise—that Christena's white-blond hair was already wildly tousled about her face—a look that certainly suited her but was at odds with fashion and decorum. *At least,* Flora noted to console herself, *her boots are still on and laced up!*

Flora never tired of watching her daughter, especially when she was in motion: her energetic little body was strong and wiry as a spring and always ready to leap. It filled Flora with awe to see this vivacious and independent creature and remember that it was something that had come through her body, something she and Antone had—albeit unwittingly—created together.

But not everyone had the energy to keep up with Christena. Smiling, Flora went to rescue Matty. "Why, here's my little apricot," she said as she reached them. "Would you like to see my room, Steenie? Where I slept when I was your age?" Christena nodded in her most enthusiastic manner—which made her hair float like a wispy cloud all around her head—and Flora told Matty, "Thanks, I can take her now." No sooner had the child released his hand and taken Flora's than Matty was besieged by young ladies bent on gaining his attention.

Flora led the way into her old room and took a few moments to look around and touch a few items: the crocheted ivory bedcovering, the rose-patterned basin with the chip in its rim, the silver-backed brushes from Dubrovnik.

"What's this?" Christena asked, picking up something beside the dresser.

"Why, that's a concertina. Your grandpa used to play it."

"How does it work?"

Flora took it in her hands and explained its basics, fingered the keys and worked the bellows just a bit. She laughed self-consciously and said, "I was never very good at it myself."

Christena regarded her with those riveting blue eyes of hers and said, "I can!"

"Oh, can you?" Flora laughed, but she should have known better. From her very earliest days, Christena seemed to have a very real sense of exactly what was within her power. The four-year-old hands couldn't touch all the buttons properly but she got the bellows to make some rather convincing noises. "I'm impressed!" Flora told her. "It will work better for you when you're a little older, but would you like to have it for your own? Take it back to San Francisco with us and learn to play it when you're ready?"

Those blue, blue eyes widened. "Oh, yes, Mama. Thank you!" And she put her complete attention on experimenting with the instrument.

Flora turned—at last—toward the window. She had been avoiding looking at it, but when she did, there, on the sill, was the amber bottle. Her mother had filled it with bright roses and used it as a vase. How ironic, Flora thought, wondering how often it ended up in this window, signaling across the street to Antone, but neither one ever came to the bower now. Flora went to touch the glass and pull aside the lace curtain and gaze across the street. There were different curtains in that window now, and no green glass signal. Still ....

"Would you like to take a walk, *janje?*" she asked.

Again the enthusiastic nod, and Christena carefully placed the concertina on the bed where she could find it later. Then she went to her mama and took her hand, ready for an excursion.

Flora and Christena slipped out the front door, moving in and among the chatting guests till they could get down the steps and into the yard, then quickly out to the edge of the orchard. The trees were heavy and fragrant with ripe fruit, and the ground beneath was littered with windfalls. It was the height of the harvest, and the only reason Philomena and Matty had agreed to take this day off for the party was that they'd have extra help for the next few days to make up lost time.

"Tomorrow," Flora reminded her as they walked, "you'll join your first apricot harvest."

"Will I get to stand on the ladder?"

"No. You'll start out gathering the fruit underneath the trees."

"Why?"

"Because that's how children start out. That's how I started."

Christena nodded as if that was good enough for her and then darted in under the nearest tree and picked up one perfect apricot to hand to her mother.

"Thank you," Flora said, brushed away some bits of dirt, and twisted it open.

Watching, Christena said, "I can't do that yet."

Flora handed her the half without the seed and assured her, "It will come."

Eating the fruit, they walked all the way to the end of the orchard to the strip of grass grown lush and wild without Dolce there to crop it. Flora had thought the bower might be gone, that perhaps Matty had torn down the brambleberry canes or that they had been washed away in a time of floodwater. But from the top of the creekbank, it looked much the same as she remembered it had looked that other June—leafy green and starred with white blossoms. Seeing this and remembering the other time it had looked this way, Flora realized today was the very day of the summer solstice.

"Want to see a special place?" Flora asked, and she could hear the tightness in her voice. Christena must have heard it too, because she studied her mother a long, solemn moment before nodding.

Flora led the way down the path and, barely breathing, pulled the bramble curtain aside. "Oh!" Christena breathed with delight. "A secret room!" and she scrambled on inside. Flora followed. It was much changed. Of course all traces of blankets or candles or bottles were long since gone, and the inside was altered by new growth and flood tides and time. But it was enough the same that Flora felt her eyes fill with the bittersweetness of the memories.

"I like it," the child declared. "It feels good in here. How do you know about it?" She was always one for discovering the how and why and where and when of things.

"Matty and I used to play here when we were children," Flora answered. *And*, she thought, *five years ago tonight your father and I made you here*. The memories flooded in of that most magical night, and for a moment, she forgot she was not alone.

"Mama?" Christena asked, and Flora answered distractedly, her mind full of all she had loved about Antone.

"Mama, do I have a father?"

Shocked back to the present moment, Flora stared at her daughter and said, "Yes. Everyone has a father, even if they may not be together."

"Then where is mine?"

Flora had known these questions would come some day, but she hadn't expected them so soon. She had thought a great deal about what to say and hoped to be able to satisfy the child without hurting her, scaring her, or lying to her. "Why do you ask, sweetheart?"

"I heard some people talking at the party. They said my papa was dead."

Flora sighed. "The truth is, we don't know where your papa is. I think he's alive, but I don't know for certain."

"Then why did they say he was dead?"

Flora said, "This is a very complicated thing. Can I tell it to you as a story?"

Christena knew that meant her mother would leave out some parts that she wouldn't understand until she was older. She nodded. "Don't leave out anything important. All right: once 'pon a time …."

"Yes, once upon a time there was a Croatian girl with red hair named Flora. She fell in love with an Italian boy named Antone."

"Is that my papa's name?" Christena interrupted excitedly.

"Yes, and he was very beautiful—both to look at and also in his soul. A very gentle man who never tried to hurt anyone. Antone and Flora loved each other very, very much and wanted to be married, but they were forced to wait, because their families were so different. Croatians and Italians had different customs…ways to do things. The Croatians thought they were better than the Italians, and the Italians thought they were better than the Croatians, so they didn't want their children to marry."

"That's silly," Christena declared.

Flora reflected that this child was growing up raised by a Croatian woman, an Italian woman and two Greek men. She was fluent in her mother's language, and spoke Italian with Isa and the Greeks. All of them were still learning English. Christena was certainly a child of the future.

"Yes…silly," Flora agreed. "That's what Antone and Flora thought, and you know what they found out loving each other?"

"No, what?"

"That they really weren't so different after all. And that many of the older people were wrong about what they believed, but before they could convince the older people, something terrible happened."

Christena leaned forward, her eyes alight as the story unfolded. "What?"

"Well, there was a very bad man—someone hurt and angry—who hated Antone. One night he tried to kill both Antone and Flora, but Antone turned out to be a very brave man, and he saved their lives. But there was an accident and the bad man died."

"That's good, isn't it?"

"Well, it's good that Antone and Flora weren't hurt, but then Antone was scared he'd get in trouble about the accident, so he went away to hide."

Christena nodded. This she understood all too well. The very thing had happened to her. She'd only a week ago gone into hiding when a glass vase accidentally got broken. "And he's still hiding?"

"I guess so," Flora answered. "I think he's just lost and can't find his way back." She watched her daughter mulling all this over and waited for the next question; it wasn't anything she expected.

"Why doesn't my papa love me? And don't say he does, because if he did, he would come to see me."

"Oh, sweetheart, he doesn't even know about you. When Antone went to hide, you were still a secret inside me, and now no one knows where he is so no one can tell him."

"I want him to come back."

"I want that too. Maybe someday he will. And if he knew, I promise you he would love you **at least** as much as I do. Now, we've been gone a long time; we'd better go back to the party."

As they crawled out into the sunlight, Christena asked, "Then why do people say my father's dead?"

"Remember how Antone and Flora had to keep their love secret, because the Croatians and the Italians didn't trust each other? Well, we still need to keep my love for Antone secret, so we pretend that your father was a Croatian man named Antal Bogdonovich." As they walked up the path, she asked, "So do you think you can help keep all this secret?" Christena nodded with great seriousness, seeming lost in deep thought.

At the top of the bank, Flora looked back at the little bower and all its sweet memories. "Let's go back a different way," she suggested and started to walk toward the road, paralleling the creekbed. Any traces of the path Dolce had worn carrying Antone to the bower were long gone now, but Flora would never forget the spot where Gregorio had lain dead in the moonlight.

When they reached the road, they turned north on it and started back toward the houses. It was a peaceful walk, listening to the birds welcoming the summer season, catching the scent of Mama Philomena's roses on the breeze. Faintly, too, came the hum of voices from the party, like an evening *korzo* in the streets of Dubrovnik.

Up ahead, on her right, was her childhood home, and on the left, Flora could see the Mellini property. She reflected that little had actually changed here on Page Street. The Italians and the Slavs kept to themselves and each looked upon the other with doubt and suspicion. Her mama and Matty had very little to say to the Bruno Mellini family, and the reverse was also true. This was doubly strange since Theo and Demetri remained close friends with both families, as did the Fortunallos. *Perhaps,* Flora thought, *Bruno blames me for what happened that night.* But there was nothing she could do about that, and she was tired of trying to puzzle out why everything had turned out the way it had.

"Mama?" Christena said after her long, thoughtful silence, squeezing her mother's hand to make sure she had Flora's attention.

Flora glanced down. "What, *janje?*"

The face turned up to her—blue-eyed, delicately boned, with a scattering of freckles and the sweet curve of Antone's mouth—was a face full of conviction and the inner peace that can bring. "I think," the child said, "my papa will get un-lost someday and come back to find us."

Quick tears stung Flora's eyes, and she answered in a husky voice barely above a whisper, "I hope so, Christena. I hope so." She squeezed the strong little hand clinging to her own, and drew strength from her daughter's conviction, and they walked on up Page Street together.

ORDER FORM

SEND POSTAL ORDERS TO:

ABALONE PUBLISHING COMPANY
P O BOX 3138
HALF MOON BAY CA 94019-3138 USA

PLEASE SEND_____COPIES OF PAGE STREET TO:

COMPANY NAME:_____

NAME:_____

STREET ADDRESS:_____

CITY, STATE, ZIP:_____

QUANTITY ORDERED	PRICE	TOTAL PRICE:
	@ $9.95	$
TAX: CALIFORNIA RESIDENTS ADD APPLICABLE SALES TAX.		$
SHIPPING: BOOK RATE - @2.00 FOR THE FIRST BOOK: $.75 FOR EACH ADDITIONAL BOOK. AIR MAIL - $3.50 PER BOOK. SURFACE SHIPPING MAY TAKE 3 - 4 WEEKS.		$
	TOTAL:	$

PAYMENT:　　　□ CHECK □ MONEY ORDER
PLEASE SEND ORDERING INFORMATION FOR *APPLE PIE* AND
THE SEQUEL TO *PAGE STREET* (WHEN IT BECOMES AVAIL-
ABLE IN SPRING OF 1994). I'M ENCLOSING SASE (SELF-
ADDRESSED, STAMPED ENVELOPE).

About The Author

Mark John Boskovich was born in Santa Clara in 1950, two blocks from Page Street. His parents raised him—along with three sisters and twin brothers—in a traditional Roman Catholic atmosphere.

Some of Mark's loves are: baseball, the redwood forest, the ocean, animals, literature and watching children grow and learn.

At present, Mark works at a privately owned nursery in Half Boon Bay, California.

He is most happily married to a beautiful Cherokee lady named Charlotte, with whom he shares the joy of raising three precious daughters: Misty, Cassandra, and Christena.

Mark is working on his next two books: *APPLE PIE* (a collection of short stories about a young boy growing up in Northern California's Santa Clara Valley in the 1950s) and the sequel to *PAGE STREET*.

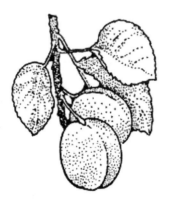